ural

IMPERIAL BLUES

IMPERIAL BLUES

GEOGRAPHIES OF RACE AND SEX
IN JAZZ AGE NEW YORK

FIONA I. B. NGÔ

Duke University Press
Durham and London 2014

© 2014 Duke University Press
All rights reserved
Printed in the United States of America on acid-free paper ∞
Designed by Heather Hensley
Typeset in Minion Pro by Tseng Information Systems, Inc.

Library of Congress Cataloging-in-Publication Data
Ngô, Fiona I. B.
Imperial blues : geographies of race and sex in
jazz age New York / Fiona I. B. Ngô.
pages cm
Includes bibliographical references and index.
ISBN 978-0-8223-5524-3 (cloth : alk. paper)
ISBN 978-0-8223-5539-7 (pbk. : alk. paper)
1. Arts and society—New York (State)—New York—
History—20th century.
2. Immigrants—New York (State)—New York—
Intellectual life—20th century.
3. Minorities—New York (State)—New York—
Intellectual life—20th century.
4. Imperialism. I. Title.
F128.9.A1N46 2013
305.8009747—dc23   2013025466

CONTENTS

ACKNOWLEDGMENTS

First, I'd like to thank the folks at Duke University Press for all their help in getting this project into shape, especially Ken Wissoker, Jade Brooks, Danielle Szulczewski, and Heather Hensley. Jeanne Ferris is a great copyeditor, and this book reads better for her hard work. I also wish to thank the Crisis Publishing Co., the publisher of the magazine of the National Association for the Advancement of Colored People (now known as the NAACP), for the use of the material first published in the September 1928 issue of *Crisis Magazine*. Sean Metzger, Gina Masquesmay, and the folks at Lexington Books published an early version of my first chapter in *Embodying Asian/American Sexualities*. Thomas Wirth generously provided access to Richard Bruce Nugent's manuscripts and art and introduced me to the Negroni, Nugent's drink of choice. I would also like to thank all the archivists and librarians at the Lesbian Herstory Archive, Columbia University Oral History Archives, New York City Department of Records and Information Services, New York Public Library (NYPL) Center for Humanities, NYPL Performing Arts Library, NYPL Schomburg Center for Research in Black Culture, Beinecke Rare Book and Manuscript Library at Yale University, Bancroft Library at the University of California (UC), Berkeley, and the University of Illinois at Urbana-Champaign.

I would also like to thank the students, staff, postdocs, and faculty of the programs and departments that have housed me during this long process: UC Irvine's History Department, Loyola Marymount's American Cultures Program, the University of Oregon's Department of Ethnic Studies, and the Department of Gender and Women's Studies and Department of Asian American Studies at the University of Illinois at Urbana-Champaign. All the help—from answering my inane questions about where supplies have been moved to and making sure that my documents arrived on time to encouraging my intellectual development—has been indispensable. My dissertation committee, whose members may not even recognize this project at this point, consisted of Alice Fahs, who has been a wonderful model for me in navigating my job; Jon Wiener, who keeps the political import of the academy alive; and Bob Moeller, who taught me how to be a patient researcher and how to teach. I would also like to thank all the incredible students I have had over the years, including Ma Vang, Kit Myers, Margarita Smith, Lezlie Frye, Khanh Lê, Chris Finley, Angie Morrill, Leslie Riggs, Beverly Zoll, Mark Padoongpatt, Ari Divine, Christine Kolb, Héctor Miramontes, Michael Eaves, Katie Barry, Bess van Asselt, Angeline Shea, Ashley Zamora, Eric Roth, Sarah Phillips, Ashley DeGroot, Christa Kivarkis, Stephanie Murphy, and Liz Verklan. All these students and many others have sustained me, pushed me to learn new things and become more articulate, and reminded me why education is still important.

A number of folks have been kind enough to read parts and drafts of this manuscript. Their comments, advice, and acumen have made the book better in every way. Thanks to Roderick Ferguson, Sherrie Tucker, Chantal Nadeau, and Jerry Gonzalez. Emily Skidmore gave me great comments on a draft of this book and also worked as my research assistant. I can't wait to read her book! A big shout out to Siobhan Somerville and Moon-Kie Jung, who not only have read earlier forms of this book, but have taken time to mentor me and teach me how to exist ethically in institutions.

This book would not have been possible without the love and support of my friends and family. Both my parents have done time in various capacities in academic institutions. Their love, support, guidance, and advice have helped me through some of the most difficult of times. So thanks, Mom, for all those hours-long phone calls and for making me do times tables while rolling meatballs! And thanks to my father, whose exploits at trad jazz basement shows in mid-century London serve as proper inspiration for this project. My brothers and their families have served as inspirations because they are so smart, creative, and nice. Thanks, Ian, for buying my first guitar. It turned into this book. I have cherished some of the most confused, funny, and heartening phone calls with Nalini, Caden, and Asha. Caden's drawing of a hammerhead shark floating in air next to a tree reminds me to think against regimes of common sense. Asha's punk performances make me long for modes of resistance. Robin, you are one of the smartest guys I know. Amazingly, you always seem to know everything about everything. Whenever I see Kathy and Nigel, warmth fills my heart. Nigel's enthusiasm for, well, every single activity reminds me to live joyfully. Colin in particular did hands-on work for this book, telling me that what I thought was a clarinet was in fact a soprano saxophone, and helping me transcribe music. He and the incomparable Aimee generously let me stay at their place whenever I had research to do in New York. You two are the best, or maybe just the best eaters.

My friends, who often seem like family, have gotten to witness this project develop on a (sometimes almost painful) daily basis. They have provided me with food, love, laughter, incredulity, and even places to stay and airline tickets when I was down and out. They have also taught me how to vacation and how to work without going crazy. Beth Stinson is one of my oldest friends. We have joyfully collaborated as bandmates, coeditors, and coconspirators. She often knows what I am thinking before I do. Thanks, especially, for taking a first run through my footnotes and bibliography and for staying up all night with me to turn in drafts. Mariam Lâm is super smart and generous, and seemingly has endless energy. It has been a genuine pleasure to collaborate with her. She is always welcoming and full of warmth and cleverness. The perceptive Mike Masatsugu provides me with another model of what it means to be a good person. Here's to the everyday! It was great to be a postdoc with him and Chris Lee, super genius. Jennifer Allen made me into a mind warrior. That takes a lot of skill. Robert Martinez kept me sane with his willingness to always hit the court. Bruce Manning and Blake Manning Wong, may the force be with you. Thanks for using your powers for good instead of evil. Dustin Allred has not said "no" to writing a book with me. I am always impressed that he can discourse on art, survive in a forest while eating ants, and fly planes. That's cool. Max is cool, too. Ian Sprandel has given me some of the most vaguely positive and useful advice I've received, and is always welcoming, loving, licking, and cooking. Also, Luciano looks like a keeper. Stephen Hocker, what a tart. Seriously, he is a great pastry chef and a great friend, a gentleman and a scholar. David Coyoca really tried to make me a better writer, and when that didn't work, he made me a great cocktail.

I have also been blessed with the best writing companions *ever*. The ebullient Mireya Loza cheers for everybody. Karen Flynn has finally joined the (grading) party! Ruth Nicole Brown is creative and productive, and often chooses to do things the hard way. In short, she inspires. Yutian Wong smiles and demands the best and most work from me in a way that makes me want only to thank her. She also knows everything about everything and has the best real and fake ideas for book projects. I hope to join her someday at the Giant Bonsai Institute because her intellect touches so much of my own work. Isabel Molina has always opened her home to me, has provided career guidance, and, most importantly, has been an admirable example of how to cheerfully destroy institutions from the inside. Unfortunately for Lisa Cacho, she's the one I consult and lean on when I'm totally wrecked. These moments often call on her broad set of skills, her intelligence, and her patience. She is one of the smartest people I know, and she never holds that against me. Soo Ah Kwon has sat down with me almost every day for almost two years. She starts the clock so that we both get work done. She is levelheaded, has a can-do attitude, and has given me insight into how the popular kids live. I really, really could not have finished this book on this timetable without her.

Mimi Thi Nguyen is that rare combination of public intellectual, academic, and punk as fuck zinester. I am glad all over that she is in my life, and would like to thank the Council of Magical Creatures for sending her to the Land of Time. Her raw intelligence sustains me, and her presence reminds me that I am free to fight. She always indulges me, even when it is difficult. In addition to that, she is the most beautiful, bravest, smartest, and kindest person I know. Morton is second.

"Folks, now here's a story 'bout Minnie the Moocher / She was a red-hot hoochy coocher" is the beginning of one of the most famous songs of the Jazz Age. Cab Calloway and His Orchestra first recorded "Minnie the Moocher" in December 1930, while Calloway was presiding over Harlem's world-famous Cotton Club in the absence of Duke Ellington and the club's regular orchestra, who were then touring and making films in Hollywood. Perhaps the most famous "black and tan" nightclub, where white patrons reveled in black pageantry, the mob-owned Cotton Club has come to represent the sundry delights of the Jazz Age.[1] A New Woman and New Negro, Minnie signified an age of newfound freedoms. The story Calloway's song spins about black womanhood, however, is multiracial and spatial in nature. Minnie's exotic, erotic dancing—named the "hoochy coochy" in the song—was a fusion of "authentic" and fantastical forms of belly dancing borrowed from an imagined Orient, and in the course of her adventures, Minnie travels the length of Manhattan and finds herself in an opium den in Chinatown. This song, then, provides a complicated snapshot of Jazz Age New York, in which we find not just the Harlem of black entertainers and white interlopers, but a complex, multiracial, imperial cityscape.

In Jazz Age New York, exotic tropes of empire had captured the imaginations of city denizens. Nightclubs featured performances and décor inspired by idyllic dreams of island paradises;

cabarets, speakeasies, dance halls, and the sheet music of Tin Pan Alley teemed with jangling tunes infected with orientalist themes and images. Even the Cotton Club, renowned for its "high-yaller girls" and great orchestras, traded in other forms of exotica. Furbished with a plantation façade, palm trees, and other signposts of warmer climes, the club's interior simultaneously recalled the U.S. South, Africa, Latin America, and the islands of the Pacific and Caribbean. "Minnie the Moocher," with its reference to belly dancing, and other popular tunes such as "In Harlem's Araby," "Palesteena," and "The Sheik of Araby" contained fantasies of Arabia, made popular in part through Hollywood spectacles. Performed nightly in New York's speakeasies, cabarets, and nightclubs, the hoochy coochy marked its dancers, like Minnie, as sexual creatures with an exotic allure. One titillated vice investigator, describing a performance of the hoochy coochy, observed that the dancer stood in "one spot for about five minutes and simply wiggled her body around the middle from her waist down to a little below her hips, in such a way as to suggest that that part of her body was a universal joint."[2] Calling on an imperial language of strangeness and sexual aberration, the disturbed vice investigator reported these movements as an oriental corruption that "released" dancers from bourgeois respectability. Indeed, for many New Women, orientalist forms became signs of self-possession, a way of mastering their bodies and their fates through a mastery of the Orient. However, such performances also brought some women to the notice of disciplinary powers, which perceived such women as perversely intimate with racialized wickedness. This imperial logic was thus double-edged. Minnie is described as "the roughest, toughest frail," but by the song's end, she is strung out on opium, a pitiable figure ("Poor Min, poor Min, poor Min"). In some versions of the song, she is left for dead. The same imperial markers that attract the listener to her also bring her to her end.

The musical scene set by Calloway's signature tune includes other questions of travel, and not just white adventurers journeying to Harlem's Cotton Club to encounter black performers. Not only were nightclubs filled with the sights and sounds of distant continents and tropical islands, but travelers from around the world — including the multiple outposts of the United States — made their ways through the city streets and spaces of nightlife. New migrants from the Philippines, Cuba, Puerto Rico, Hawaii, Mexico, Japan, and China crossed paths with black Harlemites and white "slummers" in dance halls and speakeasies. Such movements traversed the city, but as one consequence of imperial reach, they also reconceived its ordering through more complicated racial and spatial schema. Though New York was often imagined as a city of discrete neighborhoods whose cartographies delineated racial boundaries—black people in Harlem, between 110th and 142nd Streets; Chinese migrants in Chinatown, around Mott Street; Jewish families near Delancey Street on the Lower East Side; and so forth—this song, like other cultural productions of the time, demonstrates that such boundaries were indeed traversable by neighborhood inhabitants, across the island of Manhattan. This is a simple fact, but one that troubles often presumptive racializations of neighborhoods that design and desire separable and static racial and national categories. Minnie's tale begins with a hoochy coochy in Harlem, but she travels downtown with her lover to an opium den in Chinatown: "Now she messed around with a bloke named Smoky / She loved him though he was cokie / He took her down to Chinatown / He showed her how to kick the gong around." Here, and in the later song "Kickin' the Gong Around" (slang for smoking opium), Chinatown is a foreign destination, where lawless people find pleasure in illicit deeds. In such stagings of multitudinous travels across oceans and over thoroughfares, gender and sexual forms are transfigured not only through interracial mixing, but also through the transnational production of space as it remaps the imperial city.

These strange encounters present a novel account of the crucial presence of empire in Jazz Age New York. *Imperial Blues* offers a study of empire at home, one that critically rearticulates urban history and possible stories about race, gender, and sexuality in the United States in the early part of the twentieth century. This book suggests that without a new consideration of how empire circulated in everyday life to inform and transform national subjects and their understandings of the categories that defined their conceptions of home and away, friend and stranger, we cannot comprehend the complexities of how race and sexuality in the United States were lived in the interwar years that comprise the Jazz Age. For the most part, discourses of race in Jazz Age New York are framed around black and white dichotomies.[3] In regarding the city not as a discrete object of study but as a global center for economic development and creative labor, *Imperial Blues* moves beyond the "black and tan" to examine the considerably more complicated borders and border crossings of the Jazz Age. Studies that investigate intersections between Asian American and African American cultural practices and political discourses are proliferating, though these studies base their categories on the U.S. context.[4] Taking Jazz Age music cultures as both a cue and a circuit, this book pursues those intersections that are transnational in nature. I ask, for instance, how did immigration from Asia, the Caribbean, and Latin America transform city living and the imagination of artists in this critical interwar period? Furthermore, how did the imperial reach of the United States—or, indeed, its ties to other empires—shape these vibrant metropolitan cultures? How did the increasing prominence of eugenics and sexology as sciences of biological distinction and management traverse national and other borders? How did political upheavals surrounding women's suffrage and continuing racial antagonisms manifest in Jim Crow and anti-immigration legislation influence governance, particularly in relation to imperial gendered, sexual, and racial formations? I propose that the traffic in these bodies and the crises of knowledge about them serve as evidence that the United States as a nation, an ideology, and a concept has always been permeable and heterogeneous across its populations and perimeters. *Imperial Blues* thus argues that the domestic or national organization of race and sex during the Jazz Age, and in New York City as an exemplar of this period's sensibilities, cannot be understood except in the context of the growing ambitions of modern U.S. empire.

For me, empire must be a central analytic rather than simply a context for understanding Jazz Age New York because it was an everyday reality of changing urban demographics, and it played a large part in the creative imagination that guided the design of interiors, the making of music, and even the naming of spaces within the Empire City. Although imperialism brought people and ideas into a complicated mixture in the city, imperial logic served as a basis for meaning making. Imperial logic forms concepts of distance and intimacy. The connections between peoples and places produce complex conditions for contact, through which a nation or an empire relates stories of its past and establishes the cultures of its diverse subjects in the present. At stake in the mobilization of imperial logic are a breadth of concerns that pertain to the conception and organization of space and subjectivity, especially wrought through unstable categories of race, gender, and sexuality, which often serve as a way to envision and wield power.[5] Revisiting the Jazz Age through the lens of imperialism renders visible (as well as audible) previously underacknowledged connections and collaborations between domestic and imperial discourses of race and empire. I demonstrate that the domestic and the foreign are intertwined, and that modes of transgression and regulation emerge through their dense linkages. By approaching the cultural landscape of Jazz Age New York through the logic of empire, it becomes possible to analyze formations of identity within the nation by understanding both the influence of New York beyond its borders and more intimate circumstances through the movements of bodies in the city.

Imperial logic labors through a sometimes contradictory flow of signs. My contention is that it manifests itself through the complex workings of referentiality, and that the spaces, objects, and bodies that act as signs of empire are mutable. In other words, a geographic marker of China or Hawaii or Cuba might be repositioned in the city through a club's interior design, the placement of silk pajamas or pillows in a bordello, or the naming of a cabaret or restaurant. While this spatial reorientation may seem insignificant, these kinds of renamings and replacings were modes of exoticization and titillation designed to lure clients off the streets and into these places of business through signs of empire. Imperialism, then, was a way to understand pleasure, consumption, and sexuality. Furthermore, the mutability of signs might also mean that imperially derived meanings could be transferred from one type of body to another. For example, although we might be used to thinking of Asian bodies as orientalized or orientalizable, white, black, and brown bodies could also be orientalized. Artists such as Martha Graham, Ruth St. Denis, Richard Bruce Nugent, Wallace Thurman, and countless chorus girls from Broadway and nightclub floor shows might put on the accouterment of the Orient for various purposes: to subjectivize or eroticize themselves, to build narratives of resistance to empire, or to prove their cosmopolitan sensibility. Importantly, then, not only were the markers of imperial logic peripatetic—attaching themselves to various spaces, objects, and bodies and then detaching themselves again—but the meanings created through their circulation rendered them unstable.

At stake in the mobility of meaning is the way that power structures people's life chances and access to subjectivity, as well as the way it valuates difference, whether it is racial, spatial, gendered, national, or sexual. Part of how imperial logic works, I argue, is through the belief in a model of power that presents colonizing and imperial nations as stronger or morally superior to those nations being colonized, a model that justifies colonization. But the meanings enacted through these understandings of spatial and national relationships are not uniform, as the power structure offers diverse modes of narrative identification that help produce particular subject positions within social systems. These subject positions include those of a dominant citizen, a resistant artist, a social and moral outsider, a knowledge-producing collector of artifacts and songs, and an artist exploring a historical racial past, depending on whether one identifies with the colonizer or the colonized and how one understands that identification. Because a complex of meanings is produced through imperial logic, the use of imperial imagery in aesthetic production often speaks both to the modes of resistance and, simultaneously, to the limits of that resistance through regulation. For instance, the logic in a song like Porter Grainger's "In Harlem's Araby" might signal the sexual and gendered freedom of a neighborhood space by comparing it with an imagined Orient, but through this signaling it might also hail regulatory bodies to that space so that it might be policed. The logic, then, both in resistance and regulation, relies on making city space and its inhabitants strange through ideas of distant (and distancing) imperium, even while one celebrates that difference and the other attempts to control it. The narrating of imperial difference and its valuing become the basis for how people might be treated in these spaces and gives rise both to a discourse of internal colonialism and to a language for sexual and racial experimentation. Furthermore, as imperial logic is domesticated, it helps to make sense of the continuing need for imperial and colonial practice. In other words, the circulation of imperial logic at home helps to justify, and even make necessary, continuing and new colonial and imperial projects in the West and overseas.

Imperial Blues considers how jazz cultures are a particularly useful site for investigating these connections, working as a contact zone for a multiplicity of discourses and practices anchored in imperial logic. This book defines jazz cultures broadly, as places where nightlife, music and dance performance, art making, and novel writing collide with newspaper reportage, the scientific discourses of sociology and sexology, vice reports, and policing, and it draws the uneasy parameters of subjectivity and subjection, resistance and assimilation. Although this text is about jazz cultures, my focus is not always on the music, but often on spaces of musical performance. In order to understand the modes of racialization, sexual expression, regulatory regimes, and the imperial imagination, I interest myself more broadly in the context in which jazz is played in public; the dances that might accompany jazz performance; floor shows; novelty songs; theatre; yellow journalism reporting on the chaos of the Jazz Age; music-oriented fiction, poetry, and graphic art; and vice reports aimed at monitoring and regulating this context. In doing so, I bring together texts and theories that may at first appear unconnected but whose discursive formations and regimes of representation often overlap, in order to show how empire informed the material and symbolic borders of the city. In this way, I hope to uncover the context that helps to make meaning for jazz. For example, in chapters 1 and 3, I examine the city's extravagant, multi-ethnic, multiracial, and polysexual ball scenes, where dancers crossdressed and wore costumes signaling imperial time and space from around the globe and throughout history. While these scenes were monitored by police and vice investigators, and the sexuality of the participants questioned in scientific reports, the mixing of people from various neighborhoods and countries created new meanings for space that simultaneously drew on and challenged discourses of empire. The alternative archive in which this book is situated provides new opportunities to work through these pro-ductive, repressive, and transgressive strains of jazz cultures as discursive inventions and improvisations tethered to the expansion of empire. Jazz cultures, I argue, are a key site for intimacies between colony and metro-pole, between the realms of art and science, between bodies across bound-aries, and the other vectors of contact and encounter that form the heart of this book.

Central to this book's discussion of the logic of empire, orientalisms made the distant proximate, the national intimate, and the domestic for-eign. Performances of the "Orient," through the hoochy coochy dancer or the cabaret's chinoiserie, brought its signs and symbols closer and ascribed to these bodies and spaces discourses of oriental sexual excess as promis-cuity, (queer) perversion, or liberation from bourgeois norms—sometimes all three at once. Orientalisms also described and circumscribed the bodies and movements of Asians and Asian Americans who entered spaces of nightlife, mingling there with other members of the city's multiracial popu-lace. Both imperial fantasies and diasporics' joint presence speak to epis-temological and material intimacies across continents. In her important essay "The Intimacies of Four Continents," Lisa Lowe uses three meanings of *intimacy* in defining the "intimacies of four continents": first, intimacy as "spatial proximity or adjacent connection," as in the case of "the political economic logics through which men and women from Africa and Asia were forcibly transported to the Americas"; second, as the biopolitical management of forms of gender and sexuality within (and without) the bounded bourgeois private sphere; and third, as "the volatile contacts of colonized peoples," including sexual, laboring, and intellectual contacts that often involved fears of racial mixture and unstable social order.[6] Lowe's schema provides a way to understand how imperial logic underlies aesthetic production in the Jazz Age, guided by new and continuing forms of empire. These frameworks are especially useful for thinking about jazz cultures through the multiple modes of intimacy that brought people together across national borders and that directed and regulated the forms of desire and anxiety circulating among them. Such intimacies between continents are brought to bear on the close encounters found in nightclubs and cabarets and balls and bedrooms, where imperial logic transformatively impacted encounters between empires, nations, and bodies.

Imperial Blues moves along these geographies to analyze the logic of empire on, first, New York as an imperial metropole and its jazz cultures, through which various racialized and nationalized groups were resignified by the circulations of imperial logic and signs, whether dangerous embodiments of sexual savagery or sensual seduction located on particular bodies in the dance hall; second, productions of knowledge about the racialized borders of neighborhoods through colonial discourses of invasion and occupation; and third, practices of local surveillance that drew on the government of empire. In this project, then, imperial logic shaped the movements of individuals and populations, as well as the construction of categories that engendered new forms of creative expression and claims to imperial selfhood.

IMPERIAL CITY

How did these intimacies come to be? What accounts for the imperial imagination in the Jazz Age? What effect did the presence of new immigrants from imperial outposts have on shifting currents of culture and politics in the city? How did they fit into a domestic racial order? How were they fathomed through prevailing and emerging discourses about sexual perversity or biological degeneration? How did the signs and symbols of the places the immigrants had left—or had never known, because so many of these signs and symbols were already hybrid in their origins—follow them to this imperial city? Together, these issues begin to explain the relations of love and hatred (and indifference), and of intimacy and distance between bodies and between continents, that played out within New York's public cultures.

If jazz cultures act as a contact zone, the first question I want to address is who is in that zone of contact. To do this, I turn to some demographic information that shows that immigration, caused in part by U.S. imperial expansion and the aftermath of World War I, made New York an extremely diverse space. The diversity of the urban landscape, however, did not mean that there was equality between participants in New York's nightlife; rather, the melting pot was set to an anxious simmer. The influx of new U.S. nationals, the movement of people of color from southern states to northern cities, and their interactions with the people already there were considered fraught with peril. Often narrated as a danger to white women, interactions between races were sexualized, criminalized, and otherwise made strange through the use of imperial logic. This meant that people at once found the city space invigorating and in need of regulation. In this section, I explore the making of this multiracial space and begin to point to the anxieties these shifting demographic arrangements caused.

Much of the great shift in New York's population during the Jazz Age was accounted for by immigrants from imperial sites and Europeans trying to make a new start following World War I. Migration internal to the United States accounted for another significant change in population, as workers from rural parts of the U.S. South moved to industrialized northern cities. New York City's population demonstrated these dramatic transformations wrought by war and industry. During the Great Migration following World War I, three-quarters of a million African Americans left the South to work and settle in industrial cities like Chicago, Detroit, Philadelphia, and New York.[7] In New York City alone, the black population grew from less than 100,000 in 1910 to more than 300,000 two decades later.[8] Furthermore, rapid industrialization as well as "massive troop deployments during imperialist expansion and occupation, the World Wars, and other military projects" moved hundreds of thousands of working- and middle-class men (and some women) to city centers.[9] In addition to these internal migrations, successive waves of documented and undocumented immigrants continued to enter the country, many from places with which the United

States had histories of economic and imperial relations. Immigrants from Canada, China, Japan, the Philippines, Western and Eastern Europe, the Pacific Islands, Puerto Rico, Cuba, and other Caribbean nations made up a growing percentage of New York City's population. Sailors and merchants from imperial outposts followed trade routes and troop deployments to new ports along the U.S. imperial archipelago. Taken together, these migrations force us to widen our understandings of race in Jazz Age New York beyond a dichotomous color line, thinking instead in terms of a larger colonial and imperial scope through which New York becomes an imperial city that might also tell stories about the Philippines, Cuba, Puerto Rico, Malaysia, Thailand, and the Pacific Islands, as well as European settlement and African diaspora.

The kinds of racial, national, gendered, and sexual contact that occurred in the city, imagined through colonial actions and brought about by imperialism, also bear the burden of representation that inscribed modernity on the streets of New York in the Jazz Age. Indeed, scholars in postcolonial studies have long theorized that the colonies were influential in shaping the metropole and have connected that influence with the production of ideas of "the modern."[10] This is an apt description of New York City in the Jazz Age. The very name of the period that began after World War I and lasted into the Great Depression—the Jazz Age, a term coined by the novelist F. Scott Fitzgerald—was shot through with such contradictions. Named for the popular music that was understood to capture the modern spirit as the U.S. empire marched across the globe, the Jazz Age usefully gathers the threads of contact and movement between parts of the world, though these were hardly experienced in the same way by everyone. The end of the transatlantic slave trade in the preceding decades had been followed by waves of "free" indentured laborers from Asia (often called coolies), arriving to work in Hawaii, California, and New York.[11] At the turn of the century, the U.S. empire swelled with the acquisition of Mexican territories, violence against and displacement of indigenous populations, and the wartime acquisition of Hawaii, Cuba, Puerto Rico, Guam, Panama, and the Philippines. These instances of both material and symbolic racial violence also enabled great leaps in technological progress and economic prosperity, encouraging the growth of industrial capital and urbanization and creating and circulating new consumer goods and entertainments. These modes of explaining, selling, and regulating the city became marks of modernity, and New York situated itself as the Empire City within a cultural and social global economy.

The production of urban space through imperial discourses and through a shifting population also provided the means for the creation of a modern aesthetic culture. That is, aesthetic production in the Jazz Age was guided through imperial metaphor, read as dangerous through interracial contact, and rendered alluring through the sexualization of space. Indeed, the development of the modern city in the early twentieth century, Raymond Williams observes, had much "to do with imperialism: with the magnetic concentration of wealth and power in imperial capitals and the simultaneous cosmopolitan access to a wide variety of subordinate cultures." "Within many capital cities," he continues, "and especially within the major metropolises, there was at once a complexity and a sophistication of social relations, supplemented in the most important cases . . . by exceptional liberties of expression."[12] These liberties of expression, I would argue, were grounded in imperial logic—a logic that might in some situations fight against the domestic social order, and in other instances might help maintain that social order. Aesthetic modernisms such as Art Deco and primitivism drew inspiration from colonial aesthetics, while the New Woman who danced the fox-trot and bound her breasts ushered in for some people a newly streamlined modern femininity, for instance. This abundance and avant-gardism was countered, however, by tempering forces, including Prohibition and other civilian and state stratagems to curb "vice," which saw a moral crisis in such rapid metamorphosis. Indeed, these shifting currents of sounds and images, politics and art, proved to be both disquieting and vitalizing.

In fact, the presence of all the world's peoples gathered together on this island metropolis was mobilized to fashion U.S. exceptionalism as a global spirit and a global culture. New York City was (and still is) understood as a crossroad of the world, and thus some of its denizens imagined themselves as world travelers, even if they did not leave the city. Especially during the Jazz Age, city restaurants, nightclubs, speakeasies, and cabarets made reference to this U.S. exceptionalism through far-flung geographic references, such as the names of the Roumanian Restaurant Inn, the Moscow Inn, the Parisian, Egyptian Garden, the Hacienda Club, Chez Mecca, the Riviera, the Coconut Grove, the International Café, Sugar Cane Inn, the Russian Palace, Bolivar Café, the Tokio, and the Little World Café.[13] These names connected city to empire as the United States stretched into the Pacific, the Caribbean, and Central and South America, and they reflected the experiences of travel and displacement of migrants and refugees caused by World War I and U.S. imperial expansion. We might observe further that these contact zones enacted a sort of racial liberalism, inasmuch as new immigrants might be perceived in what Carrie Tirado Bramen names an "urban picturesque," which contributed the "best" of the world's unique cultures to the United States as a global exemplar. In this manner, Bramen argues, "the urban picturesque was an important vehicle for transforming immigrants from social threats to cultural resources, as signs of an urban identity but also of a national one. It was part of a cosmopolitanism with modern Americanism."[14] It would be no understatement to say that the imperial imagination of the co-presence and encounter of peoples and places from around the globe within the city ascribed meaning to those people, those spaces, and New York City as a whole, although, importantly, power across these geographies of scale might be distributed unevenly.

The notion of racial and ethnic tourism that work like Bramen's relies on made sense to tourists and city residents alike, but it told only part of the story of race, ethnicity, and sexuality in New York's neighborhoods. Those neighborhoods were, and still are, marked by racial and ethnic signifiers, but the neighborhoods' boundaries were imminently permeable, and their populations were much more diverse than the schematic renderings would have one believe. Harlem, for instance, was a neighborhood marked by blackness. It was most often described as a site of black natives and white interlopers, but Asians, Latinos, people from the Caribbean, and some white ethnics also populated what was often referred to as the colony of Harlem.[15] Alongside the black and white *flâneurs* and *flâneuses* who promenaded along its avenues, Asian and Italian immigrants also carved out a niche within the bustling metropolis.[16] Harlem's black denizens themselves were quite diverse, with 40 percent being foreign-born migrants.[17] The Harlem Renaissance journalist, novelist, and playwright Wallace Thurman notes: "There is no typical Harlem Negro as there is no typical American Negro. There are too many different types and classes. White, yellow, brown and black and all the intervening shades. North American, South American, African and Asian; Northerner and Southerner."[18] In an essay on the "real Harlem," Thurman and William Jourdan Rapp observe:

Like New York, Harlem is a cosmopolitan city. Its people are as varied and polyglot as could be found anywhere. The whites indiscriminately lump them together as "Negroes" or "niggers." But they are really unclassifiable under any existent ethnic term, for the racial complexity of the American Negro is astounding. In his veins flows the mixed bloods of the Africans from whom he originally stemmed, the American Indians with whom he intermarried in pre- and post-slavery days, and of every white race under the sun. And then in Harlem this home-grown ethnic amalgam is associating and inter-mixing with Negroes from the Antipodes and Caribees, from Africa and Asia, South America and every other place that dark-skinned people hail from.[19]

Cosmopolitan and polyglot, connected to nations and peoples across the globe, Harlem's spatial and racial narration stretched to make present and proximate the multiple histories of colonialism and imperialism that constructed New York's heterogeneous population. Furthermore, imperialism, as a heuristic device, exposes the black-white binary that often characterizes scholarship on the Harlem Renaissance as inadequate to describing blackness, whiteness, or the plethora of imperial subjects visiting and living in Manhattan. The work before you, then, in lieu of presenting a stable, untroubled mapping of the racial and ethnic neighborhoods of Manhattan, suggests that the borders between neighborhoods—and, indeed, between cities, regions, and nations—is always already varied.

Restaurants and spaces of nightlife provided prime real estate for this kind of intermingling and neighborhood border crossing. Indeed, a typical space for jazz culture, like a dance hall, demonstrates how these forms of racial contact, which were simultaneously erased by the idea of racially bordered neighborhoods and monitored because those borders were never secure, caused a variety of reactions from city inhabitants and city fathers. Intertwining the presence of Asian immigrants with black creative endeavors, empire sets a context for, but is also sited in, the dance hall. The dance hall acts as one useful space I pursue in this book to investigate the multiple connections that extend across oceans and national borders, across histories of racial labor, across techniques and methods of representation, across scientific imperatives and aesthetic movements, across kinetic energies bounding between jangling limbs and pursed lips. The movements of so many people from so many places failed to escape the notice of civic authorities, who viewed such promiscuous contact as a social threat. Although the mixing of peoples and cultures allowed New York to boast of its cosmopolitan character, it also led to innumerable moral panics.

Painted as corrupting, sexualized contact between races was part and parcel of the Jazz Age's zeitgeist, which embraced the exuberance of a space like the dance hall but also controlled what was viewed as deleterious behavior. This era ushered in the pernicious passage of anti-immigrant legislation, bolstered by the eugenic sciences that sought to sharply curb the presence of supposedly inferior stock inside the nation's boundaries. Such panics about racial contamination and their attendant spatialization also led to stricter municipal regulations for the licensing of cabarets and dance halls, which were already largely aimed at spaces where people of color gathered or, worse yet, people from across the "color line." In reference to the racial and sexual dangers presented by this kind of comingling, in 1926 the Board of Alderman flatly noted that "when strangers came to New York they wanted to 'run wild'" in Harlem.[20] Multiracial dance halls, one of the contact zones discussed in chapter 1, provided police and vice investigators with volatile ground for monitoring encounters between white women and men of color. The inappropriateness of the assumed sexual proximity written not only through race but also through space demonstrates how racial others "come to embody distance."[21] The composite gaze of vice investigators, newspaper reporters, social scientists, and state authorities sought to implement boundaries of nation and empire in the city, reinforcing the understanding of Asian immigrants in the multiracial dance hall as strangers, not belonging to the places where they now lived and where empire had carried them. Jazz Age New York City, then, was constructed through an imperial logic that governed immigration and integration but also engendered modernist and avant-garde movements in politics and arts (and emerging subject positions through these movements), linked by New Yorkers' material and immaterial encounters with the sounds and signs of outposts of empire and other faraway lands.

SPACE AND SUBJECTIVITY

One of the major tenets of this book is that imperial logic is based in mutable meanings attached to stories about space. Spatial narratives provide the basis for understanding the confluence of the U.S. imperium, U.S. racialized domestic space, regulation and excess of sexualized bodies, and aesthetic production. Space, race, and intimacy together render sensible various modes of subjectivity: from reclamations of a primitivized Africa to create the New Negro to performances of orientalized dances to sustain the New Woman, from the renaming of Harlem as a "Mecca" to make the space and its inhabitants both exotic and important to the renaming of black and white men as "sheiks" to instantiate their sexual prowess or excess. Nightly negotiations over subjectivity (and its value as ascribed through imperial personhood) helped to reproduce modes of empire, whether performers and artists reclaimed Africa's past, imagined themselves as conquerors, or performed versions of exotic and sexualized masculinities and femininities; or whether the police, courts, journalists, and vice investigators, whose supposed task was to control these types of displays, might also produce that conspicuously consumable exoticism so that these spaces and bodies might continue to be regulated. From discourses of orientalized sexual freedom to justifications for internal colonialism, the ideology of empire broke through the borders of the city to mark its inhabitants as ready for subjectivity or subjection. In this way, modes of resistance and regulation, subject making and disciplining, worked together to bolster and reproduce imperial logic across an ever-changing variety of situations, bodies, and spaces.

In the Jazz Age, to borrow a phrase from Langston Hughes, blackness was in vogue.[22] However, the meanings ascribed to Harlem and its residents were heterological. If the fact that blackness was "in vogue" means only that it was simply prized or exoticized, then this vogue does not speak to the complexities of how these two treatments might work together to produce a sense of racial and spatial difference. I suggest that the vogue of blackness was more complex and that it was informed, at least in part, by imperial logic's creation of a spatial and ideological distance between the rest of the city and Harlem and its residents. As an image and a style, "Harlem" traveled around the world. Indeed, North American jazz and the literature and arts of the Harlem Renaissance came to stand for the spirit of the modern age. For instance, though hailing from Los Angeles, the jazz trumpeter Buck Clayton and his orchestra were nonetheless billed in Shanghai as the "Harlem Gentlemen," so large did this New York neighborhood loom in the spatial narration of black America.[23] At the same time, between World Wars I and II the signs and objects of primitivism, which drew heavily on European appropriations (and inventions) of African aesthetics, became symbols of the avant-garde in European modernist culture. Such negrophile movements spoke in celebratory terms about all things *nègre*—an expansive category that combined North American jazz and the literature of the Harlem Renaissance with African and Oceanic carvings and Josephine Baker's delirious performances—at the same time that they sought to preserve the primitive as such.[24] As moderns searched for new and novel forms to arouse the senses, stereotypes about the racial other that had long been coupled with civilizational backwardness and moral depravity became symbols of authentic freedom and spontaneous creativity. Such an aesthetics was duplicitous for, as Simon Gikandi notes, it is instead the modern who comes to understand or fashion his or her personhood, a process in which the racial other is used as both "raw material" and counterpoint: "Savagery and the artistic sensibility would intimately be connected in the aesthetic of modernism; however, it did not follow that the moderns were willing to give up civilization to become one with the savage."[25] As with orientalism, primitivism produced a discourse about the racial other through a double bind of idealization and denigration. In either case, the racial other must stay in its place. Here collocated with imperial logic, both orientalism and primitivism transformed the imaginable range of human possibilities through modernist reinventions, while reinforcing the spatial and temporal distancing of racial others.

It is in this way that Jazz Age Harlem was a site of contradictory spatial ideologies. Often referred to as Black Manhattan or the Black Mecca, Harlem was alternately located as the seat of the aesthetic modern, adjoining but also distinct from the imperial city, and as a domestic Arabia recalling oriental and African tropes. This spatial confusion, caused by a reordering of referentiality, allows us to address the intersections of national and imperial discourses of race and space. For example, the Romanian immigrant Konrad Bercovici, in his 1924 travelogue called *Around the World in New York*, included in his chapter on Africa the nightlife of Harlem, along with a tour of its literary and political stars.[26] Such perceptions of distance and intimacy, mapped onto a distinction between a modern United States and a backward Africa, were profoundly felt in Harlem itself. Regarding the travels of black people to Harlem, Thurman and Rapp observed: "The American Negro looks down upon these foreigners just as the white American looks down upon the white immigrants from Europe. The native black man takes pride in the fact that he is a citizen of the 'world's greatest country' and is proud that he has had the advantages of a supposedly superior civilization, with modern plumbing, a system of education and high wages."[27] These remarks raise numerous questions about spatial narrations of African American subjectivity with and sometimes against the United States as nation and as empire. Spatial narrations derived from imperial logic made distinctions between black progress (made by citizens of "the 'world's greatest country'") and black primitivism (people without "modern plumbing") that were located on black bodies.[28] In similar fashion, orientalisms also presented a way for people struggling for recognition as U.S. subjects to identify with Western civilization, in contrast to the benighted other. Contrasting themselves with the oriental woman confined to the harem, and to a despotic sexual slavery, some African American women (and some white women) dancing like Salomé sought to claim imperial personhood through discourses of mastery and distance from the Arabian other, for instance. In order to claim citizenship in the present, these women relegated the material history of black women's exploitation in the United States to the past and displaced it onto the premodern, orientalist other. However, the women were circumscribed in advance of— and especially during—their performances through a dangerous intimacy with the racial other. References to imperial logic, therefore, foster myriad possibilities for self-fashioning, but as Minnie the Moocher might attest, these are not reducible to freedom or captivity through such uneven and contradictory encounters. In reconsidering what have been seen as separate realms of material and immaterial forces—nation and empire—and their profound consequences for subject formation and art making, I trace this imperial logic as intertwined with the constant negotiation involved in the story of racialized peoples' incorporation into U.S. modernity.

This book calls attention to the continuities and discontinuities between imperial and domestic categories of modern selfhood and subjection through spatial narratives of movement, intimacy, and distance. In this study, race and sex refer to mutable, "dense transfer point[s]" of power, to draw on Michel Foucault, that are embedded within histories of empire, including the transatlantic slave trade and Asian coolie labor, and also situated within national cultures.[29] These are distinct, but not discrete, realms, and this study follows a wayward path between movements and contacts between continents in order to connect the material conditions of empire and industrial capital with emerging articulations of subjecthood and cultural labor. The rise of Western imperialisms and modernisms are linked, yet, as Fredric Jameson observes, the encounter between these historical movements does not reside just in content, but also in form.[30] In this book, I hope to show that empire both opened and resolved crises of differentiation about the content of the modern, through recourse to discourses and practices about space as the way of interpreting and managing these crises.

Practices of orientalism and primitivism and the rewriting of Harlem as Mecca or Africa conjure up the relationship between spatialization and subjectivity. Thus, much of my focus in this book is on the power granted through narrations of subjectivity, and how very tenuous that power might be. Building on this sense of space and subjectivity, I foreground imperialism as a constellation of power—not simply power over, but rather a field of forces that makes sensible, and sense of, many types of relations through spatial metaphors and exercises.[31] As seen above, this takes place in the city through the renarration of space as being about power, race, sexuality, and subjectivity. My understanding of power, space, and subjectivity comes in part from the work of Michel Foucault. In the lectures collected as *The Birth of Biopolitics*, he argues that modern forms of subjectivity and subjection operate via both micropowers (which might intimately interact with the regulation of the body or create docile subjects) and macropractices (like the management of the body politic or the social body), and our critical queries as such must accommodate a variety of stops along a geographic scale, tied together through systems of thought. Foucault's intent was "to see the extent to which we could accept that the analysis of micro-powers, or of procedures of governmentality, is not confined by definition to a precise domain determined by a sector of the scale, but should be considered simply as a point of view, a method of decipherment which may be valid for the whole scale, whatever its size. In other words, the analysis of micro-powers is not a question of scale, and it is not a question of a sector, it is a question of a point of view."[32] My interest in this formulation is in Foucault's use of space, power, management, and thought. He holds that power works along geographies of scale, but that management happens in the most intimate of spaces and in the grand strokes of institutions, which in the Jazz Age might be represented by the police or the courts. For the purposes of my project, I imagine the system of thought—what Foucault calls "a point of view"—as produced by imperial logic. The spaces touched by this logic are not confined, in part because it hinges on the continuous unfolding of its "point of view" across the globe, and thus should be considered crucial to deciphering power elsewhere on the scale, which in this book is focused on the U.S. imperium; Manhattan; and its neighborhoods, cabarets and dance halls, and vice investigators and nightlife enthusiasts.

Indeed, beginning with the imperial contact coincident with the Enlightenment, discourses of race and subjectivity have been drawn from encounters with distant or intimate others. Thus, concepts of freedom and self-possession crucial to liberal selfhood are deeply embedded within spatial formations of the modern nation and empire. Charles W. Mills and Denise Ferreira da Silva, for example, both argue that race is a global idea that has persisted since the Enlightenment. For Mills, this has taken the form of "racial liberalism," as seen in Immanuel Kant's reflections. Mills writes: "Kant, the most important ethicist of the modern period and the famous theorist of personhood and respect, turns out to be one of the founders of modern scientific racism, and thus a pioneering theorist of sub-personhood and disrespect. . . . So the inferior treatment of people of color is not at all incongruent with racialized liberal norms, since by those norms nonwhites are less than full persons."[33] For Silva, such modes of Enlightenment personhood continue to persist through raciality despite declarations to the contrary: "The Subject is dead! we have been told. So why is its most effective strategy of power still with us?"[34] My answer to this query is, in part, that modes of resistance still rely on imperial logic, even as we are left with subject-effects rather than Cartesian subjects, and that modes of power that rely on racial, sexual, gendered, and national difference can continue to reproduce themselves. In fact, the dissemination of imperial logic helps promote these very modes, whether one resists them (for resistance needs to create systems to resist) or perpetuates them (for perpetuation requires the remaking of challenges to the social order).

My interest here is to understand how Enlightenment notions of subjectivity are rendered meaningful through racial reference and spatial narratives that serve to divide humanity. The Cartesian subject, for instance, did not just demarcate the seat of reason in the mind against the body (a kind of spatialization of the consciousness). In Cartesian thought, space was understood as static and absolute, against which consciousness was produced—in Henri Lefebvre's words, "as Object opposed to Subject, as *res extensa* opposed to, and present to, *res cogitans*."[35] For Kant, space became a way to know particular peoples through their distinction and demarcation, although such knowing was an extension of the (European and imperial) Subject. For instance, in his 1764 essay "Of National Characteristics, so Far as They Depend upon the Distinct Feeling of the Beautiful and the Sublime," Kant suggests that various racial populations are knowable and divisible (again, to the Enlightenment subject) according to their spatial occupations, so that Persians were designated as sensual and unreliable, and black Africans vulgar.[36] Thus does imperial contact assert that "otherwise diverse phenomena" should be grouped "into a single category or class"—again, a spatial metaphor that places objects (or peoples) together.[37] Furthermore, such placements help us make sense of the nation as a space. As Sara Ahmed explains, "the nation becomes imagined and embodied as a space, not simply by being defined as close to some others (friends), and further away from other others (strangers)."[38] We can elaborate on this understanding to note that these metaphors of "close" and "further away" also engender a point of view internal to national space: "other others" need not be outside the borders of the nation proper, but only identified or connected with extranational spaces.[39] It is in this way that space as both a physical and a metaphorical organization assigns subjectivity and subjection to particular groups and bodies. As we shall see, forms of resistance to, or preservation of, the social order or prescribed selfhood are thus intimately embodied through spatial discourses and practices.

If the terms of subjectivity that concerned Enlightenment philosophers were made sensible through both physical demarcations of space and spatial narratives, through imperial logic such terms were further wrought by trajectories of movement and contact. Whether actual traffic or imaginative metaphor, movement acts as a primary mode for meaning making via spatial logics. Movement and the contact it engenders can function, for example, as an enhancement, the modern's freedom as mobility; as displacement, the removal or expulsion of a person or peoples from one place to another; or as a contravention, the breach of safety and security by a wayward other. These are not distinct, and also not necessarily discrete, movements. Most obviously, the myth of Manifest Destiny connects the crucible of a U.S.-based selfhood with the ruthless expulsion of and continued violence against indigenous populations in the name of territorial expansion and settler colonialism. So, too, did modernist aesthetics depend on mystified metaphors of movement, signifying commercial and leisure tourism as well as elite, individualized travel in an era of expanding the U.S. reach around the world. To travel the world one need not go far; the cosmopolitan character of New York hangs on a "naturalized" mixing of peoples and cultures, and movement through the city is to experience the whole world. Yet, as transnational feminist scholars such as Caren Kaplan and Inderpal Grewal demonstrate so well, cosmopolitanism and colonialism are inextricably linked in cultures of travel.[40] Inasmuch as immigrants—not a homogeneous group themselves—provide the raw materials for the creation of the global city and give cosmopolitans in search of travel opportunities for spatial expeditions, they are not themselves recognized as cosmopolitans, or as producers of modernist culture.[41] Kaplan notes that such manifold "questions of travel" therefore operate as "signs of different critical registers and varied historicized instances."[42] Although to be modern might equate with the exercise of freedom of movement, not all those who moved could be understood as modern. And though the city was understood as modernist through movement, not all who lived in the city were recognized as modern or mobile. Imperialism and its spatial narratives spurred some migrations of less modern peoples through the forces of labor and capital and narrated some racialized groups as immobile, lending its ordering logic as a means of disciplining these wayward populations. Furthermore, some subjects experienced multiple forms of movement, such as forced migration but also pleasurable travel, whether real, imagined, or both (as in the case of Minnie in her adventures to Chinatown and on to exotic lands). As Kaplan observes, "many modern subjects may participate in any number of the versions of displacement over a lifetime—never embodying any one version singly or simplistically," and therefore "the material conditions of displacement for many people blur these distinctions."[43] What I draw from this insight for the project at hand is that real and imagined travel, both modes of imperial formation, do not necessarily signal just one meaning for any one person; rather, the meanings instilled by notions of travel form subjectivities that are multiple and changeable. This mode of subject making, then, reiterates the forms imperial logic takes as simultaneously resistant and regulatory, as complex and often contradictory.

Modes of spatial displacement—the renaming of Harlem as Mecca or Africa, travel across neighborhood borders, and travel across regional or national borders—can be used to think about how travel across empires, both actual and ideological, shaped the ordering of bodies, races, neighborhoods, cities, and nations. To establish a comparative analytic in this book, then, I consider how distance and intimacy play out both within an empire and between empires. Through the first frame, *internal colonialism* becomes for me a term of comparison, allowing linkages within a single empire across oceans or borders. Following Linda Gordon's definition of the concept, I see internal colonialism as not only denaturalizing national boundaries as proper and inevitable, but also as allowing us to recognize that some racial others are always already strangers to the national polity.[44] Chinatown inhabitants were spatialized as foreign, for instance, nearer to China than to New York and otherwise belonging to another, strange social order.[45] Harlem, too, was understood as a colony by tourists and civic-minded scolds alike; as I show in chapter 4, the former found in Harlem an exotic destination, and the latter a depraved nature. These analogies, which often depended on naturalized relations of racial intimacy, thus perform specific cultural and political labors. In seeking to understand their implications for this colony of Harlem or Minnie's Chinatown, I reclaim the term through feminist and queer of color critique and deploy the concept to understand the strength of racial discourses as their mutable and movable components as well as to comprehend the concept's gendered and sexual imbrications, in contingent and contiguous intimacies with empires.

I also reposition domestic racial and sexual classifications and concerns through the idea of comparative empire. Imperial tropes often situated in domestic racial and sexual schemata were not entirely of U.S. invention. Rather, references to Arabian deserts or Indonesian batik fabrics drew heavily on far-flung dominions including the British, French, Spanish, Dutch, and Portuguese Empires. Indeed, the fantasy of escape from bourgeois sexual norms through contact with and sometimes conquest of racial others, including Salomés, Madama Butterflies, and sheiks, was shared across European and U.S. empires and aesthetic modernisms.[46] Tropes that came from other empires, like the British or the French, found their way into the lexicon of U.S. empire through the circulation of novels like E. M. Hull's *The Sheik*; operatic performances like Henry Hadley's *Cleopatra's Night*; competitive collecting by museums of Egyptian artifacts; and travel across imperial territories by would-be adventurers, tourists, and artists. Categorical creations (and confusions) regarding sex, race, civilization, and humanity thus traveled through such intimacies among four continents, becoming transfigured as people encountered strangers in contact zones close to home, refashioned themselves through the signs and symbols of racial others from distant lands, or found themselves brought closer together in body or metaphor for various purposes.[47] Indeed, to this end Ann Laura Stoler writes that studies in comparison allow us to denaturalize the nation as a "historiographic directive," interpret metropole and colony as one analytic field, and fathom those circuits of knowledge and cultural production and governance moving between the United States and its outposts, between the United States and other spaces of empire.[48] With this methodological insight into the work of comparative empire, I hope to push the spatial boundaries of what urban histories might take as their object in thinking through the definition of city borders and the systems of thought, policing, and pleasure that occur in cities and beyond.

Jazz Age New York is thus replete with the material and metaphor of empire, crucial to the forms of subjecthood and cultural production that came to define this period's political and aesthetic modernisms. To better grasp the consequences of such material and metaphor requires histories of cultural labors that illuminate emerging and often complicated subject positions, and critical and cultural practices that are more receptive to transnational movements. *Imperial Blues* proposes paths of inquiry for some of these histories and labors, with the entangled rise of jazz and empire, by analyzing discourses of space that create new subject positions, negotiate power, and reiterate justifications for empire. Importantly, the reimagining of flexible urban borders—particularly as people and cultural objects move in and out of city space, and as artistic inspiration becomes the unbounded invention of tropical islands, East Asian royal courts, and North African desert landscapes—provides a valuable context for understanding the uneven distribution of value associated with personhood and the desire to police racial, sexual, and gendered boundaries.

INTIMATE COMPARISONS

Imperial Blues suggests a reorientation of Jazz Age New York, in multiple senses. I ask how differing orientations toward and away from the Orient, including the physical directionality of the body and its movements, might transform the meaning of race and sex in the imperial city. It would almost be an understatement to say that movement constitutes a source of both intense power and acute anxiety for the imperial management of race and space. Such movement is multidimensional or multidirectional—not just shifting resources and bodies for war or labor, but actually placing and replacing categories related to sex, race, civilization, and even humanity. This replacement—meaning substitution, settling, dislodging, and moving or redirecting elsewhere—is central to the ways through which imperial logic operates as a discourse of spatial and racial arrangement. At stake in this argument is a more complex account of how imperial logic territorializes spaces and bodies through new or transfigured orders of desire and danger, so that a subterranean cabaret in Harlem becomes an Arabian outpost, and those who are close (within the bounds of the city, a neighborhood, or the same dance hall) become materially and symbolically strange. In this I follow Ahmed, whose uses of the term *Orient* also elaborate on its multiple meanings simultaneously. "My analysis of orientalism," asserts Ahmed, "suggests that spaces become racialized by how they are directed or oriented, as a direction that follows a specific line of desire. It shows us how the Orient is not only imagined as 'being' distant, as another side of the globe, but also is 'brought home' or domesticated as 'something' that extends the reach of the West."[49] Ahmed's mode of analysis rethinks the meanings of space and how value is unevenly assigned to racialized and sexualized bodies described by different spaces. For Jazz Age New York, this analytic line intersects obliquely with analytics that imagine city space and the characterizations of urban residents as static and defined only through the immediate geography. Just as margins shape a text, what lies outside of the city also shapes our ideas about the modern city and the flappers, molls, dandies, and swells who winged their way along its boulevards.

In thinking through imperial logic's mobilization of distance, intimacy, and race, I also find it useful to turn to queer of color critique—a term coined by Roderick Ferguson[50]—as a mode of analysis, though with a difference. Because my interest is primarily in modes of imperial thought and draws heavily on postcolonial studies and postnational American studies for its methodological grounding, my use of queer of color critique necessarily joins with questions about the borders and meanings of national space. Queer of color critique itself draws on a genealogy of women of color feminisms to understand how analytic categories such as race, gender, and sexuality are related to structures of economy. In this process, Ferguson also uncovers the ways in which we are encouraged to think of these categories separately and what the cost of that kind of analysis is for social justice projects and aesthetic production. For example, racial analyses—such as those forwarded by the author Richard Wright, which do not account for gender and sexuality—retain hegemonic structures that ensure inequality. In this way, social justice projects that remain focused on one category of analysis might help reproduce modes of capitalist injustice. For my work, I foreground the aftereffects of imperial violence rather than political economy as a way to understand how personhood is drawn and valued. To do this, I extend the reach of queer of color critique to understand the relationships between nations, how those relationships are racialized and sexualized, and what that process means for the construction of identities and the policing of peoples within the borders of the United States.

It is in this way that *Imperial Blues* concerns itself with empire's repercussions in the intimate and public spaces of U.S. history in general, and Jazz Age New York in particular. Such a study must certainly include and account for Asian Americans in the racial mix of the city.[51] But it is even more critical to reframe the concept and lived experience of race through techniques and methods of rendering space, both as a politics of representation but also a practice of regulation, especially as technologies of race and racialization are founded on crises of differentiation that in turn hinge on fixed borders. For instance, Alva, the antagonist in Wallace Thurman's most famous novel, *The Blacker the Berry* . . . , is of mixed race—part white, part black, and part Filipino.[52] His movement across the city's strata as an ambivalent figuration of the Harlem Renaissance is made possible by his journey as an imperial subject to the imperial center. In contrast to a nation-based arrangement that isolates race and racialization within national borders, Thurman's Alva suggests that even domestic racial discourses of subjecthood (and objecthood) are created through transnational processes and imperial logic. The language of racial mixing, meant to guard the boundaries of race and sex in the city, often borrowed the rationale as well as the schema of empire and colonial rule to do so, imbricating the regulation of women's sexual behavior, men of color and their movements, and the distinction between public and private space and making them central to the governance of bodies. Even though racial classification itself is fraught with creative fancy, as Jennifer Brody notes in regard to racial taxonomies, "the language of purity is imprecise and impossible, as are the lines that distinguish (binary) categories."[53] Though racial (or sexual or gendered) categories are "impossible," it is still important to understand how they are mobilized and for what purposes. In Jazz Age New York, racial mixing might signal racial uplift, sexual freedom, or a reason for increased disciplinary attention. Indeed, municipal regulations even suppose that race and racialization might pass from neighborhood to neighborhood, raising the specter of contamination and degradation through zoning laws and other boundary enforcement. The language of racial mixing thereby suggests multiple forms of contact—of being touched by another, whether through sexual acts or mere proximate association—which requires further inquiry.

In the first two chapters of this book, I propose a staging of multiple, overlapping gradations of contact in order to understand the profound anxiety about the discrete otherness of racial bodies and, as we shall see, the objects appended to those bodies. That anxiety expressed itself through the policing of spaces where interracial contact could be construed as sexual, but it also created a queer black aesthetic that purposely played with and denied the expectation of stable boundaries (of race, gender, sexuality, and nation). How, then, do contact zones create crises of differentiation through a crisis of referentiality for imperial logic that seeks to draw distinct boundaries between bodies—those of a friend and a stranger, for instance—and between bodies and objects? That is, how is our desire for difference (both sexual and taxonomic) denied or enforced when the referent of discourses of race, primitivism, or orientalism moves across various bodies—like the orientalization of white men or women, or black men or women—rather than remaining attached to those bodies that are already coded as racialized in particular ways (like the orientalization of Asian or Asian American bodies), or are imagined as foreign and strange.

In chapter 1, I introduce the inhabitants of the city in more substantive ways. I argue that the sexual proximity and intimacy created in city spaces marked by interracial contact were presented as simultaneously alluring and dangerous. A configuration that drew readers, spectators, and customers to these spaces and stories about them also drew the attention of curious authorities like sexologists, sociologists, journalists, vice investigators, and the police. In examining the mix of bodies in these spaces, I elaborate on the concept of jazz cultures as a "contact zone," borrowing Mary Louise Pratt's formulation, to consider 1920s New York, the imperial city, as a space for improvisational encounters between empire's subjects.[54] Highlighting jazz's sensual and kinetic energies, and the discursive and performative productions of these energies, I argue that such contact is manifold. That is, jazz as a site—or an assemblage of spaces—draws bodies and movements together with popular and scientific discourses of racialized sexualities and across genres of cultural labor, including sexological studies, newspaper reportage, vice investigations, pulp fiction, and experimental literature. Jazz is therefore a contact zone struck through with desire and danger. From the dance hall where Asian immigrant men were thought to hold young white women much too close and the sensational reporting of the unsolved murder of Vivian Gordon, a former chorus girl thought to have been killed by variously racialized men—either a sheik, a Latin lover, or a "darktown gigolo"[55])—to Thurman's mixed-race queer characters in *The Blacker the Berry* . . . , I pursue the multiple discourses about race and sex that jazz cultures summon.

In these encounters we find Foucault's "especially dense transfer point[s] of power," through which imperial logic reverberates across domestic realms of gender and sexuality. Orientalisms in the popular cultures of the 1920s and 1930s borrowed from, and subsequently transformed, imperial signs and symbols to generate new cultural forms of sexual expression and popular entertainment as well as new languages of control about foreign bodies and domestic bodies made stranger. In thinking through these new forms and languages, I argue that the contact zone, subject to medical, hygienic, and regulatory gazes, is also a zone of ontological indeterminacy. In the sexological and eugenic sciences touched on in the book's first two chapters, mixed-race bodies and queer bodies metaphorically occupied such a zone as admixtures of supposedly discrete, but unstable, categories of race and sex. I argue that orientalisms have a significant effect on gender and sexual forms even in the absence of actual oriental bodies. Because orientalisms act as the signs and symbols of imperial projection, attached to particular bodies but not essential to them, the signs and symbols are mutable and mobile, repeating a crisis of referentiality that founded such imperial logic in the first place. The music, movements, and accouterment of spaces or bodies marked as oriental (including those assigned to East Asia, the Pacific Islands, Southeast Asia, West Asia, and North Africa) could easily be reproduced by—but also importantly on—cabarets and nightclubs as well as musicians and other performers in New York City. In the case studies I offer here, I argue that race and racialization thereby occur through modes of comparison and contact that are also spatial in nature— such as distance, contamination, analogy, intimacy, proximity, juxtaposition, and directionality.

In some of these cases, race and racialization may arise through an intimacy between a body and the signs and symbols of racial others from elsewhere in the empire. The body is the primary site implicated in racial discourse because race is presumed to be in but also on the body, and it is something that informs how bodies might sexually interact with one another. As Jennifer González notes, race is especially "subject to display": "There is no escape from the fact of its 'epidermalized' status; the materiality of the body is understood to offer a continuous surface of legible information."[56] Stuart Hall likewise observes—writing of the look that confirms the "fact of blackness," as Frantz Fanon argues—that "exclusion and abjection are imprinted on the body through the functioning of these signifiers as an objective taxonomy—a 'taxidermy'—of radicalized difference, a specular matrix of intelligibility."[57] With these remarks in mind, the mixed-race body renders narratively unintelligible the skin, now a suspect surface of disorienting information. Indeed, as I discuss in the first chapter, Thurman's Alva is one such figure, someone whose materiality confounds categories even as his depiction relies on the imperial logic based on those racial taxonomies. Because race as a category is struck through with sexual meaning—race might signal exotic and erotic pleasure, hypersexuality or sexual excess, or frigidity—the boundaries of race might also inform the boundaries of sexuality, and vice versa. This is certainly the case for Thurman's Alva, whose racial mix signals his bisexuality. For Thurman, the mixed-race body follows sexological knowledge that renders it simultaneously queer. In this way, expected connections between race and sexuality, and between the nation and the city, contribute to the meaning of bodies in the city and what dangers and pleasures their proximity held. The combination of unease and heightened desire for this kind of racial mixing, then, could produce a range of reactions: newspaper articles that breathlessly retold the story of intimacy, police raids and other forms of internal colonialism, and aesthetic portrayals intended as social commentary about the difficulties and joys of negotiating these various boundaries.

This kind of play between meaning and context, between danger and pleasure, and between race and sexuality, could, then, serve multiple purposes. Chapter 2, "Queer Modernities," centers on a crisis of referentiality arising when bodies imagined to signify categories that lend themselves to a stable social order within a national discourse instead refer to heterological and transient meanings conveyed by mutable and imperial geographic and ideological borders. Through the production of a crisis of referentiality, artists like the Harlem Renaissance writer, graphic artist, dancer, and bon vivant Richard Bruce Nugent fashioned a semantic, visual, and mobile vocabulary for queer black aesthetic practices. For this reading, I build on Jacques Rancière's notion of the "reconfiguration of the sensible" and the insights of queer of color critique to analyze Nugent's and Thurman's artworks as examples of their queer black aesthetic.[58] Nugent mobilized the signs and symbols of primitivism as avant-garde culture, reclaimed from the modernist movements in both Europe and the United States as particularly African, together with images and styles of the Orient, inherited from the European decadent queer canon, to collapse distances between maps and bodies. The chapter also discusses Thurman's presentation of Paul Arbian, a character inspired by Nugent, in his novel *Infants of the Spring*.[59] The figure of Arbian disrupts the boundaries of race, nation, gender, and sexuality. Thurman boldly juxtaposes and collapses these categories, referring to Puccini's *Madama Butterfly* and other famous imperial texts as a way to express the stakes involved in, and the purposeful tenuousness of, a queer black aesthetic. By commingling primitivism and orientalism, Nugent and Thurman seek to escape referential certainties, even while they rely on empire's signs and symbols. In this way, the wielding of imperial logic both set the stage for an assertion of queer sexuality and imposed limits on the representations of that sexuality.

The transgression and transformation of boundaries remain central to this chapter. Through the works discussed in it, I show that Nugent and Thurman adopt multiple strategies for confounding—or, indeed, queering—those forms of knowledge built on spatial and racial arrangements, including doubling, collocation, and collapsing. All these forms come together in Nugent's novella "The Geisha Man,"[60] whose protagonist is the mixed-race child of Butterfly and Pinkerton, Puccini's operatic lovers. Following this character, named Kondo Gale Matzuika, as he experiences various spatial and racial dislocations as a Japanese prostitute, immigrant to the United States, and queer black man reveling in Manhattan's polysexual, multiracial ball scene (which I also describe in more detail in chapters 1 and 3), Nugent whimsically fictionalizes the meanings of bodies, objects, and fantasies flowing across borders and the changes these bring to modes of identification. In doing so, Nugent questions the ontological determinacy of bodies and objects, and the use of race and sex as maps for their distinction. Through the accouterment of an Orient perceived as particularly queer, Nugent's works—including his best work, his life—seek to interrupt the referentiality of the black body and the perception of the space of that body's gestures and movements, within both political and aesthetic modernisms.

As I describe in the second part of this book, the traffic in Araby during the 1920s relied on intimacies between empires. In the final two chapters, I focus on circulations of the signs and symbols of North Africa and West Asia throughout Jazz Age New York, shifting the timeline of U.S. interest in these regions from the standard origin after 1945 into the Jazz Age. Though the United States did not have a direct colonial relationship with North Africa or West Asia in the 1920s or 1930s, it was nonetheless expanding its imperial interests in these regions through informal means (for instance, the Metropolitan Museum of Art funded and supported the excavations of the British Egyptologist Howard Carter) and through cultural and political exchanges with the French and British Empires, which did directly rule parts of these regions. These chapters thereby explore comparative practices of empire. Stories about intrepid archaeologists unearthing ancient treasures in the desert circulated in newspapers and popular magazines, and Hollywood studio productions such as *The Sheik* (1921), set in Algeria, or *The Thief of Baghdad* (1924), set in Persia—featuring enslaved princesses, irresistible princes, and rapacious sultans—all suggest contact between empires.

Looking at multiple orientations toward Arab embodiment and movement, chapter 3, "Orienting Subjectivities," focuses on performances of Salomé and sheiks by a diverse group of performers—none of them Asian or Asian American—to consider how each might embody a politics of space as particularized subjects through their world facing, to and away from the Orient and the U.S. empire. I rely here on the heuristic devices of the archive and the repertoire as discussed by Diana Taylor and Jacques Derrida in order to understand the formation of subjectivity across diverse bodies.[61] Although the collection of artifacts, even those for live performance, is associated with archivists' projects that lend a sense of distance and, in turn, mastery over the objects being created, the repertoire slides more generously into that foundation of native goods and acts for, collapsed, into, and performed. My argument, then, explores the slippages between these imperially forged categories and attempts to understand the difference that race makes in performances of empire's elsewheres. For instance, white women who sought to claim an imperial selfhood through imperial activities, such as collecting the forms and objects of civilizational others, nonetheless found themselves as performers too close to these forms and objects to be judged through rubrics of expertise. Indeed, their orientalist archives marked them as cosmopolitan, but their repertoires branded them as carriers of a moral decay. The dance, we could say, had got under their skin. In this way, orientalism as a discourse of promise and power was brought to bear even on nonoriental bodies, and the Salomé dancers' display of an exotic sensuality and the disciplinary endeavors of civic and state guardians of morality remained inseparable from one another. Here I turn to Ahmed and her conceptualization of "orientation" as a complication of orientalism as directional, and proximate, to understand how these and other performers—including African American men and women—generated heterogeneous claims that did not necessarily secure imperial subjecthood, even while such performances relied on the imbalance of power supposed by imperial structures of knowledge.[62]

In chapter 4, "Dreaming of Araby," I argue that references to West Asia and North Africa, although manifesting the foreign in the imagination, activated forms of imperial subjecthood and subjection in the domestic order of race and space. In doing so, I demonstrate that the distance between the foreign and the domestic is an ideological construct. In examining these connections further, I revise a concept of internal colonialism through feminist and queer of color critique in order to understand the uses of imperial metaphor to warrant surveillance and control in the colony of Harlem, as well as annexation into the continental West. Although some African Americans had begun to claim a national affiliation with a cosmopolitan United States, or a racial affiliation with Africa through their use of exotic images and styles, vice investigators and lyricists construed a disturbing distance between African Americans and the rest of the national body, seeing both African Americans and West Asian and North African peoples as part of an uncivilized cohort. Conversely, African Americans saw Harlem as Araby, a space of intrigue and sexual freedom. Following Porter Grainger's "In Harlem's Araby," a novelty song that traces the adventures a tourist might have in the neighborhood, experiencing its nightlife, and enjoying pleasures described through an orientalist lens to lend the space of Harlem both a mysterious and erotic sensibility. The final section of the chapter traces the use of Arab or Muslim signs and images to denote domestic spaces through strangeness and follows the courted New York traveler to Palm Springs, California, via a tourist booster tract that names this desert "Our Araby." Describing the desert in the familiar terms of Hollywood and Tin Pan Alley, while promising friendly, disappearing, and removable natives, the tract introduces a symbolic realm of Arab signs and symbols to manifest the material expansion of U.S. empire throughout western North America.

This investigation into Jazz Age New York will, I hope, make clear that the various domains and borders that seem to be distinct actually remain unclear. It may seem simple to say that empire both creates distance and breaches it, but this fact has had profound implications for our histories of and inquiries into those boundaries and the encounters that we pursue or refuse with strangers. Indeed, the accounts I have brought together here help us see that an imperial logic of distance may make people who are close to us disappear, even as the intimacies among four continents bring them closer.

In *Imperial Blues*, I pursue questions that reconfigure the meaning and management of race and sex in Jazz Age New York through the differential knowledge that bringing empire home places before us. This book is oriented toward these histories of intimacies in order to reconsider what political stories inform the categories of race and sex, and what other stories we might tell from the confusion of those categories. Toward this end, Rancière is illuminating when he observes that "the 'logic of stories' and the ability to act as historical agents go together. Politics and art, like forms of knowledge, construct 'fictions,' that is to say *material* rearrangements of signs and images, relationships between what is seen and what is said, between what is done and what can be done."[63] This rearrangement is what I hope to accomplish — to engender new relationships between signs and images, politics and art, friends and strangers, and those other forms through which we encounter empire at home and abroad.

CHAPTER ONE

DESIRE AND DANGER IN

JAZZ'S CONTACT ZONES

"Police can do nothing in this obvious menace of young white girls with young Orientals," worries the journalist Marion Carter, warning of the looming specter of racial mixing at a Sixth Avenue dance hall.[1] Marshaling her own moral sensibilities as a measuring stick, Carter baited her readers with this salacious description of the dance hall in a 1930 article, hoping to incite shock and horror at the spectacle of interracial impropriety: "A langorous [sic] and fragile blonde floating gracefully in the arms of a Filipino! A little black haired flapper in the close and questionable embrace of a Chinaman! A Negro orchestra blaring out jazz tunes. All around, Orientals—Filipinos, Chinamen, Japanese dancing with white girls for ten cents a dance! The only white men in the place the three managers."[2] In this titillating passage, Carter presents Asian men as a powerful threat. These men have crossed great distances and now cross great boundaries to insinuate themselves in "close and questionable" embraces with "langorous," "fragile," and "little" "young white girls." Neither these white women, depicted as tractable victims and being of easy virtue, nor Asian men, understood as carnal predators, fare well at the hands of the journalist. While denigrating both groups as immoral and lascivious, one by association and the other by nature, Carter makes it clear that the dance hall facilitates acting on both association and nature. The dance hall as a quasi-outlaw frontier, with the "Negro orchestra blaring out jazz tunes" as its medium, makes such embraces possible. For Carter, the presence of a few white men and the limited laws present an inadequate defense of white womanhood. As she scornfully observes, "so long as the law on ages and conduct in the dance hall is observed," the authorities could not further control this racialized sexual (though notably legal) threat.[3] Carter's article was one of many that pointed to the dangers of profiting—the "big money lure"—from interracial sexuality in spaces of New York's nightlife and the limits of the law in stopping this kind of societal scourge.[4] Carter sought to bring the manifest danger of interracial sexual unions to public attention, and in her denunciation of them help restore an imagined social order. In doing so, however, she rehearsed the heightened eroticism and taboo thrill of encounters across racial and imperial borders, relying on the same excitement of forbidden contact that made interracial dance halls thrive.[5]

These and other scenes (actual, fictional, and in between) of racial mixing were expedited by the rapid spread of U.S. economic and imperial power around the globe—particularly in the Pacific, the Caribbean, and Latin America—during the second half of the nineteenth century and into the twentieth. The reach of U.S. empire shifted demographics at home, forcing the renegotiation of racial, gendered, and sexual borders as waves of immigrants from new possessions such as Hawaii, Guam, the Philippines, Cuba, and Puerto Rico—as well as from China and Japan, where the United States intervened at times—reached the United States. Such global influence had pervasive and often perverse implications for the national imaginary, in particular for the constitution and governance of public urban spaces, as forms of regulation and transgression sought to keep pace with changing racial and national formations.[6] New York City is a key site for understanding the consequences and entanglements of imperial states and domestic civics through new improvisations of regulation and transgression, subjection and subjectivity. "Modern cities, especially major ports," Caren Kaplan reminds us, "function as crucibles where identities are formed, transformed, and fixed. Such identifications not always self-chosen, welcome, or advantageous to the newly arrived, but they do play roles in the formation of literary and artistic canons as well as the deployment of political interests on the part of state institutions."[7] In the Jazz Age, empire, immigration, and racial mixing served as vital contexts for understanding aesthetic production, nightlife, and the city's imagination of space and sexuality. The traversable lines of the cityscape invited both policing and transgression in modes created through histories of imperial diasporas.

The task in this chapter is to think of jazz cultures as contact zones, with all the spatial and somatic dimensions this implies. Jazz's allure as well as danger hinged on an extemporizing series of analogies and affinities with and across imperial formations and racial classifications, through which jazz denoted codes for border crossing. I borrow the concept of the contact zone from Mary Louise Pratt, who in her coinage redefines the zone of colonial encounter against ideas of sustained borders of time and space between peoples, and instead argues for spatial and temporal copresence and "interactive, improvisational" contacts within asymmetrical relations of power.[8] Instead of challenging frontier mythologies at empire's outposts, however, I use the concept of the contact zone to argue that the nation is continuously created through racialized and sexualized contact with purported strangers even within its borders, as those frontier mythologies— along with peoples from empire's outposts—are brought home. Spaces of urban nightlife drew attention to the anxieties caused by the increasing breadth and breach of national borders (now redrawn precariously around the globe), with particular attention to the concomitant unsettling of gender and sexual formations. Configuring contact zones between Asian, Latino, Caribbean, and Eastern European migrants and "native" African and European Americans, spaces of nightlife thus prompted the emergence as well as the entanglement of new discourses and practices of racialization that describe much more than merely domestic race relations and their relays of power. These multiracial spaces provided opportunities to flout social norms and state regulations, and for that very reason they attracted both formal and informal surveillance from people interested in reinforcing and restoring order. Carter's article and similar written works told a manifold tale of racial mixing, produced by but also contributing to national debates about African American and Asian (and other) immigrant urban cultures. The dance hall is not incidental but crucial to this tale about the public character of the imperial city, as the scene for so much movement of bodies.[9] Reporters, police, and vice investigators patrolled those public spaces that also served as microsites of imperial logic made intimate and thereby dangerous. The discourses and documents created to describe jazz as a contact zone, like those in Carter's article, addressed themselves to complex triangulations of Asianness, whiteness, and blackness; moralistic allegories and also supposedly scientific assertions about distinctive racial formations of gender, sex, and sexuality; and a multitude of anxieties about national borders and imperial volatility. Thus the power of movement coded in the syncopated jazz that flowed from the bandstand to the dance floor was necessarily transnational in nature.

Traversing geographies of scale, from transnational and international to national and metropolitan, and further to commingling bodies, as I argue happened in Jazz Age New York, the imperial logic of regulation and subsequent resistance—both too often violent—took place not only abroad but also in the heart of the metropole. Expressions of identity and subjectivity in jazz cultures helped challenge gender norms and racial formations while using imperial logic, albeit often for different ends than those of the civic and state institutions that sought to police those norms and formations. In this way concepts of space crucially informed differing claims of subjectivity and subversion. I intentionally use terms such as *boundaries* and *borders* because these terms speak to the spatial dimensions that create and challenge the categories and vocabularies of various epistemological authorities on racial and national difference. As we shall see, forms of resistance to, and preservation of, the social order are embodied through spatial discourses and practices. Travel, whether actual movement or imaginative metaphor, is a primary way to make meaning via spatial logics. Travel, especially across borders, can function as an enhancement, the modern's freedom seen as mobility; or as a contravention, the breach of safety and security by a wayward other. For some people, world travel demonstrates their achievement of modern subjecthood. Others, such as those Asian immigrants who peopled the dance hall, were subject to monitoring and surveillance as carriers of moral but also biological threats to city dwellers. Likewise, the metaphor of travel is often assumed to transmit both liberating prospects and vectors of contagion. Narratives and performances of passing and crossing, and the border figures that incarnate these movements—whether via racial passing, appearing in drag, racial miscegenation, or bisexuality—rely on the epistemologies and methodologies that inform spatial logics and their signifying economies.[10] In this way, ideas of resistance and discipline, of possibility and power, produce themselves through conceptualizations of space and the differences these make.

Because of their compelling connections between music and immigration, race and sexuality, jazz cultures act as key sites for understanding the machinations of scientific discourses, immigration legislation, imperial fictions, and racial classifications in the give-and-take of identity making. That is, jazz is also a contact zone for multiple ideological and institutional schema addressed to technologies of the body. Therefore this chapter juxtaposes a range of cultural texts often separated in popular and scholarly accounts of the construction of Jazz Age modernity. In doing so, I examine how imperial logic worked across and between genres of aesthetic production, such as novels, music, and dance—as well as analogous documents of vice investigations, eugenics, sociology, and sexology—to map the city and the movements of the body (and its parts) through an economy of distance and intimacy. The first section of the chapter investigates the multiple interpretations of jazz as a contact zone to describe the sexual transgressions invited by the dance hall. In that context, sexological discourses that described interracial sexuality as aberrational seeped into vice reports that provided evidence of aberration, thereby confirming the stakes of surveillance. I argue that the imperial logic, which informed immigration legislation and national security, was also imposed on the bodies of immigrants and other city dwellers, especially in these contact zones, to police and monitor their sexual activity. The second section of the chapter addresses the imposition of imperial fantasies of the contact zone onto the city's nightlife, through which white women's sexuality was policed in relation to the looming specter of racialized masculinity. In reporting on the murder of Vivian Gordon, a former chorus girl, I argue that the yellow journalists of *The New York Evening Journal* used conventions of the domestic pulp novel (especially those tropes of the urban underbelly and the fallen woman, who had even further to fall) in order to produce a story of sexual danger dependent on imperial logic's racialization and nationalization of men described as threateningly out of place. The third section brings these vice reports and their sexological counterparts to bear on Wallace Thurman's description of Harlem nightlife in his best-known novel, *The Blacker the Berry. . . .*[11] In this novel, Thurman explores the nightclub as a site of possibility, thwarting expectations dictated by compulsory heterosexuality and monogamy through the particular provocations of interracial contact.

These profoundly dissimilar documents present cross-racial sexual activity as an imperial matter, gesturing toward an alternate history of negotiation between racial formations and national borders in a new age of empire.[12]

JAZZING EMPIRE: IMMIGRANTS AND SCIENTIFIC DISCOURSES IN THE DANCE HALL

The multiracial character of Jazz Age New York presented city residents and visitors with myriad possible encounters and contact points at which manifold boundaries were nightly negotiated. A constellation of racial and sexual discourses targeted jazz in particular as a powerful medium for contact and encounter in the imperial city. Though we well know that the port city is a juncture of empire, I argue that imperial logic augmented and transformed the port's domestic racial logics in shaping intimate relations of power. Operating across geographies of scale, discourses and practices aimed at controlling the movements of bodies were themselves peripatetic, sliding from empire's outposts to the imperial city where those outposts' outlaws lived, from the peripheries to the center and back again. The dance hall in particular drew the regard of sociologists and vice investigators alike as a place where new Asian and Latino immigrants, African Americans, and white adventurers met; at the borders and on the streets, the presence of these immigrants both provoked and justified new legislation and policing measures at the national and local levels, meant to protect the nation's whiteness.[13] Jazz was a contact zone for concerns as well as creations materializing from transactions among immigration control, local legislation, sociology, eugenics, sexology, vice reports, and aesthetic modernisms such as primitivism and orientalism. Although jazz cultures are imagined to provide freedom from social constraint, they also occasioned new discourses of restraint.

Pieced together by multiple migrations originating both inside and outside the expanding territory of the U.S. empire, the multiracial character of what could be understood as its key metropolis was a cause of concern for some. Sciences including eugenics, sexology, sociology, and psychoanalysis found fertile ground to emerge and become established in the empire's dislocations, discerning there the specter of racial miscegenation, sexual perversion, congenital criminality, and other forms of pathology. Addressing the diagnosis and management of these pathologies, these fields informed imperial rule as well as national legislation, such as the Johnson-Reed Immigration Act of 1924, which included the National Origins Act and the Asian Exclusion Act. An addendum to the Immigration and Naturalization Act of 1917, which immigration restrictionists had come to consider too lenient, the 1924 Act was passed with the support of work in eugenics, which warned of the racial threat posed by inferior genetic material that could contaminate bloodlines. Although such immigration legislation had a powerful effect on limiting the presence of supposed undesirables in the United States, the application of such scientific discourses for the control and curtailment of possible incursions into the body politic did not end at the national border.

Within the limits of this imperial city, sociologists, social workers, vice investigators, and police officers worked to delineate and demarcate the character, and in some cases the pathology, of neighborhoods. As the presence of new immigrants sparked concerns about danger and degeneracy, scientific and state authorities sought to create comprehensive maps of the constitution of the national and civic body. These new sciences, committed to Enlightenment notions of personhood, created racialized epistemological frameworks for knowing the city and its diverse inhabitants.[14] Although some denizens could be construed as cosmopolitan in their movements, others were marked through racial and imperial schema as out of place. For example, as Henry Yu argues, sociologists labeled whole swathes of the city as alien: "Chinatowns and Japantowns were delineated as distinctive geographic and cultural spaces within America. Because the definition of Oriental culture was tied to an opposition between American and non-American cultural traits, Oriental communities became equivalent to foreign places within America."[15] (Harlem was also seen as outside Manhattan proper, as I discuss in chapter 4.) These scientific formations sought to further delineate and demarcate bodies through vectors of contagion and congenital abnormality. Eugenicists measured craniums, lips, and foreheads to denote innate racial differences and promote theories of racial degeneracy,[16] while sexologists measured labia, nipples, clitorises, and hypothalamuses to understand the congenital aberrations of the homosexual.[17] Physiological models like these rendered bodies as series of somatic signifiers that then grounded certain biopolitical discourses and practices for city, nation, and empire. Nor were these unrelated pathologies. Siobhan Somerville connects the significance of scientific racism to the invention of the sexual deviant, and Nancy Ordover observes that anti-immigrant legislation also denied entry to anyone who had been convicted of, or had confessed to, crimes of so-called moral turpitude, including prostitution and other activities deemed to be sexual perversions.[18] In this case, such scientific discourses became powerful instruments for people seeking to identify whole racial groups as criminal elements prone to perversion, and to police neighborhoods and spaces of leisure through the ostensibly authoritative language of science and security.[19] Though varied and often contradictory in application, an imperial logic often underpinned these border crossings and the fields (and forces) of knowledge used in their explication, through which spatial difference operated as a significant medium and metaphor for racial and sexual transgression.

Accompanying these scientific explanations of pathology and modes of classification were regimes of policing and social research. One organization established to carry out investigations of unlawful activity, particularly focused on wayward women and their sexuality, was the Committee of Fourteen. The vice investigators employed by the Committee of Fourteen provided some of the most detailed firsthand accounts of spaces of New York nightlife from 1905 to 1932, which have become an important source of information about the history of sexuality—despite their authors' biased belief in the need to control women in public spaces.[20] The privately funded Committee of Fourteen worked alongside city police to investigate prostitution, women working as hostesses in dance halls, the phenomenon of sex in moving taxicabs, the sexual perils of cabarets, and queer relations within the city's ball scene, among a multitude of other potentially sexually transgressive spaces and activities. The Committee researched, compiled, stored, and published thousands of reports regarding civic sexual dangers of all manner—illicit, legal, private, public, and consensual. Its vice investigators often were proactive in collecting data. They entered cabaret spaces looking for and noting, among other details, the number of hostesses and other female employees who could be seen, the number of hostesses and other female employees seen who admitted to being prostitutes, the number of other prostitutes seen, the number of other questionable women seen, and the number of exploiters and go-betweens seen.[21] In addition to using these schema that mirrored sociology's craze to classify, the Committee also employed at least one investigator who was a student at Columbia medical school and who showed an interest in sexological discourse. In these ways, the Committee melded the language of sociology and sexology with the compelling discipline of the police force. Indeed, working hand in hand with law enforcement and the judiciary, the Committee's vice investigators sought to uncover women they suspected as being prostitutes and could request or recommend the women's arrests. Thus, those interested in controlling women's sexuality and their contact with men, in general, and with men of color, in particular, had official means at their disposal to carry out their wishes.

These discourses of restriction came together as ways to understand emerging forms of nightlife, especially as jazz became an entry point into public culture and a contact zone. As perhaps the most obvious impetus for movement in jazz cultures, music intimately connects power to subject formation at the somatic level of the body and movement. As Susan McClary observes, "the music itself—especially as it intersects with the body and destabilizes accepted norms of subjectivity, gender and sexuality—is precisely where the politics of music often reside."[22] Music thus functions as a compelling example of how Foucauldian analytics of subject formation and subjection can be brought to bear on popular forms and their sensate, somatic effects. McClary further elaborates on theories of the body as a site of power, mediated through Foucault as well as Teresa de Lauretis, writing that "music is foremost among cultural 'technologies of the body,' that it is a site where we learn how to experience socially mediated patterns of kinetic energy, being in time, emotions, desire, pleasure, and much more."[23] And like other discursive forms, music can shape relations between bodies; this power was well known to nightlife patrons and those bent on policing them.

At the dance halls, patrons were treated to some of the finest and most popular jazz bands in New York, as the songs that emanated from the bandstand came from the orchestras of Duke Ellington, Chick Webb, Cab Calloway, Jimmie Lunceford, and Paul Whiteman.[24] These groups might mix imperial and sexual themes in novel songs such as Chick Webb's "Swinging on the Reservation," Fletcher Henderson's "He Wasn't Born in Araby, But He's a Sheikin' Fool" (1924), Duke Ellington's "Swingtime in Honolulu" (1932), and Porter Grainger's "Hula Blues."[25] Songs like "Swingtime in Honolulu" and "Hula Blues" profited from the craze for Hawaiian sounds that began in the Jazz Age and continued beyond it. One of the most recent U.S. acquisitions, Hawaii took hold of the U.S. imperial imagination, inspiring music, dances, and nightclub routines. Indeed, ambiguously named Hawaiian Orchestras—either orchestras from Hawaii or orchestras with instrumentation meant to sound Hawaiian—also played at places like the Bluebird Cabaret.[26] Additionally, sheet music arrangements were often sold to accommodate the single ukulele player, as home sales of ukuleles skyrocketed. Reportedly, Hawaiian music "sold better than other music in vogue" in Jazz Age New York.[27] Hawaiian music, as played in both New York and Hawaii, was marked by the popular music of the time—jazz—and vice versa. For instance, Sol Ho'opii and His Novelty Quartet's recording of "Hula Girl" uses conventions associated with Hawaii, like Hawaiian language singing and steel string slide guitar; those associated with the pop songs of Tin Pan Alley, like a pronounced use of ninth chords; and those associated with jazz, like the slide guitar mimicking a jazz violin performing the instrumental melodies between verses. The heterogeneous nature of jazz itself already expressed empire's contact zones; in the case of music performed at dance halls, this was often achieved through a rhythm suitable for physically intimate fox-trotting.

Vitally important to the study of jazz as a contact zone for multiracial New York are its associations with sex—the sort of movement and contact, infused with "kinetic energy, being in time," that inspired the most anxiety about jazz. Though its origins remain obscure, etymologies of the word *jazz* suggest that it functioned as a euphemism for or an allusion to sexual intercourse. Some speculative accounts even propose that the relation of the term *jazz* to sexuality predated its connection to any musical form. One contemporaneous commentator notes: "Used both as a verb and a noun to denote the sex act, . . . 'jazz' . . . has long been a common vulgarity among Negroes in the South, and it is very likely from this usage that the term 'jazz music' was derived."[28] The ethnomusicologists Alan Merriam and Fradley Garner observe that "there is a certain degree of logic in the assumption that the musical use of the term was derived from its sexual use," but the etymology remains unclear.[29] Whatever the word's origins, the intimacy and intercourse between jazz and sexuality is undeniable. This intimacy was also connected to race, and blackness in particular. Through its association with race and sex, jazz was construed as a kinetic discourse of unbounded and dangerous sensuality. Artists and musicians further associated jazz cultures with primitivism, a modernist aesthetic that sought in the signs and symbols of the African "primitive" a way to resist the stultifying tempo of a disciplined life. "Inspired by Freud and others who documented the repression presumed endemic to Western civilization," the jazz historian Kathy Ogren argues, "twenties artists and intellectuals invested primitive culture with 'uncivilized' virtues—particularly sexual freedom."[30] These associations also suggest an intimacy with emerging sexological discourses, particularly those that assigned a range of sex acts to distinct civilizational times and spaces.

What we could call jazz's constellation of multiple technologies of the body is further reified by its distinction from other modes of dance music. One vice investigator, reporting on his experience at a jazz-filled dance hall, describes the wildly uneven distribution of sexual energies and emotions that emerged in response to distinct musical forms: "While dancing with Helen a second time a waltz was suddenly struck up by the orchestra and I observed about 25 men leaving the floor. I said 'What is the matter, the dance is not over is it?' She replied 'No, the cops are here.' I said 'How do you know that?' She said 'That's the signal. Just as soon as they come we get that and we are ordered to immediately break into a waltz.'"[31] According to the same report, the "six piece colored orchestra" had been playing jazzy fox-trots before breaking into the staid waltz after the unexpected arrival of the police. The quick-time rhythms and looser motions of the fox-trot are themselves the reason for unwelcome surveillance; the waltz, on the other hand, though at an earlier time considered shocking for its mandated embrace, had become respectable and morally faultless (unless, perhaps, one were dancing to Chick Webb's rendition of "The Naughty Waltz" at the Savoy Ballroom in Harlem). Performing a waltz was intended to cleanse the dance hall and its patrons in the eyes of authority.

Jazz thus transmitted a series of codes for rebellion—against respectable sexuality, racial segregation, and even civilization—though these codes often had a troubling provenance. Furthermore, its kinetic music was seemingly infectious. Jazz threatened to spill forth from the nightclubs and cabarets, seeping onto the street but also stimulating and entering the body.[32] Jazz was thus perceived as a primitivizing, uncivilizing technology of the body, inasmuch as the body would be compelled by its music toward promiscuous movements, emotions, desires, and pleasure across boundaries of a multiple nature. Accordingly, jazz appeared to require concerted surveillance from sometimes conflicting, sometimes collaborating, institutional and ideological apparatuses. One article in the *New York Evening Journal*, for instance, described a sax player who had been wooing women with his jazz music. He was so successful, according to this account, that he had seven wives. The story of the "Sax Tooter" relied on jazz as a signifier for non-normative, aberrant sexual practices—in this case, the article drew a direct line between jazz and contemporaneous public debates being waged about "free love" and polygamy. This immoral situation was resolved through juridical action—with the law unleashed on the hapless musician, the "Sax Tooter" was sentenced to two and a half to five years in Sing Sing.[33] Of course, this disciplinary action did not only establish a prohibitionary discourse. It and other acts, such as the publication of the article by Carter cited at the start of this chapter, reified jazz as the scene for those illicit activities that these actions sought to limit, thus circulating and possibly inventing a context for linking jazz and perverse intimacies.[34]

The threat of racial mixing and sexual encounters, mediated by jazz, proved to be so threatening that New York City's government created new juridical discourses and practices in order to curtail its menace. Indeed, many of the public spaces associated with jazz culture were so fraught with racialized sexual tension that the Board of Aldermen sought to regulate those spaces where jazz moved bodies. In December 1926 the board required "any room, place or space in the city in which any musical entertainment, singing, dancing or other similar amusement is permitted in connection with the restaurant business" to apply for a cabaret license from the city.[35] In this way, city fathers hoped that they could legislate the morals of the cabaret scene. Many of the instruments and combinations thereof named in this legislation were used to play jazz. We can surmise from this that the regulations were aimed specifically at spaces of nightlife guided by the jazz ethos.[36] Indeed, though the ordinance was commonly referred to as the "cabaret laws," it also applied to dance halls.

As one particularly disturbing (at least to the state) contact zone, the dance hall brought together itinerant populations of U.S. empire with imperial economies of distance and intimacy. The dance hall was specifically given to encouraging close encounters of a sensual kind, and it functioned as a multiracial locale for adventuring as well as a cause for concern for authorities.[37] Multiracial dance halls were fairly common across Manhattan, and they included Roseland Dance Hall, St. Nicholas Rink, Happyland Dancing Academy, Moon Dancing Studio, Lincoln Square Dancing, Romey Dancing School, Rose Danceland, Roma Danceland, Mayflower Dancing Academy, the Cathedral Ballroom, the Sunbeam Dance Palace, and the

Bamboo Inn.[38] Many dance halls had male patrons hailing from all over the world—the consequence of imperial expansions. For instance, Yeaple's attracted a varied, multiethnic crowd including men identified as Chinese, Japanese, Filipino, Cuban, and the amorphous "Spanish."[39] Dreamland, run by Morris Goodman, also boasted a mixed patronage of Italians, Spaniards, Greeks, and "Latins," and its patrons reportedly expressed joy over the fact that Dreamland was unlike the Royal Dancing, where "Chinks and Japs" might be found.[40] In the remainder of this section, I argue that the dance hall makes clear the multiple technologies of the body that were brought to bear on empire's racialized masculinities. Through scientific and state schemas of colonial and domestic racial classification and sexual categorization, as well as these schemas' intercourse with jazz discourses of primitivism and free movement, the new immigrants carried with them a double contagion. Together these technologies interpreted the new immigrant, the Asian man from empire's outposts, as a vector of danger—to U.S. borders, the integrity of white women (and, in turn, white manhood), and the civic honor of New York City.

Empire and city were spaces of both possibility and limitation: where there existed discourses of freedom and defiance, there also existed the desire—on behalf of city administrators, police, and reformers—to manage the shifting population in this urban contact zone. Furthermore, prevailing social codes and inequalities among patrons and managers also found their ways into the heterogeneous space of the dance hall. Doreen Massey notes that "the spatial has *both* an element of order *and* an element of chaos."[41] This was certainly true of New York's spaces of nightlife: while these spaces organized new social relations, allowing interrelations and interactions, they also ordered the limits of those relations, keeping their outcomes unpredictable. The simultaneous presence of so many differently racialized people in clubs and dance halls did not testify to equal access to public space, because racialized borders and other striations of power continued to operate there. As the jazz historian Sherrie Tucker argues, interracial nightclubs were not signs of democratization; rather, race, gender, and sexuality were negotiated in uneven exchanges within those spaces.[42] Public places that included so many peoples from so many places were also predicated on the necessarily antidemocratic acts of empire that provided the contexts for how, and why, those people were "here." These antidemocratic grounds further transposed themselves into multiple readings of the wayward bodies that moved through these quasi-outlaw spaces. Jazz cultures, as such, provide a novel means to examine the movement of bodies as a marker of how anxieties over borders manifested on the dance floor and in public space.

If imperial logic brought certain racialized bodies from the empire's possessions to the metropole, it also helped name those racialized bodies as they entered spaces of public entertainment. Specifically, the logic that names racialized, imperial masculinities as unsophisticated and uncivilized could be used to understand bodies in the urban core: racialized masculinities posed a threat in a distant "elsewhere," and this threat was multiplied in closer proximity to "our" women "here." Discourses of containment thus sought to both control and temper the so-called yellow peril. Bruno Lasker, a researcher and social worker from New York City commissioned by the American Council of the Institute of Pacific Relations to address the issue of Filipino immigration, noted that it was "widely conceded, among those whose business it is to watch their behaviors, that the Filipinos are unusually considerate in their dealings with women." This consideration, Lasker explained, facilitated Filipino men's success in the dance halls, an intolerable situation for authorities. In order to diminish the specter of Filipino sexual prowess, Lasker attributed their success less to virility than to gullibility. In doing so, he argued that women who frequented the dance halls were probably prostitutes, or at least women interested in Filipino men only for their money.[43] Lasker observed that "in several cities dance halls have been closed, not so much because their patrons were in danger from immoral Filipinos, but because professional prostitutes invaded these places in large numbers attracted by the presence of unsophisticated Filipino patrons, who are known as lavish spenders."[44] This formulation served a dual purpose. First, it constructed Filipino sexual luck as the consequence of an irrational impulse, spending flagrantly on morally dubious women. Second, it named white women in relationships with Filipino men as likely prostitutes.[45] Together, these assertions further served as a caution to white women to stay away from Filipino men, lest they be confused with loose women.[46] Asian American men in these scenarios are routinely described in terms of criminality, demonstrating the difference in valuation across imperial personhood.

Lasker's findings were echoed in vice reports as well, where Asian American sexuality was imagined as inappropriate, undesirable, and unromantic. Reporting on a night out at the Cathedral Ballroom in Manhattan, a vice investigator noted there were "25 Chinese and Japs, among them 3 sailors. There were 15 Philipinos [sic] and Spaniards and the only white men in the premises besides myself were bouncers, and lobby guys who are not considered as patrons."[47] His description of the racial mix of the dance hall divides the men into groups: the Chinese and Japanese; the Filipinos; whites; and, most likely, Cubans and Puerto Ricans. The presence of multiethnic and multiracial men complicated the meaning of proper white femininity, and how women should behave in public space.[48] Though this was a multiethnic space, and any of the male patrons could be seen as threatening the authority of imperial white masculinity, the investigator singled out the first group for particular scrutiny.[49] He surmised: "A white man has very poor standing here, the instructresses ignore them and prefer the Chinese or Japs who spend quite some money on tickets, drinks, and besides tip the girls."[50] The investigator divulged his worry that these "Chinese and Japs" had been able to "buy" access to white women who enjoyed their attention. The fact that Asian men had to spend much larger sums in order to have the pleasure of these women's company seemed not to have been entirely lost on the investigator, but this did little to relieve him of his worry that the wrong men were able to access white women. Again, the difference in human value is evident in the description, which here depends on the imperial logic of valuation being made mobile and brought home.

Such anxious discourse centered on notions of proper and improper sexualities, instigated by jazz's energies and movements. "Some of the dancing instructresses laid full length on the benches here," reported the investigator, "and some of the Orientals fooled with them while they were in that position. Also improper dancing was observed by girls and men rubbing bodies imitating the act of sexual intercourse."[51] The investigator made the stakes clear: he found white women engaged in sexual actions with men of color in a public space where white men were virtually ignored by women. Though this might appear to be a case of competition, the investigator painted all of the sexualities found in the dance hall with the same brush: all were cast as suspect under the sign of jazz. Asian men were sexual aggressors willing to go to extreme (financial) lengths to fulfill their perverted desires, whereas the white women were money-hungry vamps. Reports such as these (and Carter's) thereby produced Asian masculinity as simultaneously threatening and thrilling.

Although these investigative accounts give us a sense of who frequented dance halls and how Asian men embodied particular danger and degeneracy, abetted by the primitivist energies of jazz music, the style in which these "facts" were reported means that they do not offer much insight into how racial mixing and seemingly concomitant transgressions might themselves account for the appeal of the dance hall. One 1929 article centered on the Bamboo Inn, a Harlem nightspot owned by a Chinese man by the name of Lee Shu, offers a clue.[52] Described as a "transplanted bit of Mott St. whose oriental setting seems strangely out of place in the center of the capital of colored America,"[53] and reportedly boasting a significant base of Asian patrons, the Bamboo Inn's provenance certainly added to the foreign feeling of the club for the white reporter. Though the space may have appeared exotic by design, it was the racial mix that the reporter found fascinating and newsworthy: "Men of the mysterious lands of the Far East—Hindus, Japanese, Chinese, Malays—rub elbows on the dance floor with West Indians and colored folk from all parts of America. . . . [A] man of any color may walk in accompanied by a woman of any color—or with no woman at all."[54] The author's amazement concentrated on unconventional sexual couplings—not necessarily queer couplings, but those that strayed across racial boundaries. Though the article did not condemn the Harlem nightclubs that it described, and even illustrated their pleasures, the author nonetheless borrowed from the imperial schema to make sense of sights before him. In other words, by making the clubs seem all the more foreign because of the transgressions occurring there, the author reiterated empire's bounds, too—in which whiteness defined moral measure and proper civilization, with the Orient, the primitive, and racial admixture as its outposts.

The multiracial character of New York denoted both the cosmopolitanism and civilizational thinking of U.S. empire. In the contact zones of jazz cultures, eugenicist nomenclatures of racial degeneracy; sexological materials; sociological demarcations of race and space; and the multidimensional, multifunctional movements of bodies, goods, and capital across these borders shifted and converged to produce their own kinetic energies. It is as such that imperial logic described both the arts and allurements of jazz-filled nightlife as well as its dangers.

Some white women, such as the dancer and choreographer Martha Graham and the mezzo-soprano Eva Gauthier, assembled for themselves an imperial subjecthood from contact with the other that bestowed an air of cosmopolitan sophistication.[55] For others, such as immigrants and working-class women, proximity to empire's outposts could be dangerous, even fatal. Respectable women were warned in numerous ways that their entrance in increasing numbers into the public sphere—as workers in factories and shops, for instance, or as consumers of fashions and entertainments—could be dangerous, and not just in terms of their virtue. In the late nineteenth century and the early twentieth, more and more women sought some measure of autonomy inside but particularly outside the home. As Kathy Peiss argues, "many young women, particularly the daughters of immigrants, came to identify 'cheap amusements' as the embodiment of American urban culture, particularly its individualism, ideology of consumption, and affirmation of dating and courtship outside of parental control."[56] Some women sought to exercise their newfound freedoms only in leisure pursuits, but the radical shift in traditional familial authority that these exercises denoted did not go unnoticed by public officials, newspaper reporters, police officers, and civilian vice investigators. Indeed, these disciplinary bodies issued (often in concert but sometimes in conflict) dire cautions about the disorder and chaos brought about by women who publicly participated in commercial entertainments and economies of pleasure.

The likely convergence of white women enjoying jazz culture's nightlife and racialized men—some racialized through their participation in nightlife, some through more recent movement from the Caribbean, and some through histories of the transatlantic slave trade—provided the ground for a discourse of danger simultaneously meant to tantalize and to provide a rationale for regulation. These cautions, founded on the confluence of fact-finding forays by reporters and vice investigators with the genre conventions of pulp fiction, were used to spin a rationale for the surveillance and control of the movements of women, men of color, and immigrants in the imperial city. Women were warned to keep their distance from spaces of multiracial urban nightlife and the moral taint—even mortal peril—that awaited them should they enter. Newspapers often tried to proscribe and circumscribe women's movements with scandalous tales of reputations ruined and lives destroyed. Members of civic-minded organizations like the Committee of Fourteen, created to fight the so-called blight of prostitution, considered most women in public to be possible prostitutes and maintained that most men would assume the same. Though the Committee represented some of the stodgiest interests in the city, the ideological and disciplinary undertakings its members pursued and propagated helped define the parameters of acceptable sexuality within these economies of pleasure, especially because the Committee had direct contact with the legal apparatuses that could enforce these views. But sexual peril carried racial, even civilizational, dimensions—and even within the city limits. The freedom to move around the city, to be public, was depicted as a danger by dint of encounters and contact with immigrants and people of color. In these seductive cautionary tales, immigrant and nonwhite men were portrayed as hypersexual predators and violent monsters. White women risked the loss of virtue—and, worse still, life—if they had illicit contact with these volatile bodies. Indeed, women in public who had participated in the city's nightlife turned up dead at regular intervals, according to newspaper reports. These murders were often born of illicit sexual situations: women who entertained, a class of labor understood as a scant distance from prostitution; women who otherwise cultivated suspect sexual contacts in nightclubs, cabarets, and speakeasies; and women who daringly exposed themselves to the dangers of New York's underworld were at risk. But in publishing lurid tales of sex and murder, oftentimes supplied by civilian vice investigators, newspapers and their accomplices (including law enforcement officials) sought to lay these deaths at the feet of empire's others through reasoning derived from the familiar narratives of popular culture, scenarios created in the spaces of nightlife that ironically beckoned police and vice investigators to monitor those engaged in what was known as the sporting life. These stories told of the sexual danger and disorder of empire brought home to the city.

One particular murder case illustrates both how these civic and quasi-civic organizations, together with yellow journalism, sought to circumscribe and control sexuality (while reinscribing the behaviors they proposed to end) and how, in doing so, these entities re-created categories of control and condemnation that drew on the racial schemas of empire to map the city's underworld. On 26 February 1931 a passerby discovered a strangled, lifeless body in the bushes in Van Cortlandt Park, in the Bronx. The disheveled and partially exposed corpse was soon identified as Vivian Gordon, a former chorus girl, enthusiastic participant in New York's night- life, and mother. For the next four months, Gordon's morals and murder became linked objects of intense interest and speculation in the pages of New York's newspapers. As told in the *New York Evening Journal*, owned by William Randolph Hearst, the titillating aspects of the tale behind Gordon's death were found not in the precious few facts about her murder unearthed by the police investigation but in the fantastical details, presented as both real and imagined, of Gordon's purportedly wild life. Though most papers reported on some aspect of the murder and its investigation, few devoted as much space to it as the *Evening Journal*. Hardly restrained in its report- ing and editorial decisions, the *Evening Journal* deployed a purposefully thrilling and broad net of societal fears and suspicions through which to portray the murder case. Gordon's postmortem fame illustrates some of the ways in which women moved in public and illuminates the rubrics of discourse and discipline delineating acceptable and unacceptable sexuali- ties. On the wild frontier of New York's nightlife, the unfolding story of this slain beauty illustrates the many gendered transactions between imperial and domestic racial and sexual classifications that made sense of the public spaces where she moved and was murdered. As Gordon's story unfolded in newspaper pages, tropes familiar from other forms of entertainment— nightclub shows, popular songs, operas, minstrelsy, films, and novels— made apparent the marking of women in public space as both dangerous and endangered, and the marking of racialized masculinities as criminal.

The metaphors used to tell Gordon's story often borrowed from spatial discourses of empire to make sense of her transgressions, in effect engen- dering a circular logic for her death. Additionally, her story, situated within the larger story of industrial capital, demonstrated how the decades-long move of women into public space and the workforce caused the shifting of nationalized boundaries of race, gender, and sexuality. Because Gordon had dared to cross into the dark territories of the city, a journey that posed certain dangers to the body and soul, her death was not supposed to be surprising. According to the papers, before moving to New York, Gordon lived as a wife and mother in Pennsylvania under her birth name of Benita and her married name of Bischoff. Like so many women seeking to escape the strictures of small-town life, Bischoff was propelled toward the city.

Hers was not a case of an innocent lamb stumbling into a lion's den, however. Bischoff had already made her reputation as a familiar fixture in public nightspots; she had been working as a chorus girl when she met John Bischoff, the man who would become her husband. Thus in the newspaper accounts, Bischoff did not embody noir's blameless ingénue but rather her opposite: the already fallen woman. Both victim and perpetrator, her lurid adventures in the underworld guaranteed her eventual destruction. Thus the tale of her journey, from small town to big city, would encompass a cautionary (if voyeuristic) story of transgression—of the actual and imagined boundaries of gender and sexuality, family and nation, race and empire. Hers was also a story of industrializing capital, of changing economic pressures and their manifestation in social relations in the city, wrought by national and transnational shifts in bodies and labor, goods and markets. As Peiss marks the increasing number of women in the workplace at the start of the twentieth century and its attendant disruptions in gender norms, familial authority, and public space, Roderick Ferguson argues that capital "calls for subjects who must transgress the material and ideological boundaries of community, family, and nation. . . . Indeed, the production of labor, ultimately, throws the normative boundaries of race, gender, class, and sexuality into confusion."[57] Therefore Gordon's death is a palimpsest of multiple travels and transgressions. The simultaneous and overlapping movements of women, European immigrants, and laborers from the outposts of U.S. empire—along with the Great Migration of African Americans from the rural South to the industrial cities of the North and Midwest—radically transformed both work life and leisure time and shaped both challenges to and reinscriptions of these border crossings.

Gordon's early life and her skirmishes with the constraints on women's mobility were pieced together through her documented contacts with the police and the judicial and penal systems, illustrating the overlap of institutions that both create narratives of illicit sexuality and seek to reform those named as illicit. Beginning with her death, readers of the *Evening Journal* were slowly introduced to many (often fictional) aspects of Gordon's madcap life. The unfolding story suggested that her itinerant nature had long been a disciplinary problem for various state institutions. For instance, newspapers found that her husband and Andrew G. McLaughlin, a local police officer with a corrupt streak, had set her up on charges of prostitution.[58] Reportedly interested in taking her daughter away from her, the husband helped ensure her eventual conviction on those prostitution charges and sentencing to Bedford Reformatory.[59] For the newspapers and the reading public, as well as the legal system, her apparent movement from chorus girl to convicted prostitute seemed a natural progression, given that "the chorus girl as a 'working girl' was closely associated with prostitution."[60] After being released from the reformatory, Benita Bischoff renamed herself Vivian Gordon, left her husband for good, and moved to New York on her own. With the name change, and branded as a prostitute, Gordon reinvented herself as a single woman out to make a living and find excitement in the big city. Although she retained a strong love for her only child, according to the newspapers, she was determined not to be censured any longer for her taste for nightlife—and her appetites were reportedly voracious. Over the course of the next few years, Gordon broke social boundaries, traveling between New York's smart set and its lowlifes. She supported herself in fine style, even raising enough capital to become a landlord. Economic independence and mobility, the papers had it, came at much too high a price, and Gordon paid with her life. The newspaper reports invented, or reinvented, the wayward woman as public, disorderly, and hypersexual and told Gordon's story through tropes and characters lifted, as we will see, from the imperial mythologies of popular culture.

As told by the newspapers, and as modeled by a pulpish, hard-boiled blueprint of gritty realism and sexual depravity, Gordon's story carried a series of warnings against women's sexual freedom in general and included strong prohibitions against the increasingly threatening scourge of interracial relations. These cautions against sexual—particularly interracial—contact were written through the familiar logic of empire. Her affairs with wealthy white men were portrayed through orientalist narratives of sheiks and harems, while her affairs with nonwhite men (including Puerto Ricans and a "darktown gigolo"[61]) were described as an even more savage order of danger. Gordon bore the brunt of the moral fault in these tales: if she chose to approach rich white men, she was a wily woman out to score riches from easy marks; if she associated willingly with Puerto Rican and black men, she was a willing consort to treacherous men of color. Her life, encapsulated in this way, served as a warning of the dangers faced by women who moved in and out of public life. As bad examples, Gordon's life and death functioned as evidence of a general principle, and Gordon could be viewed as one of many or as any woman. Newspapers compared her with other tragically fallen figures like Anna Urbas, Louise Lawson, and Dot King, three other women reportedly drawn to the bright lights of the big city, which led to their ultimate undoing. In this way, the popular narrative of Gordon's story elaborated the principle of cause and effect, darkly illustrating what wayward women could expect from daring to transgress the rote and routine of racialized gender and sexual norms, moving from the safety of private life to the danger and excitement of nightlife.

In the stories of her travels from the small town to the big city, from the smart set to subterranean depths, Gordon played the role of a vamp, a trope familiar to newspaper readers. The vamp emerged on the stage and in film as a figure that marked women as highly sexual predators, creating an inappropriate, yet independent, woman with sexual volition. As immortalized by the silent film actress Theda Bara, the vamp incarnated the archetypical femme fatale, a seductress whose feminine charms lure her lovers into her dangerous, even deadly, embrace. "In 1922," Gaylyn Studlar writes, "William J. Robinson declared in a popular marriage manual that the 'frigid' woman was 'becoming rare,' but the greatest contemporary danger was the 'menace' of the woman of 'excessive sensuality or the Woman Vampire.' She threatened 'the health and even life of her husband.' Robinson concluded that a 'hypersensual woman . . . with an excessive sexuality' deserved 'the name vampire . . . in its literal sense' because 'out of ignorance' (excessive demands) or 'intentionally' (to kill her husband for his money), she demanded too much, sexually, from her mate."[62] As such, the vamp singularly threatened respectable and dependent femininity, especially in her sexual predations. But her wayward nature was also escalated by her racial ambiguity; indeed, one popular rumor, created by her promoters, claimed that Theda Bara's stage name was an intentional anagram of "Arab death." The vamp thereby indexed an exotic, mysterious origin that borrowed from multiple orientalisms—invoking gypsies and harems—to make sense of her unruly sexuality.

In this way the stories told about sexual transgressions in the city referenced an imperial vernacular that protested the presence of such deviations among its white denizens and instead assigned the presence of sexual corruption to empire's others through analogy and affinity. But if Gordon was more often than not portrayed as a vamp, what were her victims and accomplices? Although reporters depicted Gordon as courting trouble in any case, the men in these stories fared far differently from each other. In newspaper accounts, the vamp swindled older, rich white men, trimming their wallets whether through blackmail or payment for sexual favors. In these tales, she was a gold digger, a high-class prostitute, a predator with a plan, and she coolly and unsentimentally separated good men from their even better money.[63] In her wake, the men appeared easily duped but also uncontrollably lascivious in their tastes; in combination these qualities rendered them perfect victims of the vamp's allure. This masculine persona we have seen before, and, indeed, one narrative device used to rejuvenate these older, rich white men was contrived through empire's other masculinities. Comparisons to orientalized Arab men of West Asia and Northern Africa thus explicated both these elderly marks' moral defenselessness and their unusual sexual proclivities.

Using imperial logic to name a rich white man a sexualized caliph, a figure straight from stage and screen, one fantastical explanatory story attributes Gordon's death to her crossing of racial, national, and gendered borders as she gained sexual and economic power over this wealthy man. In writing about Harry M. Joralman, a "multimillionaire chemical manufacturer," the New York Evening Journal describes his "strange Harun-al-Raschid-like existence"[64]: "For, like some Caliph of Bagdad out of the Arabian Nights, Joralman was said to have held high court, levying with his millions upon the most beautiful of Broadway's beautiful women—surrounding himself with them, for all the world like an Oriental potentate in the midst of a harem."[65] Through such orientalist figures of both profligate wealth and aberrant sexuality, the sixty-nine-year-old millionaire was cast as a dynamic sexual force, if also a moral alien. In this instance, the name of the "Caliph of Bagdad" was familiar to readers as a foreigner, appearing in The Arabian Nights (the first French translation was published in 1704, the first English translation in 1706); François-Adrien Boieldieu's French opéra bouffe Le Calife de Bagdad (1800); Peter Cornelius's German opera, The Barber of Bagdad (1858); the novel Kismet, by Edward Knoblock (1911), and the 1920 and 1930 film versions of that novel; the film The Thief of Bagdad (1924); and the popular song "The Caliph of Bagdad," composed by Berenice Benson Bentley (1929). Such signifiers of oriental masculinity were thus regularly mobilized to explain the extraordinary sexual appetites and moral failures of elderly white tycoons. Ann T. Gibson, reputedly a "close friend" of Vivian Gordon's, told the Evening Journal, "'There was another rich old man she talked about. Said he was a banker and a regular turk, with six or eight women.'"[66] Again the sexual aberrations of Gordon's marks were made sense of through reference to orientalized masculinities ("a regular turk"). This produced a peculiar dichotomy. White men could be sexual predators, but such predation could not be attributed to the nature or culture of European or European American masculinity lest the moral, civilizational center disappear. Racialized masculinities, however, could carry the burden of such failures. These wealthy men's good standing in the imperial city (as its tycoons and entrepreneurs) could be preserved in this manner. Illicit sexuality and possible violence were obfuscated and disconnected from these men's whiteness and laid instead at the feet of orientalized masculinities that had in some frightful way contaminated these men.

Just as white men were marked through racialization that could carry implications of sexual licentiousness, reifying narratives of criminalization adhered to the bodies of men of color in fantastical stories about Gordon's life and death. Although in the accounts above Gordon courted trouble by luring some of the most powerful men in the city—indeed, in the country—into her trap, no such manipulation was necessary to entice men of color into sinning with her. Nonwhite men already tended toward the morally reprehensible in these stories, rendering any association with them immediately dangerous. Gordon's acquaintance with Puerto Rican men, for instance, was enough to cast suspicion on her associates as possible murderers. The *Evening Journal* noted that "Mrs. Halsey herself . . . is a Cuban. Thus, with her story of the two 'Porto Ricans or Spaniards' who were the flaming-haired Vivian's companions, and the fact that Zeno, the 'mystery man' of the Hamilton Apartments, likewise was described as a Porto Rican, the mystery surrounding the murder began to take on a decidedly Latin-American cast."[67] Cubans, Puerto Ricans, and other immigrants from U.S. possessions were an observable part of the cityscape, traveling from "there" to "here" as laborers or moving parts of the engine of imperial capital. In songs like the Tin Pan Alley–style "Chile Bean," Latinas in the city and in empire's elsewhere remained desirable: "You think we're full of blarney / We're full of Chile con carne," the male characters of the song sing to woo their Caribbean island love interest, named "Chile."[68] The song thus makes a case for more proper modes of choosing sexual objects through empire's lens. Unlike Latinas, who were marked as sexually available to a range of white masculinities, including the implied Irishmen in "Chile Bean," Latinos were already suspect. Their economically necessary if socially undesirable presence conjured up the continuing threat of their semitamed nature, and they were viewed as likely suspects for violent murders.[69] Indeed, it was later noted by an "expert" that "the crime seems to have a Latin touch. The fact that the woman was strangled doesn't jibe with the idea of American gangsters and gunmen. The Latins in their murders have a cruel streak, an element of torture—the garotte, the knife."[70] Not only do race and connections to the outposts of empire link these men to murderous acts in these reports, but their supposed national and racial character also betrays particular forms of sensual cruelty in intimate situations. These assertions, then, rely on an imperial logic that imagines those from the islands of empire to be uncivilized and not to value human life. As in the dance hall examples above, white womanhood is particularly threatened by racialized and nationalized masculinities.

Imperial figurations of Latino sexual prowess and violent propensities also played out in a story viewed by the newspapers as parallel to Vivian Gordon's murder. In a series of articles, the *Evening Journal* compared the brutal murders of other Broadway beauties, other women who had dared to carve out a place for themselves in public life. One article described the slain beauty Dot King's weakness for Albert E. Guimares, her Puerto Rican lover: "The girl and her lover lived a gay life and turbulent. They frequented the most bizarre haunts in town and they fought many a battle. Guimares at times beat her, punched her, kicked her, made her body an ugly picture of black and blue. But she loved him. She confided once to an intimate she could never love any man that she did not fear. And she feared Guimares, the dapper, smooth-shaven suave Porto Rican of Latin temperament."[71] In this passage, descriptions of King's life with her Puerto Rican lover shifted smoothly between the excitements and the terrors of New York City nightlife. Indeed, King's attraction to Guimares was attributed to her fear of him; his propensity for violence was portrayed as a perverse personal magnetism. His powerful physicality lent him an air of animalism that was at once fierce and enthralling. This brief excerpt thus demonstrates the imminent threat that the empire's racialized masculinities posed to the domestic order, a threat made all the more real with the crossing of boundaries— first, in Guimares's movement from Puerto Rico to New York, and second, in his associations with white women across divisions of race and in spite of racialized norms of gendered and sexual propriety.

Stories of Gordon's murder also mobilized particular notions of black masculinities, whose longer and lingering imperial histories linked them to violence, criminalization, and incivility. These complicated histories of containment and movement, tied to the all-too-recent past of transatlantic slave trading and more recent migrations from the Caribbean and the southern regions of the United States, marked black men in the cityscape. Their movements, however circumscribed in fact, also posed a danger to the racial order. One journalist, Alex Feinberg, invoked a mobile black masculinity in his invention of a potential suspect in Gordon's murder. Drawing on minstrel stereotypes, Feinberg created a character named "the Duke," a gigolo based in Harlem, a fabrication that came on the heels of the newspaper's discovery of a connection between Gordon and a black man with whom she was supposed to have had an affair.[72] In these two reports, Gordon's murder was linked not only to the manifest menace of black male sexuality, but also to the passionate, all-hours Harlem nightlife. Her journey to Harlem further challenged the racial boundaries of the city, where jazz-filled cabarets and nightclubs foreshadowed the horror to come.

The danger of transgressing the city's demarcations of safety and danger, mapped onto racialized neighborhoods and semi-outlaw spaces of jazz cultures, established the threatening milieu of Gordon's rendezvous. These accounts couple the jazz life with primitive passions, whose nature was both sexual and violent, and with the compelling force of musical rhythms and alcohol. In the initial account reporting her connection with a "darktown gigolo," Gordon was described as "tiring of the 'ordinary' pace set by her Broadway companions." To revive her interest, she "became a frequent habitué of the jazzy clubs located in the vicinity of 7th Ave. and 135th St. where 'hot' rythms [sic] and hotter hootch keep downtown patrons dancing and drinking until the wee small hours of the morning. It was in one of these places that the redhead met this darktown gigolo."[73] As with the dance hall, "jazzy clubs" were blemished by racial mixing and sexual depravity (much wilder than the Broadway scene). Multiracial nightclubs, cabarets, and "sin and gin joints" were part of an outlaw culture—here set in the heart of Harlem's nightlife district—comprised of criminal bodies and forbidden vices. Such themes of racial degeneracy and sexual wickedness, accompanied and encouraged by the sensual syncopations of jazz music, appeared in Feinberg's speculative account, which sought to offer to authorities a clue to Gordon's murder by providing a fictional version of what might have happened. Setting the scene for Gordon's imaginary encounter at a club with the Duke, Feinberg attributed a primal imperative to the persistent, perverse rhythms of jazz: "In the Blue Jazz Club, a perspiring band blared forth its maddest tunes. Jazz loud, piercing, broken, poured from the trumpets and the sax's [sic] as brown-skinned damsels, grinning, swayed and contorted their bodies in ecstatic convulsions."[74] As Feinberg sets the scene, the madness of the music was paired with the "contorted" bodies of black women dancing. Jazz music, and the movements it inspired, disordered its listeners' subjectivities at the level of the body.[75] Jazz compelled bodies into "contorted," "ecstatic" reconfigurations that contrasted with social norms of respectable comportment; jazz as presented in this brief but profoundly telling excerpt sounds like a thrilling violation of the moral order. In this lunatic atmosphere, these grotesque (to Feinberg) dancing figures strongly foreshadowed the convulsing, struggling body of Gordon as she fought and eventually succumbed to her murderer. The music was part of the joyful danger, according to Feinberg, subliminally inspiring the Duke to his primal rage. It does so first by creating outlaw subjectivities prone to perversity, and second by offering primitivist brute sensual scenes of distressed female bodies, on which the Duke might imagine imposing his murderous desires. All the while, however, the article continues to draw on the vocabulary of the adrenaline-producing Harlem nightlife that white patrons already enjoyed for years. A seemingly contradictory mode for explaining murderous rampages, the economies of pleasure represented in accounts of the Duke also tell why the air of criminality simultaneously seduced and repulsed, in a manner similar to the imagined populations of empires.

In this speculative account, the disposition of the "darktown gigolo" is drawn from pop culture figurations of black masculinity that lend meaning to our understanding of his possible role in Gordon's murder. In particular, the character of the Duke seems to come to the reader straight from the vocabulary of minstrelsy and vaudeville, both popular cultural forms that preceded and continued throughout the Jazz Age.[76] Like the dandified gentleman, a contemptuous image of black masculinity from the early nineteenth century, the Duke was a man with ambitions far beyond his station in life.[77] Feinberg's naming of this gigolo is a mockery; no one, we are meant to understand, could possibly mistake a black man for a nobleman. His act, shot through with unearned arrogance and rampant fraud, thus exemplified a serious threat to those white women who dared to wander into darkest Harlem.[78] In search of delight, they would instead find danger. Feinberg's opening description of the Duke paints a picture of the particular instruments of his deception: "'The Duke' was a picture of sartorial perfection. A green velour hat, its brim snapped down at just the right angle, adorned his head. His dress waistcoat was as snowy white as his gleaming teeth. It showed through, with its imitation pearl buttons, a suit whose color was neither quite green nor quite purple, but an eye-filling combination of both. His trousers were creased, not front and back, but sidewise in the manner of an extreme dandy."[79] This detailed description of his clothing sought to illustrate the Duke's suspicious qualities. First, his appearance was meticulous, his hat's brim "at just the right angle." He is clean and neat, but his tastes are garish and vulgar. The colors he chose are bright and "eye-filling," his suit a color so extraordinary that it defied existing categories. But his reputed perfection was strictly sartorial—set dressing, as it were: his gentlemanly appearance was an illusion, strictly tailored for a price, rather than naturally occurring in his black person. It was his buttons that gave him away most plainly. They were "imitation pearl," and the Duke himself was also imitation, in Feinberg's estimation.[80] With these few clues about his costuming, then, readers would be expected to know that this was a suspect man, an assumption predicted by their familiarity with popular entertainment that marked particular black men in this way.

Although the façade of gentlemanliness might be played for comic effect in these accounts, it only partially covered a wrathful, savage black masculinity, a racialization that marked the Duke—who could be any black man—as a likely murder suspect. Indeed, in Feinberg's fiction the man hiding behind a pretense of nobility and affected gentlemanliness was a violent creature of primitive urges. But it was not the loss of Gordon's financial support that angered him; the Duke could find "plenty of other women" who would pay his way.[81] Rather, in spite of the account of patronage that would seem to have made the Duke Gordon's dependent, he viewed her sexual being as his property. When Gordon spurned him, the Duke felt "strange uncontrollable impulses," deciding that "if he couldn't have her, no one else would. He was no plaything to be tossed aside by a woman when he wanted that woman, fiercely, with all his being."[82] Unable to deny his primal impulses, according to Feinberg's story, the Duke murdered Gordon. The fact that the Duke was fictional did not detract from Feinberg's claim that this invention might offer a clue to her death; in doing so, he suggested that any striving black man could be the Duke. Despite a pleasing exterior, and the appearance of civilized bearing, black masculinity always embodied an imminent danger because of its continuing associations with primitive sexuality. Jazz, furthermore, was the key to unchaining the beast.

Stories of Vivian Gordon as well as other women reputed to have met their deaths because of their movements into New York's nightlife—where races mixed, danced, and bedded one another—had multiple functions: engrossing, delightful tales of wild nightlife; cautionary tales; and confirmation of tales already told. As such, these stories appeared to be reform-minded, while still drawing on the appeal of heterogeneous jazz cultures and thereby luring more of the population into the sporting life, with the result that they would eventually need reform. That is, although the stories about Gordon were meant to naturalize her death, to render it inevitable because of her travel into jazz's contact zones—empire's outposts brought home—they also hinted that what was to be feared was terribly tempting. The maps and movements of empire may have denoted and described these transgressions, but these accounts drew a new chart of the city, letting readers know where and how to commit their own. In these narratives, jazz with its unbounded energies provided the soundtrack to such absorbing danger, and imperial figurations supplied the ground for comprehending jazzed subjectivities. The imperial logic used by these reports, then, provided the language of transgression and regulation, freedoms and its limits, and simultaneously served as a means of building the social order.

MIXED-RACE METAPHORS AND MEDIUMS

In February 1928 a vice investigator charged with monitoring prostitution met with Lucienne Delapazieux and Lorna Denny in a ground-floor apartment at 140 West 57th Street. Liquor flowed in the course of the "investigation," and the conversation turned to "fairies." One of the suspected prostitutes, Lucienne, advised the investigator to "read a book of homo-sexuality by Havelock Ellis, (which she wrote on a piece of paper)," according to the investigator (the influential British sexological researcher Havelock Ellis sought to shift homosexuality from the category of criminal acts to one of congenital, and thus involuntary, physiological abnormality). Lorna then offered to "stage a circus" if the investigator would pay each of the women twenty-five dollars. The circus they offered to perform would consist of queer sex acts between the two women that the vice investigator, turned prospective john, could watch. Sex between him and the women would cost more.[83] This is just one of many references to the emerging science of sexology to be found in vice reports from the era. Indeed, the traffic in knowledge between pervert and vice investigator was not unusual, nor was the sly recognition that the investigator might also be a voyeur unremarkable. One report on the Liberal Club's Pagan Rout, dated 1917, insisted that the free-love crowd were "close students of sex psychology and read every book on sex that can be found."[84] And at the highly sexualized balls in Greenwich Village, where scantily clad participants wore scandalous costumes drawing on Greek antiquities, Arab and Asian extravagances, and African primitivisms—all times and spaces distinguished in sexological and historical discourses as homosexual or so-called inverted scenes.

As with eugenics discourses of the races mingling and consequently dissolving, these reports indicate that sexological discourses marked city inhabitants and informed surveillance. They further show that some of the new supposedly scientific ideas circulated among nonscientists, including social workers, government agents, civilian investigators, and even the deviants whom the others sought to police and reform.[85] Furthermore, these reports convey fears that these same discourses produced more queer behaviors. And, as the 1917 report makes clear, the moral delinquencies of free love as well as queer and interracial sexualities can and do intersect each other, especially through the signs and symbols of imperial and civilizational divides. Here again, empire crucially informed the local demarcations of the city, its spaces, and sexualities.

This section brings together concerns from the previous two sections, in that here I am interested in the circulation of imperial logic both across the sexualized spaces of racially mixed dance halls and through discourses of racialized masculinities, as they pertain to narratives about black femininity and queer masculinities. This section turns to a novel that also took up these scientific and surveillance discourses, in order to think through the bounds of identity in the Jazz Age. The black artists and writers of the Harlem Renaissance contemplated questions of racial mixing and non-heteronormative behavior in city publics. They demonstrated particular interest in new formations of black masculinity. This younger generation, the historian Martin Summers contends, "constructed and performed their gender subjectivity through the elevation of the physical and sexual potency of the body, consumption and self-gratification, and an individual self-expression that was not confined by the black bourgeoisie's standards of propriety."[86] Thurman addressed some these experiments in self-making through the multiracial character Alva in his novel *The Blacker the Berry*. . . . When he turned his attention to the performing and policing of social and cultural identities in New York City, the impact of Asian immigrants from empire's outposts on urban demographics and the presence of Asians and Asian Americans in spaces of nightlife were not lost on him.[87] Incorporating Asian bodies as well as orientalist tropes in two of his novels, *The Blacker the Berry* . . . and *Infants of the Spring*, Thurman transformed debates about racial commingling, miscegenation, and black subjecthood.[88] In these ways, Thurman's work demonstrates connections between the making of queer black subjects, imperialism, and various scientific discourses, each of which are informed, shaped, and written against and through one another.

In *The Blacker the Berry* . . . , Thurman addresses imperial consequence and simultaneous multiracial presence through the mixed-race body of Alva, his main antagonist. As a villain, however, Alva is multidimensional. He does not simply represent the precarious social position of a mixed-race man; his multiraciality also operates as a metaphor for race relations in the city. In other words, he stands for both a phenotypical and a multivalent cultural admixture. Furthermore, rather than present his mixed-race characters as wretched or miserable, Thurman provides a more nuanced reading.[89] Additionally, he troubled dialogues about race and sex with his introduction of multiple non-normative sexualities, including queer acts and free-love ideologies, into the overwhelmingly heteronormative conversations about multiraciality and black modernity.[90] To some degree, these concerns followed from Thurman's interests in sociological and sexological studies. Although Alva's mixed-race body represents the (very literal) commingling of blood across an imperial color line, it also denotes the congenital physiological abnormality that was how most people then saw homosexuality. As Somerville so aptly observes, connections and transactions between racial science and sexual science in theories, methods, and analogies also created linkages between mixed-race bodies and queer ones. "Through notions of 'shades' of gender and sexual 'half-breeds,'" Somerville explains, early twentieth-century sexologists "appropriated dominant scientific models of race to construct and embody . . . the intermediate sex."[91] In Thurman's usage of the metaphors and analogies attached to mixed-race characters—literary and scientific in nature, but also mutually interdependent as technologies of the body—he responded to racial and sexological science in his examination of the multiple dimensions of interracial contact in the city.[92] Furthermore, he not only deployed mixed-race identities to represent the racial and national borders being drawn and redrawn in the city, but he also used these identities as instruments to pry open the borders of respectable gender and sexuality.

I argue that in much of this era's jazz cultures, the provocations of desire do not arise separately from histories of imperialism and colonialism. These histories reveal what Gayatri Gopinath calls an "erotics of power."[93] In Thurman's work an erotics of power is invoked through the bringing together of national and imperial structures of racialization and sexuality with scientific studies and the surveillance those studies inspired. By imagining the structural affinities of race, sexuality, science, and national belonging, Thurman productively created his congenitally queer figure at the scene of multiple collapses between categories. In *The Blacker the Berry . . .* (and, as I will discuss in the next chapter, *Infants of the Spring*), the metaphor and materiality of mixed-race bodies describes the transgression of distinct sexual boundaries and more. That is, Thurman also created characters that defied gender normativity, which we might call "genderqueer" from our vantage point. For Thurman, the mixed-race body as metaphor also becomes a medium for exploring anxieties about, as well as the challenges to, multiple (spatial, social, and sexual) borders.[94] The breaches and disobediences that Alva performs in the novel are instructive, demonstrating the constitutive nature of imperial logic to meaning making for interracial and queer relations in the domestic scene. Thurman, then, borrows from sexological and sociological theories and technologies in order to produce a black urban aesthetic practice of race and sex that is indelibly marked by empire.

In *The Blacker the Berry . . .*, Thurman addresses some of the concerns surrounding interracial contact in jazz cultures—including, for example, Carter's anxiety about the presence of Asian men in New York—in a fictional replication of Small's Paradise, one of Harlem's most popular nightclubs. In an early encounter between the novel's principal characters at this nightclub, Thurman illustrates the allure of the mixed-race man to a woman out for an evening's excitement. Thurman describes Emma Lou's initial attraction to Alva: "Then some one touched her on the shoulder, and she looked up into a smiling oriental-like face, neither brown nor yellow in color, but warm and pleasing beneath the soft lights."[95] Alva's racial unintelligibility is both pleasing and perplexing to her. When he asks her to dance, "Emma Lou was confused, her mind blankly chaotic. She was expected to push back her chair and get up. She did. And, without saying a word, allowed herself to be maneuvered to the dance floor."[96] In this passage, Alva's appeal is evident, due in large measure to the erotic enigma of interracial contact that he embodied as person and promise. At the same time, this mixing inspires both confusion and chaos in Emma Lou that were incited through music, dancing, and intimate interracial contact.

Thurman's The Blacker the Berry . . . is most often studied for discourses of color consciousness and consequent practices of social division among African Americans themselves, a practice that Thurman clearly abhorred.[97] Like Rudolph Fisher's "The City of Refuge" or the writings of the New Negro intellectuals, Thurman's novel destabilizes the notion of a unified and coherent black identity for Jazz Age Harlem.[98] Interrogating the primacy of skin color as the metaphor and medium for appointing value in the United States, Thurman argues that racialized identities are constructed according to demonstrably fallible categories.[99] However, this issue is more complex than simply questioning those forms of "colorism" that occur in black communities. In Thurman's novel, Emma Lou Morgan grew up in a small black community in Boise, Idaho, whose members valued light skin as a sign of status. In this community, much of the discussion of race revolved around the effort to make "good" marriages, defined by having an acceptably light-skinned heterosexual partner. Emma Lou is the daughter of a light-skinned mulatto woman and a dark-skinned black man—a pairing that the community and Emma Lou's extended family deemed inappropriate. Emma Lou's feelings about sexuality are shaped and guided by a black-white dichotomy, color hierarchies, and heteronormativity.

Worried about appearing too dark and finding a suitable partner, Emma Lou is attracted to the fairer-skinned Alva. But, of course, Alva is not just a light-skinned black man. Rather, he is multiracial. Thurman etches the transgressions occurring at nightclubs like Small's onto Alva's corporeal body and complex personhood, especially as a subject of U.S. empire: "Alva's mother had been an American mulatto, his father a Filipino. Alva himself was small in stature as his father had been, small and well developed with broad shoulders, narrow hips and firm well modeled limbs. His face was oval shaped and his features were more oriental than Negroid. His skin was neither yellow nor brown but something in between, something warm, arresting and mellow with the faintest suggestion of a parchment tinge beneath, lending it individuality. His eyes were small, deep and slanting. His forehead high, hair sparse and finely textured."[100] In this detailed description, mirroring the scientific scrutiny of the body's measurements by eugenicists and sexologists, Alva's ambiguous racial and sexual characteristics emerge. These complex characteristics, that cause anxiety in others as they traverse formerly stable categories, foreshadow Alva's queer acts, divulged later in the novel. As Somerville explains, "sexologists and others writing about homosexuality borrowed the model of the racially mixed body as a way to make sense of the 'invert,' an individual who appeared to be neither completely masculine nor completely feminine."[101] Alva's queerness is thus placed at the intersections of unsettled and upset categories, and though his queerness is disparaged by the novel's narrative structure, his liminal status nonetheless affords him access to all the identifications implicated in his particular ambiguity. A mobile figure, Alva accommodates a range of settings—from highbrow intellectualism to falling-down drunkenness and abject poverty, from heterosexual cohabitation and fatherhood to gay bachelorhood.[102] In many ways, Thurman presents Alva as the most compelling character of the novel, capable of movement and contact with many disparate people and places.

In Thurman's description, Alva's complicated racial mix (a mulatto mother and a Filipino father) produces layered unease.[103] Alva embodies a troubled triangle of race and racialization—part white, part black, part Asian—through those complicated economies of distance and intimacy that stand in for the legacy of the U.S. empire's chattel slavery and imperial expansion. As noted above, Thurman identifies Alva as "neither yellow nor brown but something in between," though his in-betweenness is not demonized at this point in the novel. Rather, Thurman uses this racial ambiguity to illustrate Alva's allure; his skin was "warm" and "arresting." In Emma Lou's first encounter with him, she notes the "pleasing foreignness of his face."[104] This blend, however, ultimately proves unsuccessful and undesirable. Though Emma Lou longs for a light-skinned man (a worry heightened by the "poor" marriage her light-skinned mother made with her dark-skinned father), Alva's skin tone proves misleading and ultimately inadequate. Though Emma Lou is also the progeny of mixed-race couplings, her multiraciality remains legible, unlike Alva's. His "parchment tinge" betrays the racial otherness that metastasized throughout his body, his blood's contamination—through its failure to be black, white, or even mulatto—of all known and legible terms.[105] Accordingly, the introduction of the Orient into a black and white equation signals new corruption. Furthermore, Alva's Asianness denotes his moral and sexual depravity as neither black nor white, saving both domestic categories from the horror and blame of Alva's despicable actions. Thurman thus uses Asianness as a character flaw to demonize Alva, even perhaps to demonstrate that lighter is not always better. However, Alva's exotic ambiguity is rendered appealing to some (albeit dangerous) degree. Though he is not rehabilitated in the story, Alva's allure is visible in his considerable knowledge of Harlem's nightlife and his social mobility as a charming guide to it.

Alva's racial ambiguities cannot be separated from their gendered and sexualized dimensions.[106] The visual markers of his racial otherness are also found in emerging scopophilic sexological discourses. This new language of sexual science, Somerville argues, "conceptualized sexuality through a reliance on, and deployment of, racial ideologies."[107] Sexological discourses created gender, racial, and sexual classifications to determine what was normal and abnormal, healthy and pathological, classifications that Thurman employs in this novel as scenes of tension. In the textual caress cited above, he deliberately confuses Alva's biological sex categorization with the origin of his sexual aberration, even before the novel's revelation of Alva's queer acts.[108] Although notions of dimorphic sex often underlie descriptions of masculine strength and bulk in contrast to feminine softness and slenderness, Alva is described as having shoulders that were simultaneously "small" and "broad." Troubling the ordering mechanisms of gender and sexual categories, these sexually ambiguous physical characteristics function to prompt further anxieties about Alva's moral character, and they foreshadow the disclosure of his queer sexuality near the end of the novel.[109]

Though Alva's gender transgressions can be understood as an instance of the feminization (or emasculation) of Asian men, Alva retains a threatening, even controlling, masculine agency that necessitates a more complicated reading of gender with race and sexuality. While Alva and Emma

Lou are married, Alva continues to have sexual relationships with many other characters in the novel, including the bisexual Geraldine, heterosexual Marie, and queer Bobby.[110] His sexual relationships deny the expectation of monogamy, instead promoting a free-love sensibility alongside his queer choices. In the climactic scene of the novel, Alva is with his male lover, Bobby. In this last relationship, Alva asserts a confident and vigorous (queer) masculinity, as Bobby appears to be a more docile partner, even going so far as to do Alva's laundry for him. While Alva's queerness, attributed to his Asianness, certainly blurs the borders of femininity and masculinity, his sexuality does not emasculate him. There is, of course, a troubling history of Asian American critics perceiving homosexual acts as a means of feminizing and otherwise degrading Asian and Asian American men. Such an argument, however, cannot account for queer acts that substantiate hierarchies of gender and sexual power, let alone challenge or embrace the idea of queerness as disruption or deviancy.[111] In the novel, Alva is still considered a sexual threat despite, or perhaps because of, his deviant masculinity. He has sex with men and women, and he dominates all of them. His relationship with Emma Lou provides him monetary resources, while his relationships with Geraldine, Marie, and Bobby function as narrative devices that reinforce his power over Emma Lou.

As Ann Stoler argues, imperial order focuses on ambiguous identities as well as the anxieties they create precisely because their features do not cohere in stable or clear categories.[112] In much the same way that necessarily malleable social and legal categories of blackness transformed the racial composition of the United States, Alva's transgressions confuse those discourses of gender and sexuality, racial thinking, and national boundaries that attempt to arrange physical and moral attributes in a hierarchical order. His ambiguous identities, then, can only be read as problematic given the conclusion of the novel. Though Alva's racial difference pleases and seduces, by the story's end it indicates his (congenital) pathology. Portrayed as being rotten to the core, the origins of his despicable nature can be discerned in Thurman's initial physical description, in both the maddening ambiguity of his visual and corporeal exterior and the muddled abnormality of his hidden interior. Alva fails to be black or even mulatto; his Asianness, as his other queer quality, taints his character and actions from the outset. That is, Alva's racial excesses gesture toward and otherwise guarantee his sexual excesses within the novel's arc. His sexual persona is marked as aberrant because he shamelessly philanders, repeatedly breaking his marital vows, and performs queer deviancy. His dangerous unintelligibility, identified as evasive and deceptive because it cannot be indexed properly, explains why he cannot be a proper lover for Emma Lou, the novel's heroine.

But to understand this danger, the tensions and outright hostilities produced by Alva's ambiguities must be read against empire, through which racial and sexual classifications emerge as ordering mechanisms. My reading of this novel brings into focus histories of colonial and imperial rule and all their racial and sexual dimensions. In this way, New York City emerges as a modern city defined by imperial ambitions and domestic struggles. Stories about new immigrants and people of color commingling in dance halls, nightclubs, and other jazz scenes thus illustrate anxieties about and also possibilities for the changing demographic characteristics of the national body, even as they extend the discourse of imperial reach. Cultural as well as scientific categories of race and sexuality, changed by encounters in multiple contact zones elsewhere, proliferate at microsites of national and imperial subject formation and forms of subjection in the city. Disciplinary rationales, incentivized by empire's encounters with racial others on the outposts, are aimed at wayward bodies within city limits. These vocabularies of race and sex, desire and danger — transported to Manhattan to underwrite the policing mechanisms of vice investigators, city legislators, and journalists and to animate aesthetic labors such as novels and nightlife — produce a complicated mesh of contacts and encounters as the grounds for negotiating freedom and control. Jazz appears as a contact zone through which imperial and domestic forms of racial thinking index Harlem nightlife as adventurous and stimulating because strange and erotic, but also unsettling and dangerous. Therefore, although the novel's outcome treats Alva's Filipino blood as treacherous, consistent with the manifest dangers associated with the yellow peril, and his mixed-race subjecthood echoes elements of the tragic mulatto (both elements common in racial thinking for the era), Alva could also be read as a more complicated and suggestively ambivalent figure. Even identified as a threat and menace emanating from empire's incursions, Alva offers a portrait of a life lived, if not beyond then beneath a stifling social order.

In this chapter, I have brought together newspaper accounts, music, dancing, performance, vice reports, sexological texts, and the specter of sociology as a way to explore how imperial logic contextualized and made sense of New York's nightlife in the Jazz Age. The racial mixing, with all it implied about empire's homecoming and sexual border crossings, was viewed as both enticement and danger. Thus, stories of these crossings were repeated across genres both as titillation and as forms of regulation. These narratives helped create nightlife participants, who could enjoy the commercialized entertainments of the Jazz Age, and suspect subjects, whose presence in public space challenged race, gender, and sexual roles and attracted scrutiny from authorities and reformers. Jazz music itself described urban neighborhoods in the United States as contact zones, where nightly negotiations of race, gender, sexuality, and nationality took place in spaces of commercialized entertainment. Participants in the sporting life challenged gender, racial, and sexual borders, the meanings of empire, and the proper use of public space. All the while, though, they gave cause for the policing of all those borders, and thus their actions described both boundary challenges and its own set of limitations. In the next chapter, I build on these ideas of transgression and regulation in an imperial context, to understand the creation of queer black aesthetic practices.

CHAPTER TWO

QUEER MODERNITIES

The cover of the March 1926 issue of *Opportunity* magazine featured a rough sketch of a primitivized black man in profile, his shoulders bared and a hoop dangling from his ear (fig. 2.1). He is posed adjacent to a palm tree, a climatic signifier for nonspecific jungles and sultry islands. This artwork accorded with other reclamations of the signs and objects of primitivism and fetishism characteristic of the New Negro intellectuals, who sought to seize and secure these symbols of modernity in avant-garde culture for the black arts—and black men—in the U.S. imaginary. The sketch is Richard Bruce Nugent's earliest published drawing, completed when he was just nineteen years old and within seven months of his return from Washington, D.C., to Harlem with Langston Hughes. Although the sketch draws on a repertoire of meanings attached to African natives and faraway landscapes, it also manifests Nugent's strategies for creating a queer black aesthetic in New York City during the Jazz Age. This particular image from Nugent's body of work brings together images of the African diaspora and narratives of the modern city to reconfigure the spaces in which we might find the African subject. Instead of remaining in the wild, outside of urban modernity, Nugent's figure confounds the boundary be-

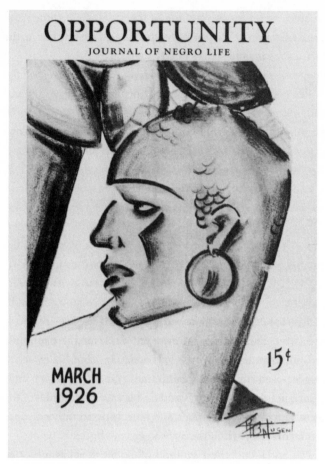

Figure 2.1 Richard Bruce Nugent, cover illustration for *Opportunity*, March 1926. Courtesy of Thomas H. Wirth.

tween the city and the jungle, the island, the faraway Eden. In doing so, he takes up various points of reference: he is an inhabitant of a remote land but also of New York City nightlife, where exotic club décor and costumed dances denoting distance also abound. In other words, this primitivized man also doubles as an urban denizen heading to a primitive ball in Greenwich Village. Thomas Wirth asks: "Is the young man really a denizen of the jungle, or is he perhaps a Harlemite in drag?"[1] The multiplicities of urban sexualities are made clear in this doubling, where the rouge on the figure's cheek and his hoop earring gesture toward queer cultures, and where the palm tree, while certainly a sign of primitivism, is also penis-shaped, a visual joke perhaps beyond the recognition of the magazine's editors, and references the sexualization of the primitive; the jungled sites of Africa, the Pacific, and the Caribbean; and spaces of city nightlife.

Through Nugent's sketch, it becomes evident that narratives of the primitive and the modern have a spatial relationship to each other and form the boundaries of the imperial city. Throughout his work, Nugent played with the solidity and surety of those boundaries of space and conceptions of geographic scale. The doubleness of the figure in this image thus locates the faraway in New York City, confounding the distance that marks both people of color as perpetual strangers and empire as a distant venture.[2] Thus, this sketch tells of the movements of peoples and ideologies in the construction of the imperial city. In the early twentieth century, public dances like Un Bal Primitiv were popular spaces of nightlife in the Village, sexually open affairs featuring partygoers dressed in jungle costumes and orientalized outfits, among whom we might find characters like the one pictured in Nugent's sketch.[3] Or perhaps the figure is a reference to those Harlem costume balls where men and women in drag received prizes for their transgendered efforts.[4] Nugent's drawing plays with these multiple mobilizations of primitivist imagery without assuming an originary point, understanding instead that these images circulate widely and carry multiple meanings to and fro as they move.[5] In this play with narratives of the primitive, Nugent blurs the boundary between the imperial city and other sites within and beyond the African diaspora.

In this chapter, I am interested in expanding the place of queer of color critique by rethinking the role that national borders, and their ever-changing configurations, play in sexual and racial formation. Artists, writers, and intellectuals of the Jazz Age insistently blurred spatial, racial, gendered, and sexual boundaries as a political strategy in the creation of a queer black aesthetic, focusing on the purposeful production and occasional (though uneven) deconstruction of nation and empire. My work here is partially in response to Roderick Ferguson's challenge in the conclusion of *Aberrations in Black*, where he invites the field of queer studies to more deeply engage with questions of the postnation in the field of American studies. Although Ferguson's call is focused on "the ways in which state and capital have achieved and continue to achieve racial dominance through discourses of gender and sexual normativity" as a means of understanding "contemporary global social formations," my methodological focus here centers on imperial aesthetic and social formations—which, of course, are affected by those modes of capital that helped found the modern city.[6] Nonetheless, I hope to take up his challenge in thinking through how imperial logic, as a system of meaning making that occurs through and across national borders and bodies, can be an important heuristic device for complicating sexual and racial formation and, more specifically, for understanding the creation of a queer black aesthetic on a global stage. In regard to the formation of a queer black aesthetic, imperial logic played a defining role in how power, social justice, the disciplining of populations, and resistance to that disciplining might take place. As artists imagined representations of bodies, city streets and interiors, and movement around the nation and between nations, the meaning of those representations was guided by empire's uneasy connections between the primitive, the orientalized, race, gender, and sexuality. In the formation of a queer black aesthetic, the instability of empire's meanings was mobilized to demonstrate the constructedness of these categories and their different social valuations.

In the instances I discuss in this chapter, these representations took both spatial and ideological form. That is, the meanings produced through imperial logic and made apparent through aesthetic practices questioned the constancy of the construction of bodies, cities, and nations as a way to, in turn, question singular modes of identity formation. I take my cue in part from Gloria Anzaldúa's landmark work in *Borderlands / La Frontera*, where she theorizes that the borderlands are spaces not only between nations but also between bodies, races, genders, and sexualities.[7] Part of how this identity manifests itself is in the organization and divisions between bodies, cities, and nations, even as these relationships are radically unstable and under constant negotiation. Anzaldúa thus intervenes in the continuous history of U.S. imperialism's assembling identities and affinities in relation to space and ideology. Imperial logic, then, brings together the material, the aesthetic, and the spatial to naturalize relationships of power. The application of imperial logic naturalizes the transference of power dynamics between these sites and creates distance where movement, bodies, and sexual desire might stand in for nations, colonies, and the desire to expand empire. This, then, also naturalizes the logic of violence against bodies engaged in desires that confound the state's enacted or legislated forms of racialization and/or desire. This logic naturalizes racial difference and reimagines imperial violence as commensurate with domestic surveillance and the disciplining of bodies believed to be aberrational in the project of the state—namely, bodies of color and queer bodies.

Although people interested in disciplining techniques might imagine the boundaries of cities and bodies to be regulatable by the police, law, and government, those who were marked as objects to be disciplined might also use imperial logic to resist those inscriptions. Aesthetic production in the Jazz Age often revealed cracks in the social order, enforced the flexibility of boundaries, or pointed out that the enforcement of those boundaries might have violent social consequences. For artists like Richard Bruce Nugent and writers like Wallace Thurman, whose work I discussed in the previous chapter, the marks of empire and the uneven relationships between nations might be used to point out differences in value across race, class, gender, and sexuality. People of color, the working class, women, queers, immigrants, and people who defy categorization along any of these lines might identify themselves in opposition to the imperium and in conjunction with those that the state considers outside of its national, social, and cultural borders. Although these aesthetic and political strategies turn the logic of the state on its head, I will show that they still rely on imperial logic to point out inequities through the mobilization of primitivist and orientalist signs that take on multiple meanings through empire. As a strategy, then, this kind of formation of a queer aesthetic practice is deeply imbricated in the imperium, even as it critiques differential valuation.

Imperial logic, therefore, provides an important context for understanding racial and sexual formation and the production of meaning for aesthetic practices in the Jazz Age. In considering the production of a queer black aesthetic through both imperial complicity and subversion, I suggest that we should ultimately see these works as articulating a crisis of referentiality and as arguing for the reconfiguration of our senses and the meanings attached to the sensible. As Helen Jun has astutely argued in regard to black orientalism, these moments of negotiation between racial and—in this case—national borders can be paradoxical and contradictory, as groups fight for inclusion through existing rhetoric and logics whose meanings may be attached to other forms of differentiation and exclusion.[8] Artists and intellectuals like Nugent and Thurman produced art and also critiqued aesthetic modernisms and the making of black art through similarly complicated and sometimes contradictory engagements with imperial logic and its demarcation and spatialization of intimacy as well as racial, national, and other boundaries. That is, through the accouterment of an Orient perceived as particularly queer, these works sought to interrupt the referentiality of the black body, and the sensual perception of the space of that body's gestures and movements, within both political and aesthetic modernisms. In describing these cultural and intellectual labors, I take my cue from Jacques Rancière. His notion of the "map of the sensible" provides a useful entry point for understanding the relationship between geographies of scale and aesthetic meaning making. He writes: "[Literarity and historicity] define models of speech or actions but also regimes of sensible intensity. They draft maps of the visible, trajectories between the visible and the sayable, relationships between modes of being, modes of saying, and modes of doing and making. They define variations of sensible intensities, perceptions, and the abilities of bodies"[9]—in the larger sense of human bodies, social bodies, the body politic, bodies of writing, and geographical bodies.[10] Rancière continues: "They thereby take hold of unspecified groups of people, they widen gaps, open up space for deviations, modify the speeds, the trajectories, and the ways in which groups of people adhere to a condition, react to situations, recognize their images. They reconfigure the map of the sensible by interfering with the functionality of gestures and rhythms adapted to the natural cycles of production, reproduction, and submission."[11] I borrow from Rancière's imagining of bodies across geographical scale, and the way it raises questions of how the map of the sensible might map onto the space of empire. I argue, then, that the map of the sensible—for the purposes of this chapter, a map that describes the boundaries of sexuality and race—becomes legible through the context of imperial logic and that this logic sets the limits on what can be sensed and known. For artists, this means that the referents for their art must, at least in part, be drawn from empire. These artists, though, are able to interpret empire, mobilize its meanings to challenge social convention, and sometimes repeat imperialist symbols, meanings, and modes.

This chapter, then, focuses on the crisis of referentiality that occurs when bodies that are meant to signify certain relationships within a national discourse take on multiple and unstable meanings brought about by the changes—often produced through empire—in geographical and ideological borders. Given the importance of the map of the sensible both in constructing the common sense of society and as a marker of the political limits of representation, considering the work of sensibility as it pertains to all those bodies Rancière had in mind—human bodies, social bodies, the body politic, bodies of writing, and geographical bodies—speaks directly to and expands the figurations of queer of color critique. Delineating the map of the sensible in this moment of ascendant empire—a geographical and corporeal phenomenon—enhances our understanding of the range of meanings of primitivist and orientalist referents (for there have to be limits, even if signifiers are loosened), as well as of queer of color formations and critiques. As I will argue in this chapter, the early forms of queer of color critique that emerge from the Jazz Age deconstruct the meanings attached to space, bodies, race, gender, and sexuality by making uneasy the relationships between bodies and disciplining ideologies of identity, bodies and imperial signifiers, and bodies and geographical space.

The chapter is divided into four sections. The first demonstrates how Jazz Age authors and artists used imperial logic to create modes of queer subjectivities. These were created, I argue, through the proximity of primitive and orientalist objects that marked those around them as queer in some respect. These artists adopted multiple stratagems for confounding— indeed, for queering—those forms of knowledge built on inflexible spatial and racial arrangements, including doubling, collocation, and collapse. In the three remaining sections, I turn to the production of a queer black aesthetic and a queer of color critique as examples of such reconfigurations of the map of the sensible in three registers. The first register follows representations of queerness in the absence of fixed and therefore knowable bodies and sex acts. Examining Nugent's infamous short story "Smoke, Lilies and Jade,"[12] I argue that he obfuscates "the functionality of gestures and rhythms" by remapping bodies and acts through another, queer order of the senses. This obfuscation directly questions the ontology of bodies and the processes by which they become attached to meanings of queerness, race, sexuality, and nation. The second register examines primitivist and orientalist objects' simultaneous abstraction from and attachment to queer bodies, and to queer of color bodies—again, with a difference. Looking at more of Nugent's visual art and a second-order representation of Nugent by Thurman, his good friend, I argue that Nugent and his literary figuration (or doubling) as a queer black artist collapsed boundaries between orientalist objects and his queer of color body through a resignification of queer European modernist tropes, heralding the productive practices of comparative empire. The mobilization of imperial markers here, I argue,

deconstructs the boundaries of race, sex, and gender as a way to formu-
late a queer black aesthetic. The third register further regards the relationship of bodies to space, as I argue that Nugent's posthumously published
novella, "The Geisha Man,"[13] thus pursues a deterritorialized queerness.
Through a reading of this novella, I argue that Nugent develops a queer of
color sensibility that expresses itself through a collapsing of geographies
of scale, where the Orient is in New York, the stability of racial categorization fails, and sexual possibilities polymorphously abound. Though each of
these strategies may not entirely succeed, we nonetheless find in Nugent's
work an expressive desire for another order of intimacy with and in contrast to the others of empire.

QUEER AESTHETIC PRACTICES IN THE AGE OF EMPIRE

Imperial logic provided a basis for modernist authors and artists to create
modes of queer subjectivities. Though guaranteed through uneven national
relationships, these queer subjectivities often signaled the author's or characters' liberalism. Because imperial logic works through modes of differential valuation, and through models of power involving both center and
periphery, the use of orientalist and primitive signs, language, and symbols
marked narratives, music, and art as simultaneously outside the bounds of
normativity, civilization, and respectability and as exemplary of modernity, as it was defined through imperialism and cultural contact. In order
to produce these aesthetic effects, which were rooted in the political, Jazz
Age artists mobilized notions of race, space, and sexuality both in opposition to and together with multiple imperial formations to explore the
bounds of sexuality and the instability of individual categories of identity,
which were implicated in the construction and destruction of other individual categories of identity. That is, the strategies of modernity and modern aesthetics already relied on imperial contact (Picasso's "discovery" of
Africa, for instance). Artists interested in queer aesthetic practices disiden-
tified themselves with these modernist strategies in the hope of producing
new subjectivity-effects for queer folks in the United States.[14] This kind of
work begins to display the way modes of Western rationality hide from
view the intersections of spaces, ideologies, bodies, and identity categories.
The form of queer of color critique supported by artists and intellectuals in
the Jazz Age—though they did not use that name for it—puts pressure on

racial and sexual formation through the evidence of empire while simultaneously creating powerful meanings for bodies, cities, and nations.

Although this chapter focuses primarily on the work of Nugent, and on a fictional version of Nugent produced by Thurman, these authors were not alone in mobilizing the modernist symbols of primitivism and orientalism as means of conveying the non-normativity of queer sexualities. Nugent's contemporaries also used primitive and orientalist signifiers to produce queerness and queer aesthetics. The articulation of queer aesthetics retained multiple purposes as sexual non-normativity and its imagined relationship to colonial outposts—the others of U.S. empire—were turned into symbols of liberalism and cosmopolitan engagement with modernity, or used to demonstrate the multiplicity of lives lived within the United States. In *Passing* (1929), for example, Nella Larsen signals the underlying queer tensions between the novel's two main characters, Clare Kendry and Irene Redfield, by placing oriental objects in both women's homes: a lacquered cigarette box on a tea table, and a Japanese print hanging on the wall.[15] Thus does Larsen use the imperial logic that interconnects race, nation, and sex throughout *Passing* to establish that the crossing of some borders of identity might also signal the simultaneous crossing of other borders of identity. Following this logic, through which these kinds of traversals appear as multiple, Larsen equates certain orientalist signifiers of nation with sexual signifiers to suggest queer desire. Larsen repeatedly refers to Clare's face as an "ivory mask": "Unrevealing. Unaltered and undisturbed by any emotion within or without."[16] Although literary critics observe that this image of the ivory mask enables her passing by hiding her blackness, it might also connect the orientalist-signifying material of ivory with stereotypes of Asian impassivity or lack of emotion. Orientalist signifiers—lacquered boxes and ivory masks—underscore the queer desire that exists between the two women, providing coded signals for readers to understand that sexuality beyond the bounds of normativity is in the offing.[17] Larsen, then, stretches the meanings of the modern—meanings often used to reassert the place of the West in relationship to the rest—by making identity and sexual practice in the metropole complicated. In doing so, she points to the cracks in the idea of the West as universal in contrast to spaces marked as primitive or orientalized. Through aesthetic design, too, she reimagines sexual normativity as a mask or veneer that hides queer sexualities existing in plain sight.

Likewise in *Save Me the Waltz*, Zelda Fitzgerald mobilizes orientalist signifiers to allude to the staging of queer sex acts, which doubly signify the liberal and cosmopolitan sensibilities of the novel's protagonist couple, Alabama and David Knight. A critique of heterosexual monogamy—subverting both the finality of monogamous relationships, even after marriage, and the expected deference of women to their husbands—Fitzgerald's novel relies on stable spatial scales to produce sexual difference. In one instance, Fitzgerald introduces Tanka, Alabama and David's Japanese butler. Tanka is marked as foreign, not just as a Japanese national but also as a non-normative sexual figure, through obvious aural signs. He is a domestic laborer whose "disquieting laughter" is obnoxious, and he speaks a peculiar English dialect: "Missy, kin see you jessy minute—jessy minute, this way, please."[18] What interests me about the introduction of Tanka is that it occurs right at the moment when two men have been discovered sleeping in the same hammock, the aberrant outcome of a presumably wild party the night before.[19] The Knights try to conceal their freethinking ways from Alabama's visiting family, but they are unable to contain their movements—queers literally creep out from behind closed doors. The orientalist signifier of the butler's intrusion onto the sleeping men is not the interruption of queer possibility, then, but a defining part of the spatial narrative of a connection and expectation of sexual experience that lies outside the bounds of heterosexual monogamy. Thus, the orientalized body of the domestic servant multiply signals queerness, liberalism, and the way segments of society can be simultaneously present and invisible.

The kinds of imperially bound figurations that mark these novels were also important to Nugent's creative works. His creative output—which included drawing, painting, dancing, and acting as well as writing poetry, fiction, ballet scenarios, and plays—provides an important entry point for thinking through the connections between modernity and modernisms, imperial logic, and queer black aesthetic practices. His relatively few publications kept Nugent from becoming a well-known author and artist of the Harlem Renaissance, but he was nonetheless a leading light of the arts and social scenes in Harlem, exercising great influence on many of the more acclaimed writers and artists of the time. While Nugent appears as only a minor character in general histories of the Harlem Renaissance, in queer histories of the twentieth century, he is recognized as a much more important figure. Born in 1906 in Washington, D.C., Nugent's mother had

Scotch, Native American, and black ancestors. A woman of many interests, she played piano and worked for the National Geographic Society and, later, as a waitress.[20] His father, an elevator operator at the Capitol and a singer in Washington's Clef Club Quartet, passed away when Nugent was just thirteen years old. Later Nugent and his mother moved to New York City.[21] As a child, Nugent pursued an interest in the arts. He was encouraged by his bohemian parents and given full access to the contents of their library, and what he read there would have an indelible influence on his life and work. His father's copy of Richard Freiherr von Krafft-Ebing's *Psychopathia Sexualis* introduced him to sexological studies while he was still in high school, helping him to give a name to his sexual proclivities.[22] His earliest, informal training in arts and letters, and as well the emerging science of sexology, would greatly influence his views on art history and unconventional sexuality. Often cited as the first African American to have published an openly queer story, he is thus heralded as a path-breaking author and artist. The central role he plays in queer literary history suggests that his work merits closer attention, especially its role in the emergence of a queer black aesthetic in the Jazz Age. Because of his place in a longer queer of color genealogy, it is also important to understand the genealogies and epistemological boundaries of his work, both as art and as criticism.

Nugent's queer black aesthetics, and the early version of queer of color critique found there, developed within and in opposition to European, African, and Asian arts and letters—that is, his body of work was engendered by the movements of signs and symbols across multiple empires. Like Nugent, most Harlem intellectuals and artists wrestled with the simultaneous admiration and domination that underwrote European negrophile movements, which had seized on the signs of primitivism as symbols of European avant-garde culture. However, the primitive, the oriental, and other did not serve as end points in this economy of new energies, but merely the conduit for multiple artistic sensibilities. Nugent's body of work in particular commented on these aesthetic modernisms, including his discovery of a queer European arts tradition and the uses of primitivism for creating avant-garde and queer subjectivities by U.S. expatriates and European writers, composers, and artists such as Oscar Wilde, Aubrey Beardsley, Erté, the British Arts and Crafts Movement, Joris-Karl Huysmans, Richard Strauss, and Giacomo Puccini. The array of European intellectual and artistic figures tells an alternate story to the one in which the work of the New Negro is made only across the Atlantic. The modes of imperialism that Nugent employed stretch across five continents and multiple empires. Even as intimacy is sought between these spaces, distance is sometimes reinstated. In his works, Nugent as artist and character considers the terms of these and other manipulations of geographies of scale for modern and modernist figurations of race and sex. In doing so, he sometimes replicates the ontological and epistemological schemas of imperial logic, even as he seeks to confound their authoritative classifications. Although I do consider his works through this duality of complicity and subversion, I ultimately argue for a reading that would see them as a crisis of referentiality, and as the reconfiguration of our senses.

For Nugent, his work depended on the circulation of meanings that guided modern art's relationship to the primitive and the orientalist. As we know, much of modern art was predicated on the uses of primitivist imagery in order to create a modernist sensibility. Nathan Huggins has written: "It seemed that the black man was being 'discovered' through his music and art, and it seemed to be his spirit which symbolized the Jazz Age."[23] And Marlon Ross argues that Alain Locke "explicitly associates the New World Negro with the artistic experimentation of high modernism. . . . Given his belief that Africa's traditional culture, correctly interpreted, represents a level of sophistication so high that Europe must borrow from it to modernize itself, it might be said that the American Negro must 'go back' in order to go forward to his already-awaiting modernity."[24] Indeed, the circulation of racialized and nationalized signs and stories was key to the creation of a modern Western self-image. These movements represented Enlightenment narratives and rationalizations of space and subjectivity that spoke to a celebratory sense of discovery and the mixing of cultures, and to the distancing operation of othering, as central to Western self-making. Travel outside of Europe, sometimes real, sometimes imagined, thus became a way to produce modern subjecthood. Furthermore, concepts of moral lasciviousness, sexual excess, and congenital deviancy that had distinguished the sexualities of colonial and imperial outposts became—in a revaluing but not a reversing of imperial logic—liberating. Empire thus became a *place* for queer subjectivity; however, that queer subjecthood is made viable and visible through imperial logic. Queer subjects like Oscar Wilde could reimagine themselves as queer moderns through an imperial discourse of travel, which marks their place within the empire, even if national belonging still eluded them.

Art making and the realm of the aesthetic, then, became an important mode of intervening in national and imperial sexual and racial politics. Nugent did not simply reiterate these terms in his own work. He knew well that the ability for people from imperial metropoles to discover and displace the avant-garde spirit of spontaneity, or even sexuality, onto the black primitive (and, as I show below, the Orient) depends on the unavailability of similar movement to those presumed to be stuck in the colonies. He was interested instead in colliding, collapsing, and confusing tropes of racialized and queer modernisms and modernities, especially in the use of the signs and symbols of primitivisms and orientalisms. Thus, he commented on the use of primitive signs in two ways. First, he provided a counterpoint to the appropriation of an imagined Africa by European arts communities, and second, he broadened the reappropriation of imagined Africas and Orients by black U.S. intellectuals to also provide a space for queer sexualities within the redefinition of blackness through language and aesthetics. Nugent's cover art for *Opportunity* provides a good example of how he understood the racial, national, and sexual markers that were circulating in art, and his view of how these markers could be manipulated in order to create conversations around the place of black arts within modern arts communities. Though he too used the tropes of African primitivism, such as the palm tree and the nude figure, Nugent's sketch is no simple reiteration of fetishistic tropes. Rather, he is at play with those tropes, and the result of that play is the creation of a racialized queer visual vocabulary, produced through the strategically mimetic repetition of primitivist iconography layered with reference to Manhattan's queer public culture.[25] Conscious of the use of primitivisms, Nugent reread stories of cultural contact to tell a different story about the place of racialized peoples within the narration of modernity. In other words, he produced an aesthetic repetition with a difference. As Gilles Deleuze observes, "repetition as a conduct and as a point of view concerns non-exchangeable and non-substitutable singularities. . . . If exchange is the criterion of generality, theft and gift are those of repetition."[26] For Nugent's work, the theft is of the primitive sign, and the singularity he makes from this theft is a queer black aesthetics. The productive heteroglossia that pervades the *Opportunity* illustration and

Nugent's other visual work denoted a genealogy of queer identities rooted not in Europe but in reimaginings of Africa and diasporic blackness. While Nugent participated in the New Negro intellectual project of reclaiming Africa to construct a powerful space for blackness in the United States, he did so with a disloyal difference, creating also a space for queers of color through a retelling of the history of queer black masculinities.

Nugent also mobilized orientalist aesthetic signs in his artwork, though they are not overtly present in the *Opportunity* cover. In some ways Nugent's mobilization of these signs follows the same logic as his dissemination of Africanized primitivisms, but in other ways his use of these signs reiterates and repeats the imperial logic of queer European masculinities and aesthetic practices, often without commenting on this logic. The redeployment in queer modernisms of imperial logic reiterated the construction of the Orient through concepts of gender and sexual perversion—what Eve Sedgwick might call a "gay affirming and gay-occluding Orientalism." [27] Yet the connections among Wilde, queerness, and orientalism are so overdetermined that when Thurman's *Infants of the Spring* references Wilde among orientalist signifiers, in relation to Nugent, those signifiers are read through a European tradition of queer arts and literature. Elisa Glick, for instance, notes that Thurman uses orientalist signifiers, but that he does so because of Wilde's influence. [28] Here, because orientalism itself as an archive of images and acts is so connected to Europe and occidentalism (as Edward Said has famously argued), the Orient becomes a complete simulacrum, associated with Europe rather than referencing actual orientalized territories or peoples. [29] Though I agree that orientalism is indeed an invention of the West, it is important to grasp how a black queer artist such as Nugent might have mobilized orientalist signifiers to manage not just sexual but also racial relations in the United States, both in the city and beyond its borders. [30] Nugent's use of orientalist imagery mapped the logics of queer whiteness onto queers of color and created a queer method for understanding what is produced through contact between racialized groups within city space. In other words, although he inherited orientalist tropes primarily from the European decadents, he repeated them for a new purpose: these tropes no longer signified a queer white masculinity; rather, they took on new meanings in creating a space for racialized queer masculinities. [31] Additionally, they provided a means for understanding immigration and diaspora through a queer of color critique, holding out the possibility of addressing the legacy of the transatlantic slave trade, Western expansionism, military and economic incursions into Latin America, and the imperial wars fought in Asia and the Pacific.[32]

Nugent's work, then, becomes a starting point for a version of queer of color critique: his interest in work across sexual, national, and racial spaces. By investigating the stability of the borders of identity, Nugent's work suggests a form of queer of color critique that retangles the strands of identity that have been separated through Western rationality. Ferguson has argued that "as social order achieves normativity by suppressing intersections of race, class, gender, and sexuality, rationality must thus conceal the ways in which it is particularized by those differences."[33] Part of the work of queer of color critique is to make those intersections visible. Nugent does so by destabilizing the relationship of the signifier to the signified. He plays with the inherited meanings of empire to show its standing contradictions. He disallows the separation of identity categories by unveiling the fact that instability in one might create instability in another. It is in this kind of geographical and ideological borderland that Nugent's work helps articulate this intervention into queer of color critique, where the modes and context of empire are paramount in the making and unraveling of meaning.

BODIES AND THE CRISIS OF REFERENTIALITY

This section focuses primarily on the interconnections between empire, the production of a queer black aesthetic, and the crisis of referentiality signaled by the representation of bodies. Because bodies, desire, and sensuality have been linked to one another in the study of queerness from early sexology and psychoanalysis to contemporary queer studies, it is important to track the ways in which bodies have come to stand in for queerness as queer objects. Nugent's work predates some of the current trends in queer studies that have troubled the easy equation of queer bodies or queer sexual practices with queer identities. His writings produce a queer black aesthetic that occurs sometimes without bodies, and sometimes with bodies that transform and work themselves into aesthetic objects, thereby desiring detachment from stable systems of scientific classification and knowledge. In thinking through the relationship of bodies and referentiality, I take my cue in part from those scholars interested in music cultures—theorists who pose questions regarding the correlation of queer bodies, race, sensibility, and aesthetic production. For example, in his exploration of the linguistic slippages and sutures characterizing *punk* as a term that refers both to queer black men and a musical subculture, Tavia Nyong'o asks: "Might we theorize the intersection of punk and queer as an encounter between concepts both lacking in fixed identitarian referent, but which are nonetheless periodically caught up and frozen, as it were, within endemic modern crises of racialization?"[34] His provocative question asks scholars to rethink the connection of "queer"—and thus queer theory—with problematically fixed queer identities. In short, it forces us to think about queer aesthetic and signifying practices, how these might contribute to racialization, and—I would hasten to add in regard to my project—how they might constitute national and other borders.[35] Also arguing against the fixity of categorization, Scott Herring provides a warning that the reconstitution of borders of identity reifies the kinds of scientism that fields like sexology and sociology establish in order to control populations. Instead, Herring works across the grain of political projects that quicken "sexual visibility and sexual recognition" in hopes of "put[ting] out of order" the means of classifying bodies.[36] Also building on this framework, Sherrie Tucker invites jazz scholars to reconfigure the burden of representation in sexuality studies from queer bodies to straight ones.[37] This move challenges the equation of queer bodies with the production of queerness, as well as the overdetermination of sexuality studies through queer bodies. Nugent's work during the Jazz Age ties these questions of sensibility and bodies as referents to empire. If empire is part of the context that lends meaning to the map of the sensible, Nugent uses that system of meanings to produce a novel subjectivity through queer black aesthetics. Losing the stability of identitarian categories, Nugent's new and mercurial vision of queer black subjectivity is purposefully mutable, constructed as the uneasy assemblage of decadence, bodies, queerness, and space. Within the context provided by imperial logic, Nugent makes bodies unstable as both signifiers and what is signified, where bodies are inhabited by sexual subjects; are replaced by other aesthetic forms, such as objects or music; and stand in for beauty themselves. This form of queer black aesthetics, then, focuses on the exotic beauty of imperial objects, even turning queer bodies into objects, and on understanding a queer sensibility in relation to those objects. Sometimes these slippages occur simultaneously, marking the various ways that imperial narratives can manifest themselves. In these ways, Nugent's work concomitantly depends on imperial logic and marshals it against itself to create new, if in some sense failed, possibilities for queer black subjectivity.

To pursue this reading, I am particularly interested in the writing of the body as a sign that both supports and delimits the logic of imperialism. Following Ferguson and others, I will explore the aesthetic and the epistemological in the formation of subjects of the state—and empire—in the language of the African American literary canon.[38] For Nugent, the body itself is often circulated as an aesthetic object that works to deconstruct the absence of queer black bodies. Although the literary scholar A. B. Christa Schwarz points to Nugent's literary sensuality, particularly in his writing of a desire for bodies and beauty, this love of bodies and beauty is arguably not about bodies as themselves, but—as Barthes suggests, in writing about the structure of Japanese—as "signs cut off from the alibi referential par excellence: that of the living thing."[39] In other words, these bodies are purposefully emptied signs, signs that work as aesthetic objects beyond the biological matter of racialized and gendered bodies. As these signs are recirculated, they rework the logic of empire, marking an epistemological shift for the production of the knowledge regimes of race, sexuality, and imperialism. In the works that I discuss below, Nugent and Thurman confuse the boundary between signifier and signified, where the body becomes in this instance an orientalized signifier. In the confusion of meaning that Nugent produces, certain boundaries between race, nation, and sexuality that establish ways of knowing are critiqued in unique ways. Using devices that seem to refer to racial and national difference in "Smoke, Lilies and Jade," Nugent produces a queer sexuality steeped in imperial logic, even while he exploits that same logic to comment on and challenge imperial intimacies' engendering of racial and sexual politics in New York City.

While he lived in New York, Nugent shared a Harlem apartment at 267 136th Street, an address playfully referred to as "Niggerati Manor," with Thurman, an author and editor with whom he often collaborated. Nugent and Thurman had a productive and mutually beneficial relationship. Their best-known collaboration was the one-off journal *FIRE!!* that Thurman edited and to which Nugent contributed "Smoke, Lilies and Jade," his most often reproduced literary work. Nugent's short story is often cited as the first piece of African American published writing to openly address queer possibility; in Daniel Kim's insightful words, "it was the first piece of African American fiction expressing an openly homosexual *sensibility*."[40] This possibility or sensibility marked a political aesthetic practice, though the honor of being the first to forward a queer black literary aesthetic could well have fallen to Thurman. According to Nugent, he and Thurman flipped a coin to see who would write a story on prostitutes and who would write a story in the manner of "the decadents." Thurman drew the former and Nugent drew the latter, whereupon he undertook to write a story in the style of Joris-Karl Huysmans's *Là-bas*.[41] On its publication, FIRE!! was openly scorned. Nugent recalled a conversation with W. E. B. Du Bois at the height of the controversy surrounding the magazine: "I remember Du Bois did ask, 'Did you have to write about homosexuality? Couldn't you write about colored people? Who cares about homosexuality?' I said, 'You'd be surprised how good homosexuality is. I love it.' Poor Du Bois."[42] Nugent's irreverence in speaking of Du Bois in this manner ("poor Du Bois") was indicative of his (and Thurman's) desire to break away from the "talented tenth" politics of the older generation of black intellectuals.[43] Such a politics, in so many ways, did not leave a space for "dandified aesthetes" like Nugent and Thurman, who shared unconventional ideas about the range of masculinities that could or should be portrayed in Harlem Renaissance arts and letters, as well as a radical notion of success.[44] As Glick argues, Nugent and Thurman's "decadent aesthetics . . . disrupts the commodity relation to African American culture."[45] Nugent's answer to Du Bois's concern also holds clues to an unprecedented queer politics, suggesting his distancing of queer acts (homosexuality) from queer identities (homosexual), a move that values queerness but does not classify and thereby "fix" bodies. Nugent's friction with Du Bois also points to how rare the combining of racial justice and queer aesthetics was, even as this combination is a cornerstone in Nugent's creation of a queer black aesthetic. Although a number of scholars have echoed Henry Louis Gates's sentiment that the Harlem Renaissance was "surely as gay as it was black," the fact remains that many of the writers and artists who are taken up in a queer genealogy were forced to use various strategies in the production of queer identity when national leaders like Du Bois were resistant to queer assemblages.[46]

"Smoke, Lilies and Jade" explores the artistic life of the mind, and the mind as an organ of the senses, as a way of defying and denying categorization. Although Nugent is interested in these forms of denial, he also relies on imperial logic that at times reasserts the differential valuation of empire's others. Following the lead of the Aesthetic Movement, Nugent references Oscar Wilde in the story's hailing of similar orientalist signs in the name of "art for art's sake," but, of course, Nugent as well as Wilde operated in a racialized political context. Sidestepping a binary of black and white relations, Nugent instead chooses to engage the racial politics of the time by depicting in his short story an interracial queer relationship between a black man and a Latino man. Nugent's aestheticized rendering of interracial queer acts informs an avant-garde mode of queer of color critique. As Rancière notes, "aesthetic acts as configurations of experience . . . create new modes of sense perception and induce novel forms of political subjectivity."[47] Shifting modes of sensibility may engender new subject positions, but those positions are still attached to a larger field of the distribution of the sensible. New modes are always still in conversation with old modes, where meaning is interpolated between many ways of understanding.[48] Nugent aestheticizes bodies, objects, and places in order to comment on the pragmatics and practices of empire. The imperial logic he deploys to break through the boundaries of possibility and sensibility at the level of the body, city, and nation, also provides its own limits, because this shift in subjectivity relies on international and imperial differences to reinvigorate the negotiation of domestic boundaries. As Caren Kaplan warns, "the modern era is fascinated by the experience of distance and estrangement, reproducing these notions through articulations of subjectivity and poetics. Yet displacement is not universally available or desirable for many subjects, nor is it evenly experienced."[49] Even as empire makes sense of queer acts, those acts still exist within asymmetries of power. Nugent's work, even as it deconstructs imperial logic, depends on it for some of its sense making, at points reproducing the modes of imperialism apparent in the genealogy of queerness and European empire.

The genealogies of imperial logic and European queer subjectivities help provide the grounds for producing novel queer black subjectivities in the Jazz Age, as Nugent references decadent artistic production as one of the keys to remapping and revaluing queer sensibility. One way that Nugent draws his readers into a worldview ruled by aesthetic sensibility is through the main narrative voice of the short story. As many authors have noted, Nugent wrote in a stream-of-consciousness style, replete with ellipses, which Schwarz connects to modern white European modes of fiction.[50] The literary critic Michael Cobb traces the production of a black and queer literary aesthetic and argues that Nugent produces an "elliptical rudeness," a form that in itself disrupts.[51] Furthermore, as Daniel Kim notes, although the story is written in stream of consciousness, it is also written in the third person.[52] The effect of a narrator describing the thoughts of Alex, the story's protagonist, creates a sense of disembodied detachment. But though the narration challenges embodiment, deflecting the burden of representation from the body, Nugent also creates a highly sensual account. He relies on sights, sounds, and feelings to produce an aesthetic vocabulary. Many objects whose colors are foregrounded recur in the story as signs and symbols. For instance, the color blue, usually describing smoke, denotes creativity and the artists' enterprise. Red calla lilies are associated with death and transcendence. Ivory, red, and green make up a cigarette holder, an orientalized object that serves as a refrain, capping each section of the story. Alongside color, music is also an important signifier for the senses. "Alex walked music . . . it was nice to walk in the blue after a party," Nugent writes, and continues:

> Alex walked music . . . the click of his heels kept time with a tune in his mind . . . he glanced into a lighted café window . . . inside were people sipping coffee . . . men . . . why did they sit there in the loud light . . . didn't they know that outside the street . . . narrow blue street met the stars . . . that if they walked long enough . . . far enough . . . Alex walked and the click of his heels sounded . . . and had an echo . . . sound being tossed back and forth . . . back and forth . . . some one was approaching . . . and their echoes mingled . . . and gave the sound of castanets . . . Alex liked the sound of the approaching man's footsteps . . . he walked music also . . . he knew the beauty of the narrow blue.[53]

In this passage, Nugent uses color, music, and space to produce Alex as a subject through his senses, through his ability to see beauty and color that elude others; to hear music available only to those of artistic temperament; and to appreciate his surroundings in a detached, critical manner. Importantly, too, Alex's body disappears into music; the body is replaced with another signifier of beauty and sensuality. For Nugent, this new aesthetic epistemology engenders Alex's novel subjectivity—the subjectivity of the artist, the queer, the man of color.

The creation of this novel subjectivity happens through a particular knowledge of space and the remapping of the sensible. In the passage above, though Alex cohabits space with others, he separates himself from the men inside the café who live in the "loud light" and cannot appreciate the night, where "narrow blue street met the stars." Because Alex exists in a different epistemological system, his mode of producing space and therefore sociality contrasts with the men in the café. They did not make *sense* of the world. They are therefore not subjects in Nugent's worldview. Conversely, Alex embodies a positivist position, repeating some of the axioms of Cartesian subjectivity, but, again, with a difference—a sensualist, he sees, hears, and feels as a mode of knowing. Through aesthetic practice, Nugent creates a new distribution of the sensible. His political call for a novel subjectivity is accomplished through a reordering and re-experiencing of space, perception, and—ultimately, through epistemological shifts—the will to knowledge. "It is a delimitation of spaces and times, of the visible and the invisible, of speech and noise," Rancière writes, "that simultaneously determines the place and the stakes of politics as a form of experience. Politics revolves around what is seen and what can be said about it, around who has the ability to see and the talent to speak, around the properties of spaces and the possibilities of time."[54] For Alex, remapping the sensible is a spatial and political project. Modes of encountering space and the multiple sensibilities of space can in and of themselves produce novel subjectivities. The queer practices of Alex's sensuality speak to the stakes of a queer politics that is simultaneously about the queer sensuality of the body and about bodies that are not necessarily sexual in the manner designated by scientific knowledge of sexuality. In this way, Alex reimagines the political boundaries of queer identification and subjectivity through playing with the map of the sensible.

As can be seen in the passage above, Nugent's epistemological shifts are created through a refiguring and revaluing of difference through sense perception. Nugent continues to work through ideas of sensuality, space, and perception where difference—and thus the mode of subject making—is borne through imperial logic and its system of differential valuation. Part of the tension and complexity in this form of subjectivization comes as Nugent collapses imperial space with New York City space through the replacement of objects and bodies in space. Like the work of Wilde, Huysmans, Larsen, and Fitzgerald, Nugent's work is peppered with objects from elsewhere as a way of creating a difference between the sensible and insensible others, a novel mode of subjectivity. The ivory and jade cigarette holder, incense, "precise courtesans winking from behind lace fans," perfume, Buddha, and Salomé all make appearances as objets d'art.[55] Orientalist modes of knowing and collecting signal an aesthetic practice that occurs beyond the ken of the limited sensibilities of others who also inhabit the city. In a twofold operation, Nugent locates the Orient outside the West as a fantasy of the exotic, and inside the West as a badge of distinction for those who can know the Orient. Orientalisms draw on Enlightenment epistemologies that often exclude bodies of color from these modes of self-making, but Alex uses them in imagining another life that would better suit him:

> he would like to live in a large white palace . . . to wear a long black cape . . . very full and lined with vermillion . . . to have many cushions and to lie there among them . . . talking to his friends . . . lie there in a yellow silk shirt and black velvet trousers . . . like music-review artists talking and pouring strange liquors from curiously beautiful bottles. . . . yes to lie back among strangely fashioned cushions and sip eastern wines and talk. . . . yes and have music waft softly into the darkened and incensed room . . . he blew a cloud of smoke . . . oh the joy of being an artist and of blowing blue some thru an ivory holder inlaid with red jade and green.[56]

This orientalist fantasy, no doubt abetted by romantic (or erotic) visions of the film star Rudolph Valentino in *The Sheik* and also "music-review[s]" from Broadway and off-Broadway, illustrates Alex's artistic sensibility. Demonstrating worldly knowledge of the Orient's (and the Orient in New York's) built environment, fabrics, and drinks, this description is both bohemian and cosmopolitan. Alex refines his subjecthood through knowing and valuing difference, but of course the capacity to know the Orient is fraught with the unevenness of imperial power and statecraft. Inasmuch as Alex avails himself of an oriental mystique to append his modernity, and deploys this fantasy to create queer space in New York, he depends on an imperial logic that would not allow bodies marked as outside the nation to participate as sovereign subjects. So, though Nugent reimagines city space through a redistribution of the sensible, he relies on more stable notions of national and imperial space in order to produce an aesthetic vocabulary.

The drawing of a queer black aesthetics from the logic of empire also betrays how Nugent valued and reiterates difference in his representation of interracial and transnational sexuality. This aesthetic vocabulary is most potent when Nugent describes Alex's flirtation and sexual encounter with Adrian, a Latino man whose presence is foreshadowed in the passage above by the sound of castanets. As Alex encounters his love interest on the blue street, imperial logic dictates an aesthetic vocabulary that literally renames his interest as an object, "Beauty," at the same time as Alex becomes a sexual subject. This encounter holds a vaunted place in scholarly circles because it marks the quintessential queerness of the text: a queer encounter between queer bodies.[57] The story's description of the Latino love interest, Beauty, was based on characteristics of the Mexican caricaturist Miguel Covarrubias; Valentino, whom Nugent had met; Harold Jackman, a "handsome West Indian man about town"; Langston Hughes; and Nugent himself.[58] Thomas Wirth also suggests that Nugent had fallen in love with Juan José Viana, the "scion of a prominent Panamanian family," while both worked at the Martha Washington Hotel.[59] These sources demonstrate how a multifaceted imperial logic of migration and mixing shaped Beauty's character. With Beauty a composite of multiple immigrants from multiple empires, Nugent is clearly playing with the imperial logic of subjecthood through queer sexuality.[60] This imperial logic creates a contradictory schema for Alex's evaluation of Beauty. On the one hand, Alex loves and appreciates Beauty; after all, beauty is the goal of aestheticism. On the other hand, because Beauty is aestheticized, he is also objectified as a means of Alex's subjectivization. The work of the body as referent, then, is quite slippery. It points both to queer acts, an imperial imagination beyond the materiality of bodies, and to aesthetic claims to objects and sensuality. The work of beauty itself is not universal or natural, but embedded within imperial and civilizationist discourse. As Mimi Thi Nguyen observes, "we can see how beauty as a measure of moral character and feeling, which has a clear geopolitical dimension, also functions to regulate moral character and feeling, especially as a geopolitical exercise addressed to the individual and the collective as power's problem and beauty's mandate. . . . When beauty is called upon to tell us something significant about the paths and places that the good and the moral might be found, the partisan nature of beauty's perception becomes all too clear."[61] Nugent revalues the imperial and racial other as beautiful, but this revaluation continues modes of differentiation, so that what is marked as strange or outside of the ordinary is materially and sexually fetishized. Imperial logic contextualizes this quintessentially queer moment—poised between queer bodies and the transformation of those bodies into empire's objects—on which Nugent's creation of novel subjectivity stands.

Clearly, Nugent's is groundbreaking work. It brings together two men of color in the shadow of a racist, heteronormative state, creating a queer vocabulary through language and aesthetics. Nugent thereby revalues racialized bodies and immigration status as ways to cross boundaries and defy social norms. He writes:

> perdone me senor tiene vd. fosforo . . . Alex was glad he had been addressed in Spanish . . . to have been asked for a match in English . . . or to have been addressed in English at all . . . would have been blasphemy just then . . . Alex handed him a match . . . he glanced at his companion apprehensively in the match glow . . . he was afraid that his appearance would shatter the blue thoughts . . . and stars . . . ah . . . his face was a perfect compliment [sic] to his voice . . . and the echo of their steps mingled . . . they walked in silence . . . the castanets of their heels clicking accompaniment . . . the stranger inhaled deeply and with a nod of content and a smile . . . blew a cloud of smoke . . . Alex felt like singing . . . the stranger knew the magic of blue smoke also . . . they continued in silence . . . the castanets of their heels clicking rhythmically.[62]

Nugent describes this first encounter in sensual detail, emphasizing color, sound, warmth, and movement. The aesthetic vocabulary established earlier in the story is mobilized here to describe burgeoning queer desire, open to the artistically sensible. This encounter situates the immigrant in the city as someone desirable and magical. In doing so, however, Nugent insists on the repetition of certain distinctions that mark the exotic other—linguistic difference, the sound of castanets, and native queerness—that enhance, by contrast, an imperial masculine self.

Even with the revaluation of the immigrant in the city, the aestheticization of Beauty's body renders him more object than subject. Although Alex is rendered as a thinking, sensitive mind who moves through the world appreciating the sights, sounds, smells, and tastes that he gladly encounters, Beauty is some*thing* to be admired and appreciated, alongside the other objects that together constitute Alex's cosmopolitanism. Nugent describes their first sexual encounter: "as they undressed by the blue dawn . . . Alex knew he had never seen a more perfect being . . . his body was all symmetry and music . . . and Alex called him Beauty."[63] Though Beauty is appreciated, he is also transformed from a body as signifier into an object of "symmetry and music," whose possession accents Alex's sensibility as a sophisticated observer and lover of beautiful things. Alex's positioning recalls the place of the imperial collector, who moves through imperial space gathering objets d'art and curios as a means to subjectivity. As Chandan Reddy has written in regard to Larsen's use of orientalist objects, "the difference between subjects and objects, persons and settings, political life and its nonpolitical limit in the public sphere, as much as in the middle-class novel, can all be rendered as a difference between varieties of speech and silence."[64] Nugent presents both imperial subjectivization and objectification, using them here as limits to show that orientalist discourse can create queer subjectivities for some but not for others.

"Smoke, Lilies and Jade" is deliciously complex. Nugent mobilizes imperial signs and symbols in ways that challenge and also uphold assumptions about spatial, embodied categories. Although he relieves bodies of the burden of representation of identity, he sometimes relies on the structure of power he calls into question. Here it is useful to turn once again to Rancière, who proposes the idea that "the arts [in 'modernity'] only ever lend to projects of domination or emancipation what they are able to lend to them, that is to say, quite simply, what they have in common with them: bodily positions and movements, functions of speech, the parceling out of the visible and the invisible. Furthermore, the autonomy they can enjoy or the subversion they can claim credit for rests on the same foundation."[65] We might therefore observe that the imperial logic Nugent relies on to draw out difference, and revalue and relocate it as magical or beautiful, also predicts and delimits a political and aesthetic form built on that difference. However, as we shall see, Nugent's works do not always negotiate difference thusly. Indeed, he also seeks to release difference from referential certainty, and to engender instead a crisis of differentiation, through his particular appetite for its signs and symbols.

PERIPATETIC PRIMITIVISMS AND ORIENTALISMS

Building on the work in the previous section, which demonstrates a crisis of referentiality as queer identities become disinterred from queer bodies and queer sex acts, this section figures the crisis of referentiality through the ways in which imperial markers of primitivism and orientalism cohere to queer bodies. Here I argue that the pragmatics of empire guided the modernist construction of queerness through the linking of empire's objects and aesthetics to queer bodies, a practice that some artists and writers of the Harlem Renaissance used to unveil the construction of race, gender, sexuality, and national identity. As I have previously shown, the crossing of national boundaries has long been imagined as a movement toward emerging queer subjectivity, or as a mechanism for producing spaces of queer activity. In this section I focus on Nugent's series of "Drawings for Mulattoes" and Thurman's fictional rendering of Nugent in his novel *Infants of the Spring* and suggest that these works disrupt—indeed, queer—the discrete boundaries between objects and bodies and the boundaries that mark identity categories.

With these objects of inquiry, I am particularly interested in how primitivist and orientalist objects are made to cohere to queer bodies and queer sexualities to generate a modernist aesthetic; and how in these works those objects and bodies that occupied a zone of ontological indeterminacy engendered a queer black aesthetic while still embedded in imperial logic. Scholarship on race has often focused on how primitivism and orientalism cohere to racialized bodies in particular, and how racialized bodies might be gendered (for example, the feminization of African Americans) or sexualized (the queerness of Asian men or the eroticism of Latina women).[66] In contrast, I focus on how primitive and orientalist objects can be associated with queerness and queer bodies that defy racial, gendered, and sexual classification. For example, in this crisis of referentiality, orientalism and orientalized objects do not act as signifiers for Asian bodies, but for queerness. Here, the distance that is carried within such objects—marking them as strange, granting them their exotic aura, and rendering them desirable—attaches itself to queer bodies to herald them also as strange, exotic, and desirable.[67] Additionally, because these queer aesthetic practices took aim at the solidity of boundaries that marked identity categories, they did not fall into the category of Afro-orientalist works that spoke to needs for alliance; rather, they worked to deconstruct the very categories of race on which notions of alliance rely. These works demonstrate how queer aesthetics and artifacts—drawn from the representational regimes of British, French, and U.S. empires; avant-garde arts movements circulating within and between these empires; and spaces of New York nightlife, such as nightclubs, balls, operas—were brought together in new spatial and racial arrangements to create a new queer black aesthetic practice that worked through the detachment of primitivist and orientalist signifiers from stable categorizations of bodies, objects, and spaces.

Nugent reimagines the relationship between the modern, the primitive, the orientalist, fact, and fiction in *Drawings for Mulattoes*, a series of four drawings completed for Charles Johnson's *Ebony and Topaz* in 1927 (figs. 2.2–2.5). These images are among Nugent's best known and most widely circulated visual works. The title of the series indicates that he used mixed-race identity as a metaphor for cultural contact and the collapse of space between the primitive and the modern, and the drawings are most often read in this way. In them, Nugent deliberately confuses the placement of the black primitive in a premodern Africa, the white modern in the urban city, and jazz culture as the border between primitive blackness and white modernity. That is, he holds up to scrutiny primitivism's invocation of blackness as belonging to Africa, outside of the United States, alongside modernity's celebration of blackness as defining the music and nightlife of Jazz Age New York. Susan Gubar reads the series as depicting an "ethnogenesis that moves from depictions of the primitive to images of civilization," but also as denoting an "illusion," because "Africa is 'always already' represented through the lens of the downtown musical and uptown cabaret."[68] She draws out the multiple layers of meaning within the series, and her reading asks us to consider the role of race and space in black aesthetic practices. To this I would add that these drawings also sought to locate gender and sexuality as central to these practices, particularly as empire intersects the city and the city encompasses empire. Remarking on those connections and connotations that bind perversion and pleasure to primitivism and orientalism, including those that informed and formed sexological studies, Nugent reinterpreted the primitive as synchronous with the modern to create a queer black sensibility—both like and unlike that of the New Negro intellectuals—in the United States. Within these drawings, Africa and New York—but also Asia, islands, plantations, nightclubs, operas, and bodies—collapse time and space within two-dimensional frames, all appearing simultaneously. I argue that this series of images provides a queer of color critique of the formation of the New Negro and, like the first figure in this chapter, does so by making use of the nexus of primitivism, orientalism, and queerness as defining terms for a black modernity under the auspices of empire.

Because these drawings have been reproduced and read extensively, I

Figure 2.2 Richard Bruce Nugent, *Drawing for Mulattoes—Number I* (1927). Courtesy of Thomas H. Wirth.

will address only the aspects of the drawings that lend themselves to this queer of color critique. Like Gubar, I am drawn to the multiplicity of meanings that proceeds from each image. The heteroglossia that composes the context, language, and purpose of the drawings is mobilized by Nugent to forward notions of the collapse of fact and fiction, of spatial distinctions, and of racial boundaries as a means of creating a sexual aesthetic. All the drawings blend elements of the primitive as aesthetic, referencing African origins as mediated by stage dressing—a move that at once plays with the assumed naturalness of black and brown bodies in jungles and the knowing fictions of nightclub performance. These works thus signal the construct-

Figure 2.3 Richard Bruce Nugent, *Drawing for Mulattoes—Number 2* (1927). Courtesy of Thomas H. Wirth.

edness of race through the assemblage of its performance—of space, of staging. *Drawing for Mulattoes—Number 1*, for instance, draws on Aaron Douglass's drawings of figures in primitivist backgrounds and thus refers to the reclamation of Africa and the primitive as a way to signal a particularly modern New Negro identity. But here the two-dimensionality of the columns also recalls a stage set with dancers appearing between the totemic pillars. Rather than calling to mind simply African origins, the drawing also benefits from the latest in stage design. Nugent's drawing becomes a third- or fourth-order simulacrum of jungles that never existed, but that nonetheless carry swathes of meaning in their representation, including those that associate race, gender, sexuality, and geographical space through the imperial imagination.

This reading, which denaturalizes the linkages between the categories created through space, time, race, and artless or natural sexuality, becomes important to a queer of color critique. Where blackness has been figured as suspect within the U.S. national imaginary, its abnormality is generated through naturalized meanings of these categories. In 1920 Sigmund Freud noted that inversion "is remarkably widespread among many savage and primitive races" and that it was also frequent "among the peoples of antiquity at the height of their civilization."[69] These two moments of inversion are present in *Drawing for Mulattoes—Number 2*, where Nugent represents queer primitivism and queer antiquity in the Janus-faced image of a black Greco-Roman head and a white Africanized head.[70] Again, while the naturalistic palm trees recall the British Arts and Crafts Movement, they simultaneously signify Africa, the tropics, the primitive, and Broadway stage sets. The buildings on the right recall Fritz Lang's *Metropolis* and the skyscrapers that distinguish the modern city, but in their flatness they too call to mind the foreshortened span of the theatre stage.[71] The collapsing of multiple times and spaces in the image thus calls into question the peripatetic place of inverted sexuality within the city by moving the primitive and Grecian antiquity into the present and confounding bearings of distance through newfound intimacy.

A similar collapse of time, space, and race occurs in *Drawing for Mulattoes—Number 3*. Here he combines a representation of an imagined Africa or island locales through the primitivized figured rendered in black on the left side with the modern city signified by the white figure on the right. This simultaneity of time and space is further exemplified in the background to this bifurcated figure: the left side holds a drawing of Constantin Brancusi's *Endless Column*, originally cast in metal, and the right side is a presentation of the intricate, naturalistic, and primitivist carvings and prints of the British Arts and Crafts Movement, or perhaps first-order representations of indigeneity rather than the British imitations of such. Combining these elements, Nugent collapses differences between various continents and islands, races, time periods, and aesthetics. Less obvious perhaps, would be his re-reading of the gendered body. While this body is feminine on both sides of the centerline, does this mean that the sexed body that these gen-

Figure 2.4 Richard Bruce Nugent,
Drawing for Mulattoes—Number 3 (1927).
Courtesy of Thomas H. Wirth.

dered referents point to is stable? What if we were to read the right side of
the body as a dancer in drag?

Nugent's work also collapses the distance between the aesthetic, the imperial, and the urban through the presence of queer bodies throughout
the series of drawings. Some figures in the series, for instance, point to the
urban presence of queer bodies that inhabited balls, nightclubs, and cabarets. The center feminine figure of *Drawing for Mulattoes—Number 2* and
perhaps the figure of *Number 3* provide an example of queer of color critique by bringing together secondary sex characteristics that confuse gender and sexuality. Seemingly female-bodied on one side and male-bodied

Figure 2.5 Richard Bruce Nugent, *Drawing for Mulattoes—Number 4* (1927). Courtesy of Thomas H. Wirth.

on the other, the figures fall in line with some sexological discourses about the bisexual being natural. But this is not all that these figures might refer to in their blurring. They, as well as the figures along the bottom of *Drawing for Mulattoes—Number 4*, further conjure queer nightclub performances as well as the clientele at masquerade balls in Harlem and Greenwich Village.

Webster Hall in the Village hosted functions such as the Bal Primitiv, the Pagan Rout, and the Golden Ball of Isis, where men wore "only a small skin that of a leopard or some such animal," "oriental costumes," robes made out of tablecloths, or the attire of Egyptian slaves.[72] One "prominent feature of these dances," another vice report noted, "is the number of male perverts who attend them. These phenomenal men dress up in the most prepossessing female attire simulating women so much as to defy detection."[73] These balls combined the cultures (and times and spaces) of the primitive and the oriental with ancient Greek and Egyptian civilizations, using Enlightenment narratives of space and subjectivity to locate the origins of queer acts outside modern European civilization, on a temporally and spatially distant link on the great chain of being. The balls thereby dismantled this civilizational divide, albeit through a reading that respatialized homosexuality or gender non-normativity within the bounds of an exotic Africa or Asia, or an always already fallen antiquity.

In many ways *Drawing for Mulattoes—Number 4* departs from the first three drawings in the series in that it introduces the Orient through an object, an Asian mask. This drawing brings to mind another set of performance references to the repertoire of the drawings: opera. With its rich orientalist tradition, the opera stage already serves as a multiply referent site of production across various empires. *Number 4* relies on a visual vocabulary similar to that of the other drawings in the series—positive and negative space, built and natural environments, and the costumed dancer who straddles these divides—but this last drawing is compositionally queer. The tidiness of spatial demarcation apparent in the first three drawings is gone. The main figure on the left, a kerchiefed head, bleeds beyond the center boundary line; the logic of the break in the figures at the bottom is gone; and the balance of the trees, here used to define the upper corners, is haphazard. Importantly, too, this piece introduces the notion of the Orient into the space of the city's nightlife through the figure of the orientalized mask on the right side of the drawing. Tellingly, the Orient is represented not by a person but by an aestheticized object that is juxtaposed and combined with familiar images of black and white sensualities. These heads not only double for the classical dyad of Comedy and Tragedy, but also for the costumes worn by partygoers to masquerade balls, where orientalist ensembles were de rigueur. The musical notes above the central figures might suggest a reference to the orientalist operas that filled music halls during the Jazz Age—*Aïda, Cleopatra's Night, Madama Butterfly,* and *Turandot.*[74] For Nugent, the introduction of the Orient further weakens the logic behind the black-white binary and points to a queer aesthetic formed from the knowledge regimes of British, French, and U.S. empires. Nugent extends the mobilization of heteroglossia in order to call into question the construction of particular boundaries, but these boundaries are embedded within the logic of empire and the desire for a queer aesthetic that transcends them.

This attitude toward the blurring of boundaries as a form of queer black aesthetic practice is also evident in Thurman's novels. In *Infants of the Spring*, to which I now turn, Thurman manipulates the arts and allure of the Orient, as displayed in objects that cohere to queer bodies, as a way to deconstruct identity categories such as gender, race, and sexuality.[75] In this novel, Thurman locates in the character of Paul Arbian, a talented but frustrated queer black artist modeled on Nugent, an orientalized fantasy within the social context of Jazz Age New York.[76] As will become clear, orientalisms (including those adopted by the character for himself) imputed to Paul Arbian the quality of an outsider, and Thurman ends his novel with Paul's climactic suicide in tribute to Nugent's love of music. That is, Paul kills himself in a manner stylistically and aesthetically reminiscent of Cio-Cio San's demise in Puccini's *Madama Butterfly*. First performed in 1904 at La Scala, in Milan, Puccini's opera is a powerful orientalist text, usually read as a tragic narrative about imperial contact between the tradition-bound East and the modern West, reiterating both the exoticism of Asian femininity and the broader feminization of Asia. The opera was incredibly popular in New York. By the time of the 1932 publication of *Infants of the Spring*, *Madama Butterfly* had been staged every year but one since its debut at the Metropolitan Opera House in 1906.[77] Thurman's use of the opera again signals the work of orientalism across empires, but it also serves to mark queer identity formation. The character of Paul Arbian lives through aesthetic practices, and—in the manner of Oscar Wilde—his theatrical suicide becomes a grand performance of queer identity, where death is presented as another form of transcendence.

Thurman's use of signs and symbols of East Asia illustrates the complexity of mixing cultures and race relations in Jazz Age Harlem, where gender and sexual ambiguity and excess are expressed through an imperial vocabulary. Paul Arbian's strangely ritualistic suicide in a bathtub in a downtown apartment, surrounded by the accouterment of Japan, reflects not only the incompatibility of his sexual sensibility with the circle of black artists in Harlem but also the usages of orientalisms to create those racial and gender ambiguities that denoted his sexual alterity. Thurman wrote Alva in *The Blacker the Berry . . .* as a biologically interracial character, but he conceived of Paul, the artist, as performatively interracial—creating his interraciality through dress, writing, comportment, and ritual. As in other discourses of the time, the orientalized figure connoted a non-normative—and here, a refreshingly complex—sexuality. In this challenge to the bounds of classification schemas, Thurman detached orientalist signifiers from Asia and Asian bodies. This mode of signification strained the allocation of stereotypes as modifiers of specific bodies and spaces. Although Thurman used these peripatetic orientalisms as a way to call attention to the porous borders of selfhood, the imperial signifiers that he employed nonetheless relied on particular notions of the Orient as fragile, beautiful, feminine, and poised for death.

In order to understand Paul's suicide and the gender and racial ambiguities that both led to his death and were created in its wake, it is necessary to first explore the underpinnings of this character's philosophy of sexuality and pleasure. Paul describes his views in an idyllic dream near the beginning of the novel, a dream that also foreshadows his death. He begins the narration of his dream in a richly wooded Eden, a utopian environment, signaled through the kinds of inhabitants that occupy that space. The reader knows, for instance, that uninhibited expression and indulgence are encouraged here, as Paul names among this Eden's inhabitants singing birds and an "ivory body exuding some exotic perfume."[78] Here, the two signs seem to be intimately interlinked: birdsong cascades down from the trees to envelope the perfumed body below. Recounting more of the dream, Paul observes a "complete merging" between himself and this other presence, pointing to his own "becoming," through which race, gender, and, by extension, sexuality are seen as processual. The presence that Paul senses in this wooded space is his own transgendered body. In an Edenic environment of unconstrained creativity, he has a dream of his transformation into a Japanese geisha. Because these tropes would resurface with Paul's death, we can surmise that the "ivory body" smelling of "exotic perfume" hints at the orientalist nature of this presence. Such racial ambiguities are also present when, in this dream, Paul grabs a "silken forelock," an element that at once conjures up an orientalist object (silk, in addition to the preceding ivory body) with and in contrast to Paul's difference. Paul's African American body is effortlessly altered.

Importantly, Paul's dream foreshadows his suicide (the two aesthetically transformative moments bookend this story) at the end of the novel, and the endings of the dream and of his life both speak to the fragile and protean nature of aesthetic production, and also to the importance of bodies' ability to transform themselves in terms of race and gender. His dream ends with the "shrill scream of a frightened woman."[79] He had been asleep beneath the stairway of an apartment house when a woman found him dreaming there and shrieked with fear or anger. The scream, however, also presages Paul's rebirth as a transgendered and transracial being in his dream. The woman screams just before Paul wakes. With his return to reality, he must immediately run to avoid capture—up the stairs, over the roof to the next apartment building, then down the stairs into the street—a glimpse into the difficult life of a queer black bohemian.[80] But the scream, occurring before the end of the dream or as the end of the dream, also prefigures Paul's final cry, a cry he makes as a woman when he commits suicide later in search of another sort of transformation.

These shifting identities highlight the ways in which Paul's sexuality depends on the breaking down of boundaries—those between Eden and the city, between life and death, between genders, and between races. Paul's proposal that race is a process of becoming is later misread by Stephen, a sympathetic white man who has taken up residence in Harlem. The difference between Paul's Edenic vision of novel subjectivity and Stephen's reading of Paul's erratic behavior is indicative of the limits perceived in Paul's boundary crossing. Stephen notes:

> Paul has never recovered from the shock of realizing that no matter how bizarre a personality he may develop, he will still be a Negro. . . . He sits around helpless, possessed of great talent, doing nothing, wishing he were white, courting the bizarre, anxious to be exploited in the public prints as a notorious character. Being a Negro, he feels that his chances of excessive notoriety à la Wilde are slim. Thus the exaggerated poses and extreme mannerisms. Since he can't be white, he will be a most unusual Negro. To say "nigger" in the presence of a white person warms the cockles of his heart. It's just a symptom of some deep set disease.[81]

In Stephen's description, however, it is clear that Paul is not performing the role of "Negro" properly, showing that Stephen comprehends race as stable and properly performable. For Stephen, Paul's misplaced intent is to become "a most unusual Negro." Again, as with Alva in *The Blacker the Berry* . . . , Paul's racial ambiguity is conflated with queerness, as connoted by the reference to Oscar Wilde. For Stephen, Paul's non-normativity is created in part through the knotty combination of his great talent, his "notorious" sexuality, and his helpless inability to be other than a "Negro." While Paul views himself as racially transgressive, Stephen enumerates those aspects of Paul's talent and personality ("the exaggerated poses and extreme mannerisms") as modes through which he simply fails to be properly black. So, though Stephen saw Paul as a transgressive being, Stephen's attachment to the permanence of racial categories imputes a differently inflected, negative connotation to such transgression. Furthermore, Stephen reads Paul's mobilization of orientalist signifiers in his dream as part of his bizarre behavior, rather than as a subversive quality.

The crisis of referentiality that follows the peripatetic placement of the Orient onto an unstably black and American body disturbs the equation of Afro-orientalisms with racial alliance or racial cooptation. Instead, Thurman's work here in deconstructing the boundaries of race questions the conceits that make alliance possible: the fixed boundaries of racial classification. Though mobile, orientalist signs and objects do not adhere to Paul's black body in the same way that they may be thought to mark properly Asian bodies, from Stephen's point of view. Instead, for Stephen, Paul's complicated racial performance is circumscribed by the very logic of distance that makes the Orient strange in the first place. For Thurman, though, Paul's worldview is intriguing, and his mobilization of orientalism is worthy of note in terms of how it exposes permeable racial boundaries. In the scheme of the novel's narrative, Paul's transformation is both a failed performance and a performance holding the performative effect of attaching the Orient to queer bodies. Here, then, the work of detaching racial signifiers from particular bodies implicates the system of race and, therefore, the system of differential valuation that rests on those categorizations. Furthermore, the loosening of the elements of the racial sign system makes room for the unbinding of the sexual sign system.

Therefore, through imperial logic the references to the Orient coincide with non-normative sexual choices. Paul's dream, with its sensual orientalism, is a mobilization of notions of sexual excess, as is evident in the responses that Paul receives from the audience to whom he recounts his dream. These questions could easily be read as pure skepticism, as they are couched in Thurman's description of one listener named Samuel, an equal rights political advocate who attempts to trap Paul with his cross-examination. Samuel's questions, however, work to validate Paul's point of view. Samuel first asks Paul if he did, in fact, have the dream. Paul replies that he did. This exchange points out not the impossibility of the dream but rather the reality of the dream, since Paul serves as its witness. Inviting Paul to confirm the fact of the dream, Samuel inadvertently implies a connection between Paul's storytelling and his reality, a blurring that continues in his next question. Samuel asks whether the presence that Paul had felt in the dream was male or female, to which Paul replies that he does not know. Though from Paul's viewpoint this gender ambiguity is Edenic, even liberating, Samuel does not quite understand how such gender ambiguity might play a part in queer sensibility. In a hushed tone, Samuel asks whether Paul had ever "indulge[d] in homosexuality."[82] Paul unblinkingly answers "certainly," profiting from Samuel's slippages to also blur the distinction between what might have occurred in the dream and what happened in the real world.

Paul's matter-of-fact admission of having performed non-normative sexual acts leads to the revelation of the interconnection, dependent on imperial logic, between the expectation of gender and sex stability with the definition of sexual object choice. Discomfited by Paul's answers, Samuel attempts to further determine, or manage, Paul's sexual preference since the gender of the presence in the dream is still in question. Samuel's assumptions demonstrate that common conceptions of human sexuality were (and indeed are) based on the stability of gendered bodies. For Samuel, there are homosexual acts performed between men, as in this instance, and there are heterosexual acts performed between a man and a woman. The introduction of gender ambiguity immediately calls into question these set categories and classifications for sexuality. Paul's purpose in answering the questions as he does is to elude the trap of these categories and classifications and to fashion instead a field of sexual variation. Samuel presses his point, asking Paul whether he prefers sex with men or women, and Paul closes the argument in opening up possibility: "I really don't know. After all there are no sexes, only sex majorities, and the primary function of the sex act is enjoyment. Therefore I enjoyed one experience as much as the other."[83] Paul's—and, by extension, Thurman's—language here is sprinkled with references to sexological discourses. Indeed, part of the weight of Paul's answer, and thus its finality, comes from the scientific tenor he employs to argue against fixed categories, which lends an air of medical authority to his argument. Paul rejects normative heterosexuality by claiming that there are not simply two sexes but a range of sexes, thereby imputing the dominance of heterosexuality not to biological but rather to imagined dimorphic sex categories. He also argues against heteronormativity in his assertion that the function of sex is pleasure instead of reproduction. Once this statement is made, Paul suggests that sexuality based on genders is irrelevant to the great variety of sexual acts, including queer acts.

The closing scene of the novel brings the boundary breaking evident in Paul's dream together with the production of a lived queer black aesthetic through the discourse of empire. Though the reader understands in these passages that Paul had an erotic dream in which he meets a "presence" of ambiguous gender marked as exotic and therefore erotic, the dream becomes legible as prophecy only with Paul's suicide:

> Paul had evidently come home before the end of the party. On arriving, he had locked himself in the bathroom, donned a crimson mandarin robe, wrapped his head in a batik scarf of his own designing, hung a group of his spirit portraits on the dingy calcimined wall, and carpeted the floor with sheets of paper detached from the notebook in which he had been writing his novel. He had then, it seemed, placed scented joss-sticks in the four corners of the room, lit them, climbed into the bathtub, turned on the water, then slashed his wrists with a highly ornamented Chinese dirk. When they found him, the bathtub had overflowed, and Paul lay crumpled at the bottom, a colorful, inanimate corpse in a crimson streaked tub.[84]

Paul believed that gender, race, and sexuality were mutable performances and that through everyday acts, he might become whomever or whatever he chose. For this final transformation, Paul clothes himself as a woman, and as an Asian other. He drapes himself in a "mandarin robe" and a "batik scarf," one recalling China and the other Indonesia, a collocation of Asian signs and objects that also reflects the complicated circuits of trade and culture throughout empire. Although batik fabric originates in Indonesia, it is also associated with Africa through its travels along Dutch trading routes.[85] It thereby becomes an artifact whose complex history unravels racial and imperial encounters. The narrator notes that Paul had designed the scarf himself, suggesting perhaps that Paul did not merely act out these identities but sought to inhabit them through his artistic labors. Furthermore, as

Anne Anlin Cheng puts it so well, "what we believe to be surface may be profoundly ontologically structuring."[86] Though Paul is clearly a collector and as such occupies a position of power, he is not resistant to influence or contamination from his objects. Indeed, the objects may be said to act on him with a formal power, to transform him in the disconcerting encounter, even to consign him to the status of another object in an imperial archive.[87]

The multiple referents for the suicide scene complicate the meanings of Paul's suicide, which then hover between life, death, subjectivization, and objectification of the queer body. The manner of his suicide purposely recalls Cio-Cio San's suicide at the tragic conclusion of *Madama Butterfly*.[88] Like Cio-Cio San, Paul was dressed in an ornate robe at the time of death and used a knife in a ritual suicide. And both Cio-Cio San and Paul had dared to want the unattainable—in the case of Cio-Cio San, a mutual, loving relationship between herself and Pinkerton, a U.S. naval lieutenant; in the case of Paul, a liberating world of sexual and gender variation and expressiveness.[89] Since the social and sexual excess of their desires marked them as outsiders, their suicides are demanded by society. Unlike the women who performed Salomé dances in the nightclubs to claim another life, Thurman took the route of operatic convention and killed his tragic heroine. The killing of a queer character as a resolution is a controversial narrative tactic, of course. Cobb is wary of the tactic because it too often relies on an "irrefutable cultural death logic of a world that would prefer to see the queer's literal death."[90] If we read Paul's suicide as an aesthetic act rather than as an actual death, however, it is a delightful act of transcendence, an exit into his Edenic dream and even into the lush world of opera. For Thurman, I would argue, the instability of meaning making is meant to be both part of that release into utopia and a beautiful tragedy.

The heteroglossia that creates intricate webs of meaning for Thurman manifests itself beyond the world of opera. Paul confirms the connection between his unattainable desires and Cio-Cio San's in the manuscript he leaves behind. Like Paul's gender ambiguity, sexual licentiousness, and interracial becoming, his manuscript is also illegible. The carefully placed sheets of paper lining the bathroom floor are destroyed when the tub overflows after Paul's death. The only pencil-written sheets that remain legible are the title page and the dedication page. Paul had fittingly named his manuscript "Wu Sung: The Geisha Man," referring to his novel subjectivity as well as his aesthetic provocations. (The title echoes that of a posthumously published novella by Nugent, called "The Geisha Man," which I discuss in the following section.) Operating within his preferred range of genders and sexualities, Paul is both excessive and queer, both a geisha and a man. This reading is corroborated by the manuscript's dedication:

To Huysmans' Des Esseintes and Oscar Wilde's Oscar Wilde
Ecstatic Spirits with whom I Cohabit
And whose golden spores of decadent pollen
I shall broadcast and fertilize
It is written
Paul Arbian.[91]

The character Des Esseintes from Joris-Karl Huysmans's *Against the Grain* sought the rare and the perverse through sensation. He loved perfume, music, painting, circus acrobats, oriental objets d'art, Salomé, and the study of medieval Latin literature. Much like Paul, he was a sensualist enamored of sex and art. "Oscar Wilde's Oscar Wilde" denotes Wilde's public performance of self. In naming Wilde's double, Paul contends that Wilde's public persona was a mutable, purposeful creation, a view echoed in Thomas Wirth's assessment of Nugent, who is Paul's double (or vice versa): "His real masterwork has been the living of his life."[92]

In these instances, imperial logic works through signifying modes that are often contradictory. Imperialism—which Homi Bhabha has noted functions through ambivalence and racism, and which Stuart Hall has noted often works through the possible doubleness of a single signifier—is able to absorb and juxtapose seemingly contradictory signs and meanings in aesthetic practices.[93] These practices are in fact established through the mobility of signs and meanings. Using the Derridean construction of the sign system—in which the signifier and the signified are detached, and multiple meanings can be produced without destroying the integrity of the sign—I argue that the various markers of empire can hold multiple meanings without destroying the form of empire itself. Indeed, the multiple meanings that are created through contradictory modes can produce a variety of politics in the spaces of empire without calling into question the institutions and ideologies that undergird it. Signs and objects meant to signify the primitive or oriental other can be marshaled as evidence that people in the imperial metropole are liberal because of their appetites for difference, but those same signs and objects could also corroborate for others (also in the imperial metropole) the need for strict social control. For example, multiracial dance halls, where people from all corners of U.S. empire might mingle, could be construed as democratic spaces or as disciplinary ones.[94] The multiplicity of possible readings demonstrates that complex ways of reading the circulation of signs and objects are vital. In this instance, a particularly complex mode must be used to understand how these incursions can happen without drastically changing imperial epistemologies.[95]

DETERRITORIALIZED QUEER

The final section of this chapter moves from considering the deconstructive principles of this early version of queer of color critique through the relationship of bodies and objects to thinking about them through Nugent's reconfiguration of the sensible, accomplished through a collapsing of space between imperial sites. Paul Arbian's novel, described at the end of *Infants of the Spring*, was based on a novella that Nugent had actually written, "The Geisha Man." Though this novella was never destroyed by bathwater, it was not published in the Jazz Age (like so much of Nugent's work, an excerpt was published posthumously). In "The Geisha Man," Nugent introduces Kondo Gale Matzuika, a queer mixed-race character. In some ways, this novella is a decadent descendant of Puccini's *Madama Butterfly*. The opera focuses on the doomed love affair between Cio-Cio San and Pinkerton, and the novella follows a character who has more in common with Little Sorrow, their child. In this way, the story of Kondo Gale follows the consequences of an earlier imperial contact. Although the story of *Madama Butterfly* is the archetypical heterosexualization of the violent imperial contact between the Orient and the Occident, Nugent recirculates this archive of orientalized signs and symbols to produces a queer black aesthetic that is also a partial epistemology of empire. Earlier in this chapter, I argued that Nugent and Thurman, through the abstraction of racial and imperial signifiers from bodies or acts, sought to reconfigure the sensible, inasmuch as such signifiers come to transform and blur the relations between themselves as minor subjects of empire and the signs and symbols as objects of empires. Because these artworks refer back to an imperial logic to produce and revalue difference, however, they operate to reinforce—and never to escape, except through extreme measures—constitutive components of imperial power. In "The Geisha Man," Nugent attempts to break down the solidity of an imperial spatial order as an ideological invention in itself. As in Thurman's work, this collapse of geographical scale is pursued through the deconstruction of other borders as well—those of gender, race, and sexuality—which makes this novella a provocative text for challenging imperial logic and its epistemological and ontological standpoints.

Nugent challenges spatial distance and distinction through a mode of "deterritorialization," a not-unproblematic term that Gilles Deleuze and Félix Guattari describe in relation to practices of imperial signification. *"The signifier is merely the deterritorialized sign itself,"* they lament, because the sign can remain despotic even while detached from the original object that influences its meaning.[96] Deterritorialization has nonetheless been adapted as a strategy for fouling the connections between signs and signifiers, between bodies and spaces and the meanings assigned to them, though such a strategy often relies on existing schemas of difference. As discussed above, some people can move out of the spaces of their signification with more ease than others. Commenting on this notion of deterritorialization, Caren Kaplan argues that Deleuze and Guattari's "metaphysical mapping of space can be read within the context of Euro-American discourses of modernism, emphasizing the benefits of distance and the valorization of displacement. Indeed, I would argue that their privileging of 'nomadic' modes relies upon an opposition between a central site of subjectivity and zones of marginality. Thus their advocacy of a process of 'becoming minor' depends upon the erasure of the site of their own subject positions."[97] Against the romance of travel and mobility, which is available to some and not others, Kaplan thus critiques Jean Baudrillard for taking up such a strategy in his postmodernist travelogue: "Thus, although Baudrillard's *America* insists upon a radical deterritorialization from culture, politics, and the social, its reliance upon a version of modernist exile poetics produces a text that is laced with Eurocentric stereotypes and other hegemonic representational practices."[98] Nonetheless, for other scholars deterritorialization remains a provocative strategy, precisely because some people cannot avail themselves of its privileges. Building on Deleuze and Guattari's writings on "nomadology," Victor Mendoza provocatively offers a productive methodological impetus: "A queer nomadology . . . can track the sexually, narratologically, and topographically wayward agent without capturing it discursively through progressive signifying practices; and it can account for the textual and material disruptions of nation-state formation and its official histories without positing these disruptions as intrinsically antithetical to state hegemony. Ultimately, a queer nomadology helps us imagine forms of resistance and critique that are not bound in binary opposition to the progressivist ideologies and forms of domination that postcolonial nationalisms often inherit from old colonial systems."[99] Mendoza's methodological interventions imagine "politically wayward resistance" in nuanced ways, tracking the enduring effects of imperialism and colonialism without overdetermining these effects as omnipotent. In this section, I combine Kaplan's necessary warning and Mendoza's hoped-for waywardness to think through Nugent's collapsing of distances between bodies and spaces in his queer of color aesthetic practice.

The story of the novella is aberrational, following Kondo Gale from the red-light district of Japan to the streets of Paris and, finally, to Jazz Age Harlem. As he traverses these spaces, he searches for his mother's lover, his father, a man who has also been his lover—a man whom he desires for more than one purpose and pursues around the world. Claiming to be "in love with [his] mother's lover," Kondo Gale catches up with his father in New York at a queer ball, where they renew their sexual relations.[100] While father and son live together as lovers, the father becomes distant, and Kondo Gale commits an ambiguous form of suicide, both fulfilling and denying the promise of every opera: the undoing of the transgressive character as narrative resolution. Kondo Gale is given to the same fate as his operatic foremother Cio-Cio San, a death inspired by the distant return of her white lover. This is nonetheless a productive repetition. As I suggested about Paul's death in *Infants of the Spring*, this kind of aestheticized death is metaphorical, a refusal of the imperial order that desubjectifies bodies that long for personhood.

In "The Geisha Man," Nugent traverses geographies of scale—from the imperial adventuring of the United States in Japan, through national discourses of race via immigration, to corporeal and stylistic articulations of gender and sexuality—in order to then interrupt hegemonic codifications of space and sociality, distance and intimacy. I first address Nugent's troubling of gender and sexuality in his figuration of Kondo Gale. As a geisha in Osaka, Kondo Gale resignedly acknowledges that "many men had bid for me, for I was the loveliest maid of all. . . . [B]ut they never stayed after they found I was . . . a man."[101] Here Kondo Gale's gender and sex appear to be mismatched, but as the novella unfolds, we find that gender and sex disruption is his ontological condition. Indeed, it is not always clear that there exists for this character a stable, because biological, referent for sexological classification.

Nugent knowingly models his characters through the kind of gender ambiguity that deconstructs the boundaries of identity by reconceptualizing the map of the sensible. After Kondo Gale is transported to New York, he muses, "If only I had been born a woman! To dress in flowing silks and silver and colors always, with a modish mannish look and gestures."[102] This passage might be read as the revelation of natural sex categories (he is not born a woman, therefore he is a man), but at the same time it challenges the parameters of feminine self-presentation. Schwarz marks this passage as transgressive insofar as this professed hope does "not fit a 'performance' of maleness"; however, she delimits this gender subversion, noting that "Kondo desires to dress in a feminine style yet wants to achieve a 'modish mannish look' in which, as might be suspected, his masculinity remains recognizable."[103] The masculinity that Kondo Gale would achieve with this "look," though, would perform a racialized female masculinity. The idea of being "modish," as in "fashionable," seems to indicate a performance of a denaturalized masculinity.[104] Indeed, the phrase "modish mannish look," recalls a famous line from Bessie Smith's "Foolish Man Blues": "There's two things got me puzzled, / There's two things I can't understand / that's a mannish-acting woman and a skipping, twisting woman-acting man."[105] In Smith's tune, the sarcastically delivered lines indicate the existence of public behaviors that denaturalized ready connections between sex and gender. Although Nugent's description appears to present a masculine body that cannot be denied ("If only I had been born a woman!"), this moment can also be read as a refusal of the secured boundaries of or policed passages between femininity, masculinity, and the body, providing queer alternatives at every turn.

Such a reconfiguration of the sensible that here troubles the borders of gender as these traverse the body can also be seen as troubling the borders of race, particularly through the transactions between the proscriptive processes of racialization and narratives of immigration that Kondo Gale encounters on arriving in the United States. As with Kondo's gender identifications, Nugent offers rough slippages between his racial identifications. In the space of a few sentences, for instance, Kondo Gale claims both that "I became a 'New Negro'" and that he is "half Japanese and half white."[106] These seemingly contradictory revelations, occurring shortly after his arrival in New York, demonstrate a fluid racial self-image, differently in-flected than a mixed-race body might be. Rather than relying on biological categories and heterosexual procreation to show that these distinctions are always already unstable, Nugent opts instead for a sense of race that is mu-table and not affixed to bodies. The writing of race in the novella, however, also speaks to the difficulties of making such claims to deterritorialized self-image, in observing those practices that instantiate the incorporation of immigrants into the prevailing U.S. racial order. That Kondo Gale be-comes a "New Negro" thus speaks to modes of racialization that do not dis-criminate between bodies of color but that only seek to mark those other bodies in particular ways. Yet Kondo Gale's initial impressions of New York demonstrate further some of the disruptions possible to this racial order, as all that is solid melts into air, and the static geography of the city—its straight and narrow streets, its distinct neighborhoods—dissolve against and into his senses. Echoing his earlier short story in his preoccupation with sight and sound as space making, Nugent creates "polyglot dreams and fantasies" to the beat of jazz rhythms—"An undulating hodgepodge of color and forms. Forms and color on a spring Sunday. And a lamb-like March oozing with warmth and rhythm on Seventh Avenue. . . . Laughing forms tinted with mad colors jumbled with jazz rhythm."[107] This passage's mad rush of colors that infect Kondo Gale's perceptions and his means of being also allude to the multiraciality of the city that he will experience, a city filled with the "four beautifully modeled men . . . headless . . . headless and beautiful . . . and one was red and one was black and one was yellow and one was white . . . and each body glistened like lacquer . . . like satin with a light cast on it"—the men he had dreamed of while still in Japan.[108] This excerpt at once refers to multiraciality and recalls the aestheticization and objectification of male bodies in Nugent's "Smoke, Lilies and Jade." His reconfiguration of racial sense, then, is part of his queer black aesthetic, which reaches back and forth across national borders.

The novella repeats the mobilization of signs and symbols through which queer subjectivities are made possible in imperialist narratives of modernity and cosmopolitanism, echoing writers—such as Wilde and Huysmans—who collect and catalog objects of empire, though to a new end. In New York this collecting and cataloguing includes those people who make up the signs and sensations of the queer public—or counter-public—of jazz culture. Although Thurman's Paul Arbian hoped that he might dress and undress himself in various bodies and identities, as practices of disruption, we saw that these leave behind a residue, what we might consider a second skin. In "The Geisha Man," such imperial vestments are more difficult to leave behind. Nugent describes a ball scene:

> The ball. We arrived late, and the dance floor was a single chaotic mass of color. Abbreviated ballet skirts of pink, blue, silver and white dancing with Arab sheiks in fantastic colors . . . Turks with bright ballooned trousers, curled pointed boots and turbans with sweeps of brilliant feathers and sparkling glass gems . . . pirates in frayed trousers, bloody shirts, headbands, earrings and tattoos . . . houri girls . . . fashion girls . . . Apache Indian, Spanish, Dutch and Japanese girls. One man resplendent in the third-dynasty costume of a Chinese bandit king. Court dresses of Louis XIV . . . hula girls and boys . . . clowns and deaths and pirouettes . . . India temple dancers . . . evening gowns and the black and white of full dress. Boys dressed as girls and simpering sadly. Girls dressed as boys and bulging in places. . . . Bathing beauties and Greek Gods. I recognized an Eastern prince as an Armenian acquaintance.[109]

Whereas these queer costume balls do reveal a mode of dressing up that reinvigorates troubling narrations of modern and cosmopolitan subjecthood, enhanced through real or symbolic travel through empire, Nugent also points to the ball as a nexus that brings together migrants from all over the world, a reflection of New York's demographic composition at the time. That is, although Nugent certainly reiterates some of the problematic poetics of modernism, he also insists on the immigrant presence as agentive in the creation of such public cultures. Caren Kaplan warns: "Neither political refugee nor exiled artist, the immigrant, in such a mystified and unified characterization, cannot participate in the terms of Euro-American modernism and cannot be recuperated or professionalized in terms of cultural production."[110] It is therefore in the context of these terms that Nugent's ball names those outposts of multiple empires, U.S. and otherwise, while also locating immigrants from those outposts within the imperial city, as inhabitants and even innovators of its avant-garde sensibility. The "Eastern prince" who appears at the end of the passage, for instance, is Armenian; and while Kondo Gale also dances with a "handsome Turk," this ambiguous naming leaves it unclear whether his dance partner is merely wearing a Turkish costume or has indeed emigrated from Turkey.[111] Nugent, at play with the confusion of signs and sensations reflecting the uneasy relations between race and nation in the production of culture and space, reimagines the immigrant as a necessary participant in the project of modernity, as well as experimental cultures. At the same time, such unease is foundational to these relations and must be considered within the logic of empire that guides, in the words of Reddy, the "collision of diasporic groups and U.S. space."[112] Indeed, by the end of the novella, Nugent has made it clear that these spaces are also patrolled and circumscribed by the same logic of empire that makes them possible.

The tension between Kondo Gale's collapse of boundaries between spaces and bodies and the ready ways in which the state revises and reinforces those boundaries through surveillance, classification, and exclusion, even as those borders threaten to waver and disappear, is structurally similar to the ways that death can be read at the close of the novella. "All women in opera die a death prepared for them by a slow plot," reflects the French feminist Catherine Clément, "woven by furtive, fleeting heroes, up to the source, to the curtain-raising, where, in words that are often trivial, the death is fore-shadowed."[113] Not unlike Clément's reading of troublesome, independent women in opera, queer characters cannot be allowed to survive the end of fiction; their inevitable doom has been often cited as a troublesome trope.[114] Because of the operatic origin of "The Geisha Man," a death at the end of the novella is no narrative surprise, but Nugent forestalls an actual death by following Kondo Gale through the city as he meditates on death and its multiple, sometimes contradictory, meanings. Rather than killing off his character as a resolution, Nugent may be signaling something other than an ending; indeed, this stream-of-consciousness reverie lends ambiguity to the death of the character, and the death of his love. "*And then maybe death is only another existence in which one 'lives' and 'dreams' and confuses the two and decides that 'death' is the sleep one was refused in that existence.*"[115] Kondo Gale considers these and other possibilities as he walks about the city—down Broadway, down Fifth Avenue, past Child's Restaurant, past the New York Public Library.[116] His meditations on death provide a map, coupling his sensual reconfiguration of the city around him with the transcendence of death and thereby transforming space and time. For Nugent, death becomes a way to refuse a particular existence organized by "a policeman. . . . Two policemen. . . ." and "a Special policeman," as Kondo Gale observes near the end of his musings.[117] As in the case of Paul Arbian (perhaps Kondo Gale's twin as well as Nugent's double), death becomes a dream of peace and continuity, eliminating the body's experience of the sensible in order to elude the disciplining presence that produces and polices the spaces in which it moves or is denied movement. Thus does Nugent hope to confound those categories built on the certainty of distances between them — "Life or death or life and death or life or . . ." — in order to transcend the social order that seeks to permanently mark him as a particular body with a particular meaning and place.[118]

By the mid-1920s, the United States had many colonial possessions and imperialist contacts in Asia, the Pacific, Latin America, and the Caribbean. As contacts abroad and at home, in the forms of new waves of immigration and an ignited imagination of these other spaces, forced a renegotiation of national boundaries, other forms of identification were also called into question. Collapsing the distance between the United States, Africa, Asia, and the Pacific and confounding signifying practices of race and sex in order to fracture an imperial imaginary of other bodies, Nugent created a queer black aesthetic through the process of cultural contacts and multiple border crossings. He reimagined these contacts as sites for new configurations of gender, race, and sexuality within New York and jazz culture. Nugent produced a black queer aesthetic through two means. First, he constructed a queer iconography in the interstices of a primitivism as avant-garde culture, reclaimed from the modernist movements in both Europe and the United States as particularly African and therefore the legacy of African Americans. However, he constructed it not as modernity's other, but as its founding self. Second, Nugent mobilized preexisting notions of the Orient — inherited from the European decadent queer canon, including works by Wilde, Beardsley, Huysmans, and the orientalist operas of Strauss and Puccini — to create a queer black aesthetic.[119] In other words, Nugent used an existing imperial logic to understand and also generate new sexual and aesthetic formations. But while these contacts produced spaces of creation and renegotiation, especially in their reframing of primitivism as a black modern, these formations also relied on exotic images of the oriental other, found in both sexological studies and queer aesthetics, that reproduced an imperial logic. Indeed, queer identities were not created outside of U.S. culture or empire, but through those cultural practices and ideologies. As a complex practice of repetition with a critical difference, Nugent's black queer aesthetic offers us a means of understanding the creation and circulation of modernisms and modernity, from the mixing of cultures and bodies to the collecting of exotic objects and being collected in return, through the logic of empire.

Nugent and Thurman, in his figuration of Nugent, identified the black body as central to the emergence of modernism not just as spiritual object but as an author and innovator. At the same time, Nugent and Thurman reconfigured this black body as what Rancière calls a "quasi-body," not an organism but "blocks of speech circulating without a legitimate father to accompany them to their authorized addressee," to "introduce lines of fracture and disincorporation into imaginary collective bodies."[120] Nugent and Thurman follow a tack advocated by many contemporary scholars in attempting to release the burden of representation from actual bodies, understanding the formation of categories as a creation that could be modified, rectified, or defied. In their attempts to imagine new epistemological, ontological, and sensible fields, some of their strategies fell within the bounds of imperial logic, while others challenged the grounds of that logic along the geographies of scale that help constitute it. In the following chapter, I continue this inquiry into the complexities of subject making through orientalist discourses.

CHAPTER THREE

ORIENTING SUBJECTIVITIES

"Palesteena," belly dancing, Salomé, snake charmers and sheiks—such orientalist signifiers were used to fashion selfhood and agency among diverse populations of artists and performers in Jazz Age nightlife. The resulting performances often betrayed a desire for national belonging through the particular ingress presented by the emergence of the United States as a world power, pursued through an implicit (or sometimes explicit) correspondence between crossing gender, racial, and sexual boundaries and the imperial license to tour and travel.[1] However, not all those who sought to fashion for themselves claims to imperial selfhood through such crossings did so uniformly, or easily. In the examples that follow, people attempting to reach longed-for forms of selfhood as archivists, experts, or sexual progressives through contacts and encounter with Arab forms faced distinct barriers and possibilities because of imperial logic.

This is the first of two chapters that reimagine the timeline for U.S. contact with the Arab world through the heuristic device of comparative empire studies. Most scholarship begins to tracks U.S. involvement in West Asia and North Africa following World War II, when—in the aftermath of Europe's devastation—the

United States established a more powerful geopolitical influence in the region. Such a timeline follows the work of Edward Said, who remarked in 1978: "Since World War II, and more noticeably after each of the Arab-Israeli wars, the Arab Muslim has become a figure in American popular culture, even as in the academic world, in the policy planner's world, and in the world of business very serious attention is being paid the Arab."[2] This chapter, however, observes that orientalist performances of West Asian and Arab signs and symbols were plentiful in the Jazz Age. Furthermore, these performances drew on the prevalent logic of empire, borrowing racial and sexual cues from European imperial lexicons such as the British writer E. M. Hull's novel *The Sheik*, Oscar Wilde's *Salomé*, Richard Burton's translation of *The Arabian Nights*, and the operas of Giuseppe Verdi and Richard Strauss. Adapted from British and French cultural works, these orientalist performances, made possible by multiple empires, generated much more than derivative stereotypes of Arabs (though these too were in evidence). Rather, the performances created new means for fashioning a U.S. imperial selfhood through economies of distance and intimacy with Arab bodies and their signs. In this regard, I draw on Melani McAlister's relocation of "epic encounters" between West Asia and the United States to an earlier era, in order to argue that an imperial archive was marshaled across national lines to manifest dreams of Enlightenment selfhood for—in this chapter—those not acknowledged as full, self-possessed subjects in domestic orders of race and gender.[3]

Many postcolonial scholars have noted, and earlier chapters of this book show, that by the early twentieth century orientalisms of one sort or another had become a means for claiming and creating Western subjecthood.[4] In Jazz Age New York, the answers to questions of cultural production raised by imperial logic thus hinged on spatializing strategies for rendering such claims and creations. To some degree, the outcome appears obvious. Orientalist performances (and their policing) relied on cultural forms and practices generated by the uneven and violent relations of power and knowledge production undergirding empire and imperial imaginaries. In particular, siting desire and sexuality in orientalist performances often provided a way for Western subjects to orient themselves.[5] That is, in assigning both desire and danger to the other, the West might come to know itself, though in the absence of Asia and Asians, the story of power remains indeterminate; part of the fantasy wrought through orientalisms is the belief in Western dominance. This knowledge formation is twofold. It marked a desire for self-possession, enacted through an achievement of agency dependent on imperial logic and the spatialization of race; it also marked a desire for the other, to collect and to catalogue its signs and forms and thus to assert mastery in the name of preservation or guardianship. Timothy Mitchell argues that the Western imaginary of the Orient fathoms the other as a series of commodified gestures, whether appearing in museums, fashions, educational literature, or, in this instance, the cabaret: "Everything seemed to be set up before one as though it were a model or picture or something. Everything was arranged before an observing subject into a system of signification, declaring itself to be a mere object, a mere 'signifier' of something further."[6] In Jazz Age New York, that "something further" was manifold, as men and women sought to become recognizably modern subjects within the U.S. racial and gender order through well-trod routes of imperial travel and touring, archiving and appropriation—sometimes of versions of the others' movements or energies. These replacements both assumed a geographical and cultural distance between nations and national bodies and sought to collapse that distance through empire's often forceful "intimacies of four continents" in order to claim power and personhood at home in the imperial city.[7] Although of course orientalisms are brought to bear on Asian bodies, this chapter continues the previous chapter's focus on how orientalism, as a mobile sign system, also made meaning for non-Asian bodies. For instance, white women in the imperial city center might perform Salomé dances, mastering Arab dance forms to secure their places as collectors and archivists of an orientalist repertoire. But these white women's success in claiming subjecthood through imperial practices of knowledge could be temporary, especially in performances of these dance forms in the speakeasy, where male clients might be invited to imagine themselves as collectors as well. When the dancers performed the movements of an Arab other, they might find themselves "arranged before an observing subject," turned into "mere objects," an orientalist "'signifier' of something further."

Part of the work of this chapter is to understand how these strategies operated in Jazz Age New York, but I will theorize not just about the problems inherent in availing oneself of orientalisms to fashion an imperial or cosmopolitan subjecthood, but also about the limits of such operations contained within subjecthood's own logic. As this chapter's themes intimate, the performance of orientalisms does not necessarily secure full subjecthood, even if the performance relies on the imbalance of power supposed by imperial structures of knowledge. Therefore, part of this re-thinking of peripatetic orientalisms relies on the reference to space in their usages. That is, in addition to economies of distance and intimacy, in what other frames might we consider these movements? If, as Yutian Wong argues, "In the case of Orientalized bodily practices, Asian bodies are not necessary for their continued existence," then how do we conceptualize what orientalism means as it travels across national and racial borders?[8] Here I turn to Sara Ahmed and her conceptualization of "orientation," a complication of orientalism as directional, national, and sexually proximate. In *Queer Phenomenology*, she productively brings the imperial qualities of orientalism together with the intimate practices of the body: "We could even say that Orientalism involves a form of 'world facing'; that is, a way of gathering things around so they 'face' a certain direction. By thinking of orientalism as a form of world facing, I want to suggest that orientalism also involves phenomenal space: it is a matter of how bodies inhabit spaces through shared orientations."[9] Ahmed's use of orientation, then, is useful for thinking through the semiotic and geographically relational aspects of staging orientalist performances, and how these performances both strive for sexual subjectivity and circumscribe agency through their wielding of imperial logic.

In this chapter's discussion of performances of Salomé and sheiks, I consider how the performers position themselves vis-à-vis these orientations, how each might embody a politics of space as particularized subjects through their "world facing," toward and away from the Orient. Although performances and artistic renderings of the Orient certainly call to mind debates about cultural appropriation, this chapter remarks on such appropriation to understand these performances and renderings as generating heterogeneous claims to signification and selfhood. In this chapter, I build on Ahmed's notion of "orientation"—a multivalent concept that describes ideological orientation toward the East; physical orientations, both embodied and geographical; and sexual orientation—to understand the creation of imperial, but not necessarily abstract or ideal, subjectivities through orientalist narratives and tropes. Holding all these relationships in tension helps us understand the myriad usages of orientalisms. It further suggests that different bodies might have qualitatively different relationships both to the signs and symbols of the Orient, here denoting West Asia, and to space and power in the United States. That is, I am interested in the possibilities of and limitations to fashioning imperial subjecthood through these enactments, and the performative effects of their orientations.

This chapter considers the uses of these peripatetic orientalisms for reconfiguring sexual subjecthood in four parts, each examining a variety of musical and dancing performances, as well as artistic and novelistic renderings. The first considers orientalist performances by and about Western white women, whose collecting and staging of orientalist dance forms often fell into a subjectivity gap between imperial selfhood and embodied interpretation. The useful but also troubling intimacies between imperial logic and African American performance is the concern of the second part. Black women were marked in advance of the orientalist performance as racial others, and this marking determined their ability to access narratives of imperial selfhood through such performances. Black dancers had to account for their racial bodies' narration of their performances; some performances then were described through the collapsing of distances—where Africa could be West Asia, and Arab women could be black women—while others were seen as suggesting the performer's similarity to women inhabiting other parts of the world's empires. The chapter's third part returns to Richard Bruce Nugent, to consider queer mobilizations of Arab signs and symbols in paintings and performance, particularly for feminine or ambiguous gender possibilities. The usages of the term *sheik* as a description of aberrant characters, both to condemn and to celebrate them, is the concern of the fourth and final part. Though the figure of the sheik was characterized by sexual excessiveness and moral shortcomings, conjuring up this figure in Jazz Age New York nonetheless implicated diverse sexualities and racial identifications. This chapter thus follows the argument that "orientations" toward the Orient produced a range of gendered, sexual, and racial subjectivities in the United States. In this way, the Orient adhered to bodies in performance—a sort of "kinetic energy, being in time,"[10] in the act—and to some more than others.

ARCHIVE AND REPERTOIRE

White women performers of orientalist dance forms found themselves in a tenuous position between the archive and the repertoire, and it is in this gap that claims to imperial subjectivity both were formed and failed. According to Diana Taylor's brilliant study, the archive contains "supposedly enduring materials" that resist change and "sustain power."[11] The repertoire, in contrast, consists of embodied practices and "enacts embodied memory."[12] Taylor explains that "the repertoire requires presence: people participate in the production and reproduction of knowledge by 'being there,' being a part of the transmission. As opposed to the supposedly stable objects in the archive, the actions that are the repertoire do not remain the same. The repertoire both keeps and transforms choreographies of meaning."[13] Taylor's argument in *The Archive and the Repertoire* shows that although these two forms of creating and transmitting knowledge overlap, the archive is aligned with the West's push to know and thereby to dominate new spaces and peoples, while the repertoire is associated with the non-West—those spaces and peoples imagined to be the objects of imperious ways of seeing rather than the purveyors of it. Indeed, in writing about the archive, Jacques Derrida notes that it connects command and law, the "jussive" and "nomological principle."[14] In other words, the archival act bespeaks and naturalizes authority over something through laws of naming and classification. This power over something, however, does not always prevail because the performers' tenuous subjectivity is built through too intimate a connection to the Orient and to the objects being collected, which, in performance, include their own bodies. In these instances, it is not always possible either to distinguish between what is being named and classified and who is doing the naming and classification, or to speak to the complicated meanings created through the mobilization of the Orient as a polyvalent trope in a mutable archive.

In this first section of the chapter, I examine white women's performances of an Orient most closely associated with Islamic and Arab movements and positions, including a song about American women travelers in Palestine, "The Dance of the Seven Veils," and other performances of Salomé. In these performances, drawn from intimacies between empires (those of Britain, France, and the United States), white women sought to narrate themselves as authorities over Arab cultural forms, collecting dances and songs to demonstrate their imperial selfhood through expertise and self-possessed sexuality. As Ahmed notes, "the Orient provides the object, as well as the instrument, that allows the Occident to take shape, to become a subject, as that which 'we' are around. . . . The reachability of the other, whether the Orient or other others does not mean that they become 'like me/us.' Rather they are brought closer to home, but the action of 'bringing' is what sustains the difference: the subject, who is orientated toward the object, is the one who apparently does the work, whose agency is 'behind' the action."[15] For these performing women, "bringing" the Orient home was an imperial activity—collecting its objects, mastering its forms, producing and ordering new knowledge about the Orient—and undertaking it would grant them imperial subjecthood. I argue, however, that for them the distinction between imperial subject and imperial object often became blurred. Because they also embodied these oriental forms in movement, slippages occurred between the collection of performances, or the archiving, and the actual performances, or the repertoire. Thus, these white women were often read doubly through imperial logic—as authorities from the West, but also as women from the Orient. Their performances sometimes racialized them as orientalist objects and activated in audience members and vice investigators a disciplinary or dominating orientation.

I consider first Frank Crumit's rendition of "Palesteena," a Tin Pan Alley ditty recorded in 1920 that introduces the difference that orientalism makes in music.[16] This musical exoticism, achieved through tones and chords, operated as an effect through which a song's performers sometimes identified with and sometimes opposed themselves to the Orient. Power and selfhood were at stake in either formulation. "Palesteena" tells the story of a white woman traveler who performed in the Orient as a musician, a story similar to those told in other songs about dancers such as "Becky from Babylon" and "Rebecca (Came Back from Mecca)."[17] "Palesteena" describes a complex relationship between the imagined Occident and the imagined Orient. Meant to poke fun at Western women who traveled to the Orient and adopted its cultural peculiarities, or who took up oriental performances without leaving the United States and thereby "found" themselves, the song's narrative depends on multiple and simultaneous registers of imperial logic. The song follows Lena, a girl from the Bronx, who travels to "Palesteena" and finds success as a concertina musician. Her terrible performances—"She awfully played one song / She played it all day long / Sometimes she played it wrong"—nonetheless thrilled the ignorant natives. A civilizational divide clearly produces a primitive, backward Arab population and, even through one of its worst representatives, an urbane and modern United States. Though this is a familiar story in some respects, its details require further investigation. This story of travel conjures up multiple gendered, racial, and sexual identifications, all of which are simultaneously activated and limited by way of the encounters and exchanges within the story. Forgoing an explication of the distinction between real and imagined contacts, I want to understand the consequence of contact through its friction—described by Anna Tsing as "the awkward, unequal, unstable, and creative qualities of interconnection across difference," a moment of fettered, though unpredictable, possibility.[18] That is, I want to understand the generative gap created between Lena's collecting of Arab culture and her performance of it.

It is important to consider the specific musical forms that portray this contact, both to find clues as to how the ciphers of contact are created and to understand how racial and national signs and symbols are mobile and translational, detachable from the objects they purport to describe and capable of assigning new meaning to bodies that usually possessed other national or racial identifications. In Crumit's "Palesteena," the juxtaposition of Western and orientalist musical modes throughout the song assert that the aesthetic judgments of the former are superior to those of the latter, reinforcing the deficiencies in the musical abilities of the Palestinians (as described by the lyrics). The song musically illustrates the frictions of contact. Mixing Tin Pan Alley progressions and orientalized countermelodies and themes, it creates a sense of Western dominance—but that dominance is incomplete. In other words, the music itself is an allegory for the clash of contact and the changes that result. Unlike the major pentatonic scales that were meant to recall East Asia, major scales augmented with a flatted third suggested West Asia and North Africa. This is true in "Palesteena": though the chordal progression of the song followed standard American pop conventions—1–4–5 with an occasional relative minor third—the major scale would sometimes be augmented with a flatted third. The extra note existed outside of the standard scale, an example of how racialized codes took the form of excess within the logic of the music. It is also important to note that the flatted third was a note that mimicked a minor scale; in this sense, the orientalized measures had a weaker tone than the themes played in a strictly major scale. This difference produced a recognizable scale that signaled West Asia, the same scale that might be recognizable in the familiar cinematic mise-en-scène in which a charmer coaxes a snake out of a basket with a simple recorder, a tune popularly known as the "Swamee Song." As one might expect, and as juxtaposed against this exoticized scale, the moments used for the major scale during "Palesteena" are moments in which the lyrics present an imperial narration of the Orient. Through this melding of musical themes, their interdependence troubling a clear distinction between scales, we might first observe that the imagined Orient is a Western production. We might also note, however, that this musical composition subsequently informs the uneasy achievement of selfhood by Westerners like Lena. On the one hand, Lena may imagine herself as achieving an imperial agency through her travels. Furthermore, the natives of "Palesteena" appreciate her musicianship as masterful. On the other hand, Lena's performances are awful according to the higher, more sophisticated standards of home (and to the narrator). This negotiation, then, spells out the power and the limit of Lena's search for imperial subjectivity through orientalist performance. Even as the song muddles boundaries, and anxiously so, it resolutely marks West Asia as always inferior to the United States, even though—or even because—it might provide the potential for white Western women's mastery or achievement of selfhood.

Lena from "Palesteena" traveled abroad to revel in the sights and sounds of an exotic locale, but she need not have wandered so far from home. Displaced and replaced, oriental tropes could be mapped onto other geographic locations closer to the imperial metropolis, as well as onto its racially diverse dwellers. I consider next orientalist performances of so-called Salomé dances by white—and, in subsequent sections of this chapter, black—women and men in Manhattan nightclubs. Popularized following the controversial ban of Richard Strauss's *Salomé* at the Metropolitan Opera in 1907, Salomé dances were titillating exercises.[19] Here, deviant sexuality, a pathology associated with the Orient, could be flaunted for the purpose of perverse entertainment. In this way, Salomé dances became staples of burlesque theatre and cabaret floorshows. Though contemporaneous descriptions of these dances are unfortunately vague, Salomé dances seemed to involve sinuous movements either identical or very close to what were elsewhere called Hawaiian dances and the hoochy coochy, usually variations on belly dancing and the shimmy.[20] The key difference was not movement but costuming; Salomé outfits referenced fantastical Arab themes, made popular through the "Dance of the Seven Veils."[21] These dances and connections between white women's performance, African American expressive culture, and the Orient were made in cabarets and dance halls, as well as more formal settings for performance such as the Ziegfeld Follies.[22]

The hoochy coochy was popular in the Jazz Age at least partly because the dance had been performed in the United States for so long. For example, at the 1893 Colombian Exposition in Chicago women attracted viewers while belly dancing outside the Egyptian, Persian, and Algerian exhibits, raising eyebrows and objections just audible over the roar of crowds.[23]

Because the Salomé dance was a sensual one, many scholars argue that white women achieved a sense of affirmative sexuality and feminine agency through its performance. The dance, according to these scholars, became a mode of both personal exploration and social rebellion against the gendered restrictions on both sexuality and women in American (and European) society.[24] Indeed, Gaylyn Studlar argues that dance in and of itself "was associated in the early twentieth century . . . with feminine desire to escape bourgeois domesticity's constraints and to create other, transformative identities that were convergent with those qualities of the New Woman that disturbed social conservatives. Thus, dance played on the imaginary Orient's symbolic value to Westerners as a place where personal identity is liminal, where identities are lost, transmuted, recovered."[25] Such a bold claim to sexual selfhood through dancing Salomé, however, was secured through a less bold claim to imperial personhood, which was dependent on the mastery and domestication of otherness. This is an orientalism that must make actual Asian and Arab bodies disappear, with the traces left behind becoming immobile objects set within the Orient and brought overseas in the dances and other performances that allow non-Asian women to first displace—an imperial prerogative—and then inhabit their alterity. Racial, class, and national differences all become commodities through which Western consumers, either the female performers or their usually male audiences, might differentiate themselves as rebels, cosmopolitans, outsiders, or individuals. Using travel as a means of escaping the circumscription of their lives, the performers nonetheless reinforced through performing their superiority and freedom in being able to pick and choose orientalist accouterment—or, more concisely, reiterate their imperial belonging—as evidence of an adventurous, mobile spirit. Thus, white women performers' claims of sexual subjectivity depended on their distance from actual Arab women, a position from which they could perform Arab dances via expertise and mastery rather than natural ability. The logic of consumption and imperial distancing that guided the performances, however, also set their limits.

In the same historical discourses that describe these salacious staples of New York nightlife, civilizing the Orient could easily become corrupting of the Occident in general, and the female performers in particular. As nightclubs and other performance spaces mobilized orientalist signifiers, in some cases as a challenge to social and sexual respectability, disciplining institutions took notice. These spaces, like many others discussed in previous chapters, were surveilled by the police, civic-minded vice organizations, city legislators, and other instruments of the law enforcement system. The imperial logic that located these spaces for negotiating multiple identifications—as Western travelers, like Salomé—also became evidence that these spaces required supervision. Certainly, the experience of entering the orientalized nightclub deliberately mimicked an imagined experience of entering a harem, offering the male patron as traveler the symbolic privilege of imperial penetration. Although the sign of the harem signaled release and freedom for some female dancers, and their allure and sexual availability for male patrons, for the vice investigator it demanded surveillance and censure. About such multiple positionings, or orientations, Ella Shohat usefully observes: "The intersection of colonial and gender discourses involves a shifting, contradictory subject positioning, whereby Western women can simultaneously constitute 'center' and 'periphery,' identity and alterity. A Western woman in these narratives exists in a relation of subordination to Western man and in a relation of domination toward 'non-Western' men and women. The textual relationality homologizes the historical positioning of colonial women who have played, albeit with a difference, an oppressive role toward colonized people (both men and women), at times actively perpetuating the legacy of Empire."[26] The police surveillance provides a clue that the bounds of sexuality were being stretched. At the same time, though, the modes of empire circumscribed how much those bounds could be altered. Through policing and imperial logic, then, women's sexuality was demarcated and delimited, emerging unevenly through bodies in performance.

One 1919 performance reported by a Committee of Fourteen investigator reiterated that proximity to the perverse Orient—even if just in spirit, not in body—might trigger contamination. According to this report, one number at the Coconut Grove, a Pacific island–themed rooftop club off the south end of Central Park West, featured a bevy of exotic beauties dressed as, among others, Cleopatra, Helen of Troy, Carmen, and Salomé, women the investigator describes as "The Vampires."[27] Here, the audience was treated not only to a number of exotic, and no doubt titillating, West Asian and North African costumes, but also to a cast of characters that immediately calls to mind the many films of Theda Bara—the original silent screen vamp, around whom swirled rumors of mysterious, Arab origins[28]—as well as some of the most famous women of opera. Indeed, all these characters had been performed at the Metropolitan Opera in the last decade, where they also vamped their ways across the stage, enticing men with abandon and meeting their inevitable deaths.[29] Just as wayward women were punished in opera's conventions, so were women performing in nightclubs.[30] Though white women performers strove to break the bounds of gendered performance by reclaiming their sexual agency on stage, such possibilities as the imperial circuits afforded also involved dangers—a proximity to racialization, the creation of a kind of intimacy across imagined bodies and continents.

These women, like archivists, may have collected orientalist signs and symbols and produced from them new performances of imperial femininity, but in doing so, they also drew the attention of authorities. These epic encounters writ small on the stage engendered new vocabularies of surveillance through these women's performances of their repertoires. That is, the remapping of imperial tropes through the dancers' defiance of sexual propriety was not lost on audience members or vice investigators. Those tropes that rendered Salomé performances sexually liberating also informed circuits of sexual surveillance. Consider this vice report, in which the entrance of scantily clad performers incited a raucous reaction among the nightclub's patrons: "old men rapped on the tables with their little hammers given by the management, mouths hung open and tongues out in amusement, apparently at the wonderful beauties."[31] Certainly we might note that the women performing defied sexual conventions; but imperial discourse shaped this defiance. If their performances of sexual transgression were made possible by the Western expansion of rule into the Orient and relied on an imperial geography that designated some bodies and spaces as available for conquest, it should not be surprising that conquest also informed the performances' reception.

In this repurposing of imperial registers of both unbreachable distance and volatile contact tinged with desire, cabaret and nightclub performances disrupted boundaries between performers and patrons, moving along geographies of scale to draw analogies between veil-clad white women and uncivilized lands and primitive peoples. These spatial reconfigurations, bringing the oriental other into the West's sphere of influence, created a frisson of forbidden intimacy between performers and the audience. Floorshows would often occur in an open area without a stage, between tables.[32] Patrons were not required to remain in their seats during the entertainment; they might be standing at the bar or dancing themselves. Indeed, patrons often interacted directly with the performers, both during and after the performances. A vice investigator's report from 1919 testifies to this interaction and its sexual nature:

> Then May Leslie came out as Salome, with a few beads on, 99–100% naked, and did a "vamp" wiggle "hoochey koochey" which elicited this from Ed Wynn, "May, for God's sake, don't do that" at the same time endeavoring hard to control himself from seizing her. It was a great sex appeal for the sexually impotent old birds present. They applauded noisily. She continued to "hootch" whereupon Ed says, "May, for God's sake, be reasonable, be reasonable, don't do that" (meaning the "enticing" wiggle). Finally, Ed takes off his coat in sheer desperation, unable to control himself any longer, then eventually has to leave the stage because no longer controllable. Some rot!

The investigator offered his own reading of Ed Wynn's comments:

> It amounts to as much as this, "If you keep that up, May, I'll have an orgasm in my trousers"; or else, "I'll have to rape you May, if you don't stop it." It was crude stuff and hardly worthy of a place such as this or any place. It was evidently suggestive—it was everything saving the ___?___ in plain words.[33]

The perception that these women performers were readily available for sexual activity may have been heightened because they had adopted and embodied racializing signifiers of sexual transgression. Indeed, the comedian Ed Wynn's pleas of helpless rapaciousness, typical banter between the master of ceremonies or comedian and the hoochy coochy floor show, invited other patrons to identify themselves as imperial conquerors. The forbidden intimacy of cabaret and nightclub entertainments not only disrupted boundaries between performers and patrons by drawing on the imperial logic of conquest and contact, but it also promised further danger off the dance floor. Ahmed's multiply signifying notion of orientation is useful in drawing connections between ideologies that mark the Orient, bodies that mark the Orient, and sexual orientation, but here these multiple referents do not necessarily work in concert with one another. The ideologies that mark orientalized bodies as sexual also mark the women performers, who might share in those ideologies (indeed, the show is entertaining because of the exoticization of their bodies through costuming and naming) but are also prey to them. Here becoming sexually objectified is part of the entertainment. Reformers and vice investigators warned that the sexual improprieties of the stage show would not stay within the performance; they warned women away from the stage, and from public spaces in general, because the nightlife would not just foster their moral degradation— one of these rapacious patrons unable to distinguish between performance and reality might subject women to further, irreparable violation.[34]

Thus did orientalizing have both selective but also perhaps unintended consequences. If white women sought and accessed what Said calls an "ephemeral 'positional superiority'" through their usage of oriental signifiers—mapping these onto their own bodies and movements to defy sexual convention and bourgeois respectability—they were not the only ones.[35] The same imperial discourses that gave them these alternate images of untamed femininity also produced accompanying narratives of masculine conquest and penetration, of unruly dangers (men who would not be able to help themselves) and civilizing imperatives.[36] Though the shows continued to have semilegal status, their allusions to and analogies with the Orient raised warning flags among dismayed community members and suspicious vice investigators, for whom the dancers' performances of even fake oriental sensuality were as dangerous as the real thing.

As archivists and performers, mastering but also moving through their repertoires, these women occupied a precarious position. Just as they sought to exercise an imperial expertise, they were marked as possibly criminal and sexually aberrant. In their embodiments, however, we could argue that these white women represented a threat to the construction of imperial masculinity that presumes a solo command of law, Derrida's nomological principle. Part of this imputed failure, or challenge, begins immediately in the epistemology of the archive itself: the archive of dances and songs that these women sought to perform. Derrida's reading of Freud is instructive here. Commenting on the phallogocentrism of Freud's creation of psychoanalytic archives, Derrida writes: "Well, he perhaps inscribes, perhaps (I am indeed saying *perhaps*), as if he were signing his name, a discreet but energetic and ineffaceable virility: *we* the fathers, we the archons, we the patriarchs, guardians of the archive and of the law. I say *perhaps*, because all these questions remain as suspended as the future."[37] Derrida reminds us that the creation of archives and the ordering of knowledge is understood as a masculine preserve. Women performers—dancers, choreographers, and singers—challenged the naturalization of these categories of knowledge production even as they narrated their subjectivity through their wielding of imperial logic. Modes of gender disciplining, however, also mobilized imperial logic in order to foreshorten the careers of these would-be archivists.

BLACK SALOMÉ

As New Women and New Negroes, informed by social movements that sought to claim full personhood for them, black women in the United States and Europe also adapted orientalist performances of imperial femininity at the beginning of the twentieth century. In James VanDerZee's photograph *Dancer, Harlem* (fig. 3.1), for instance, a young black woman poses in the customary elements of orientalist costume. Her loose-fitting harem pants and elaborate beaded belt are made for the lithe movements of belly dancing. The translucent material draped over her arms evokes veils that simultaneously hide and reveal what lies beneath. But though these performances drew on a vocabulary of orientalist signifiers similar to that used by white performers, and attracted like forms of sexual surveillance, these were nonetheless dances with a difference. For black women, the peripatetic Orient rendered their bodies through racial otherness and spatial distancing in immediate and intimate ways.

The black woman performing Salomé had a more precarious claim to empire than a white performer. Although black women too invoked an imperial positional authority in their performances, the civilizational distance between the metropole and the empire appeared much more indiscreet. That is, their black bodies were sometimes read, and sometimes presented, as already too intimate with those spaces of primitiveness and darkness, as already enclosed in the exotic genealogies conjured forth in these dances. The boundaries that marked the spatial arrangements of empire were blurred at the site of blackness. Black women's claims to Ameri-

Figure 3.1 James VanDerZee, *Dancer, Harlem* (1925).
© Donna Mussenden VanDerZee.

can imperial personhood were therefore circumscribed, and the women were denied access to discourses of mastery and expertise and ascribed as the racial other, always already in advance of their performances. Thus, although I do not argue that a natural affinity existed between women and men of color in the United States and women and men in colonial sites, I do believe that such affiliations, given the transatlantic histories and criss-crossing routes of empire—or those intimacies across continents, to call on Lowe once again—were sometimes chosen, sometimes given, and very often applied for various purposes.[38] These affiliations did not guarantee one set of meanings, but many possible ones. Racialized preconceptions were only one of many that formed the heteroglossia that situated black women's Jazz Age performances.

Already rendered vulnerable through legal and social means (including

Jim Crow, poverty, and prejudice), black women and their performances of the Orient could be interpreted through both domestic racism and imperial logic. Although working-class white women endangered their whiteness through performance, black women's bodies, already marked through racialization, became the locus of discourses of empire as they entered the gap between the archive and the repertoire. That is, black women's subjectivity, as apprehended through the mastery of an orientalist archive of performance, could be read a priori as part of that archive itself, as always already intimate with the forms found there. Thus do disparate readings of black women's orientalist performance—on the one hand, enacting affinities between people of color in the United States with the peoples of the Orient and, on the other hand, naturalizing a harmony with these performances because their ancestors may be imagined to have come from those same regions of Africa and West Asia—rely on this confluence of domestic racism and imperial logic.

This mode of racialization is marked through a spatial understanding of the racialized body as existing outside the U.S. nation. Ahmed brings this reading to bear in describing whiteness as "proximate": "While 'the other side of the world' is associated with 'racial otherness,' racial others become associated with the 'other side of the world.' They come to *embody distance*. This embodiment of distance is what makes whiteness 'proximate,' as the 'starting point' for orientation. Whiteness becomes what is 'here,' a line from which the world unfolds, which also makes what is 'there' on 'the other side.'"[39] For these black women, racial otherness already assumes a distance that is read back on the orientalist performances as a naturalized spatial logic. That kind of national distance enables exoticism and foreignness to cohere to the bodies of women of color differently than they cohere to the bodies of white women. These narratives attach themselves to black women in advance of the performance because these women are assumed a priori to belong to these discourses of empire.

The stage star Aida Overton Walker was perhaps the most famous black performer of the twentieth century to dance Salomé both in the United States and in Europe, and as such she makes an excellent example to use in exploring the construction and limits of subject making through orientalist performance.[40] From 1907 to 1914, as a choreographer and performer of this feminine orientalism, Walker exemplified the confusion over racial boundaries inherent to such a performance. She strongly identified with

West Asia and North Africa, even changing her name from Ada to Aida, after Verdi's famous opera character.[41] Daphne Brooks characterizes Walker as "at heart a cultural nationalist," interested in pan-Africanism (extended in the case of Salomé to include Palestine).[42] In her brilliant study of early American black women performers, Brooks imagines Walker's Salomé performance as having "transformed the subjectless, dancing female body into a stylized figure who was narrated by the dancer herself."[43] Through the lens of pan-Africanism, Walker's bid for a modern, black feminine subjectivity can be interpreted as mobilizing imperial logic differently. Rather than creating a narrative of travel that depends on a racial distance between the performer and the body proper to this dance, Walker's performances collapsed (or perhaps skipped) such distance and its accompanying imperial spatialization through a specifically racialized identification with the character of Salomé. Although this kind of identification illuminates the multiracial makeup of West Asia and North Africa, it does so at the expense of making Arab women disappear altogether. In a sense, this uneven identification again depends on an imperial discourse of epistemological and even ontological dominance, with the erasure of Arab and Asian women as "subjectless" and the recovery of their geographies done in the name of black feminine agency in the United States.[44] As Jayna Brown argues, Walker could "remain American" in her performances, "distancing herself, as a modern dancer, from association as a hyper-sexualized primitive."[45] As such, Walker introduces us to the complicated mix of subject making and narratives of race, empire, femininity, and performance.

Although Walker may have identified with Salomé through pan-Africanism, her performances also highlighted further axes of intimacy and distance between constructions of Arab and U.S.-based black femininities. Walker performed a particular orientalist fantasy of Arab femininity, but her blackness (like white women's whiteness) was not erased as part of the performance. In fact, her blackness gave her both more credibility as a "legitimate interpreter of native dances" and more reason to explicitly distinguish herself from this national other, this oriental primitive.[46] The slippages between Arab foreign bodies and black domestic bodies, was guided by what Hazel Carby describes as a social imperative to police black women's bodies, which were characterized as "sexually degenerate and, therefore, socially dangerous."[47] Thus Walker's performance was necessarily vexed: it simultaneously signaled a racial alliance with people involved in colonial struggles against empire and a craftswoman's correspondence with white choreographers and modern dancers. That is, her pan-Africanist politics created certain anticolonial modes of alliance, but her insistence on her own hard-won expertise over oriental forms brought her in line with white modern dancers. "Her art," Brown argues, "was the result of training experience and talent, not instinct or nature. Her *Salome* was part of her larger argument for stage performance as a respectable profession for artistically inclined 'intelligent and talented' black women."[48] As was the case with white dancers like Ruth St. Denis and Martha Graham, for Walker an imperial distancing between the body of the performer and the bodies of actual Arab women (for whom such dancing might be imagined as a natural inclination) created claims of both expertise and respectability. At the same time, Walker differed from women such as St. Denis and Graham: her blackness was called on (by herself and others, at different times) to reinscribe the authenticity of her racial performance of the oriental other—another order of imperial intimacy, born of histories of contact that are also histories of violence, that informed her success but also demanded an insistence on a distinctly American selfhood.

Though black women dancers such as Walker wielded forms of American exceptionalism, they nonetheless were caught in the mesh of multiple empires' intimacies, racisms, and histories of rule. At the juncture of an always already transnational domestic racism and the imperial logic of the Orient, black women were marked as strangers in advance of their performances, the distance between the heart of empire and its outposts intimately inscribed on their bodies. "Strangers are not simply those who are not known in this dwelling," writes Ahmed, "but those who are, in their very proximity, *already recognised as not belonging*, as being out of place. Such a recognition of those who are out of place allows both the demarcation and enforcement of the boundaries of 'this place', as where 'we' dwell."[49] As this type of stranger, black women in their performances created a dialogue within this national story that sometimes changed it, sometimes reiterated it, but always marked their bodies as spaces of negotiation, discipline, and creativity.

QUEER CIPHERS

As an apparently elastic signifier, Salomé also informed modernist modes of queer subjecthood. Salomé (and Arab womanhood in general) as a peripatetic orientalist signifier, could take on multiple meanings to critique the construction of race, gender, nationality, and sexuality, particularly where these identities depend on one another. To illustrate this form of critique, I turn to three drawings by Nugent. As shown in the previous chapter, Nugent worked both with and against the grain of imperial logic to find queer possibilities. Indeed, his creative labors often remapped imperial logic onto black bodies to secure queer subjecthood. To do this, Nugent collapsed geographies of scale and space to bring closer empires' multiple racial others, in something like a queer intimacy between continents. Although white and black women were often caught in the gap between archive and repertoire, finding there the limits of self-creation, Nugent situates the act of fashioning subjectivity in another breaking point. Imagining bodies and spaces in new ways, Nugent assumed that these were always simultaneously predetermined and undetermined. Queer renderings of the Orient, then, rely on and reiterate the exoticism of the national stranger but play with the expectations created through imperial logic to critique the imagined stability of identity categories.

As the previous chapter demonstrated, discourses and performances of queer sexualities often depended on diverse imperial histories in their formulation. Jazz Age images and performances of Arab signs and symbols also drew on European histories and maps, following from earlier queer cultural productions such as Oscar Wilde's rendering of Salomé and André Gide's depictions of sexual tourism in *The Immoralist*, borrowing across empires long before more modern forms of queer tourism.[50] In *Desiring Arabs*, Joseph Massad assembles compelling arguments about queer desires for Arabs, outlining queer sexual ontologies and genealogies of queer Europeans in the Muslim world. Massad notes that Richard Burton described versions of queer sexualities as "repugnant to English readers" in the essays in his 1885–86 translation of *The Arabian Nights*. Simultaneously, the "Stotadic Zone" marked a fascinating queer geography of Arab lands and the Orient for Burton and the "Orientalist and Anthropologist" to whom he addressed his essays.[51] Beyond these scholars, however, the circulation of Burton's text also provided queer artists in the United States, such as Nugent, with a vocabulary for defining, expressing, and coding their own sexualities. In the Jazz Age, artists like Nugent might tap into the European genealogy of such renderings in order to establish alternatives to racial and sexual discourses available in the United States.

One of the ways in which these alternatives are brought to the fore is through understandings and misunderstandings created by notions of veiling. If the use of veils signals exoticism, eroticism, and mysterious femininity, than the redeployment of the veil to critique the markers of those categories—female, racialized, foreign bodies—also contrasts the stability of those categories with their constant construction. The three drawings I call on here perform this kind of work by playing with Salomé as an orientalist queer signifier. In 1928 Nugent published a drawing in *Harlem: A Forum of Negro Life* titled *Salome: Negrotesque I* (fig. 3.2). Nugent was inspired by Aubrey Beardsley's illustrations for Oscar Wilde's 1895 *Salomé*, but in this drawing he also seems to produce new discourses for Salomé based simultaneously in queer European and in African American significatory practices. The literary critic Nina Miller makes connections between multiple modes of signification within the African American context when she argues that "Nugent's drawing targets both the theatrical and the feminine ideal in renaissance discourse, but his 'Negrotesque' is more than doubly devastating, for she exploits mercilessly the contradiction at the ambivalent core of racial uplift: that between bourgeois dignity and public display."[52] I enjoy Miller's suggestion here of a doubleness of meaning, and I would like to suggest a third possibility—that, in referencing the figure's sexual lasciviousness (also understood at times as a liberation from bourgeois propriety and the politics of respectability), the drawing also produces and works through the queer potential of Salomé. Like many of Nugent's drawings, this rendering of Salomé is produced through mixed-gender characteristics. In this portrait of the "Dance of the Seven Veils," much of the gender ambiguity rests on the veils and their multiple significations. The veil as an imperial signifier for the Orient conjures sensual beauty, social liberation, and sexual anticipation. Writing about Verdi's *Aida*, Said notes that in considering the case of colonial Egypt, "the Orient as a place of *promise and power* is very important."[53] The promise in so many of the performances of Salomé is the revelation of the body as a site of sexual sanctification. The promise, however, can rarely fulfill the thrill of anticipation—the removal of the veil, and what is uncovered, does not always match what is promised. That is particularly true, in this instance, where the promise is of sexualized power over the veiled bodies. For Nugent, the veils conceal exactly the parts of the body that interrupt and anticipate heterosexual fantasies of the Orient. In the drawing, the lanki-

Figure 3.2 Richard Bruce Nugent, *Salome: Negrotesque I* (1928). Courtesy of Thomas H. Wirth.

ness of the limbs gives the figure a sense of androgyny, and it is what is or is not beneath the veils that tell the story of gender, and, by extension, the remarking of the imagined viewer's sexuality. For instance, the placement of the veil draped over the shoulder obliterates one breast entirely (there is not even a suggestion of the other breast beneath it), and the genitals, visible through the veils, are also ambiguously rendered as possibly a penis with a pudendum or testicles. The removal of the veil, in this instance, would negate the promise of the dance—the promise of a feminized, sexually available Orient. Rather, the revelation of a gender-queer body, while still depending on a desire for an exotic perversity, disrupts the heterosexual presumption that usually accompanied performances of the "Dance of the Seven Veils."

The drawing further portrays Salomé with a mask-like face (perhaps an echo of Picasso's discovery of Africa, or rather the primitivist art movement, shown in his 1907 *Les Demoiselles d'Avignon*). The mask, like the veils that trail and waft about the body in Nugent's drawing, may in fact hide more than it reveals. Although the veils make gender and sexuality mysterious, and the possible revelation of the body tantalizing, the mask arguably does other work. Miller suggests the mask signals that "Nugent weighs in as more [an] international modernist than a citizen of Harlem."[54] Rather than arguing for one over the other, I am interested in the operations of such a spatial distancing that would distinguish between the international and Harlem as distinct spheres, when it would appear that the two were well acquainted. Nugent and Wallace Thurman were well known as critics of the often-restrictive forms that racial uplift took within the New Negro movement. The literary critic Stephen Knadler points out that, according to Thurman, "it [was] those most adamant in promoting racial purity who are secretly subverting the color line at night by acting on their 'natural impulses.'"[55] To Nugent and Thurman, in lively disagreement with the New Negro's call for a respectable black masculinity to disrupt the color line, it appeared that black masculinity's queer potential might disrupt that racial order as well. This is also hinted at in the title of Nugent's drawing. The "grotesque" suggested by the title may refer to the Theatre of the Grotesque, a performance and poetry movement occurring at the time in Italy. This movement questioned both positivism and naturalism in theatre and preferred irony and the macabre. It might have led Nugent to rethink the supposedly natural relationship between race and racial performance. When removed, then, the mask may reveal a black body, but there is no reason to assume what that blackness means in advance. Furthermore, the placement of the mask throws into confusion what lies beneath, even after its removal and the revelation.

The question of masculinity, literally as a cipher in this drawing, adds further dimension to the mask in another fashion. Like some of Nugent's other work, it includes in its numerous referents queer life in New York City. The drawing refers to the masked balls that took place in Harlem and Greenwich Village, which often attracted several hundred participants. These balls, elaborate affairs in which men and women often wore masks and revealing costumes, were spaces notable for their queer displays.[56] One vice reporter noted that the attire was "bizarre and grotesque" and that "usually the less [there was] of costume the better." The reporter observed that "Egyptian costumes are very popular with just the diaper effect and the rest of the body painted." Such exotic, orientalizing costuming was hardly the only notable aspect of the balls. The reporter continued: "One prominent feature of these dances is the number of male perverts who attend them. These phenomenal men dress up in the most prepossessing female attire simulating women so much as defy detection. They wear expensive gowns, employ rouge[,] use wigs and in short make up an appearance which looks for everything like a young lady. These men seldom dance with others save men and with each other. These are the commonly known 'fairies.'"[57] The queering effect of dress certainly played a part in Nugent's portrayal of Salomé. Dressing in costumes fit for cabaret and nightclub stages was not unusual at such cosmopolitan events as the balls, and Nugent's reference to them broadened the range of masculinities that could be performed in support of the racial justice. Removing the mask may reveal more intimacies, then, between both continents and bodies than many other New Negro intellectuals would have hoped for.

In 1930 Nugent offered another performance of Salomé, or an alternative to it. Although again relying on imperial discourses of the sexual excesses of the Orient, Nugent here suggests further modes of queer identification through orientalist signification. Certainly *Salome: Negrotesque I* suggests national cross-dressing, and Marjorie Garber observes that the adoption of (imagined) Arabic dress affords an opportunity to explore the bounds of gender, because of the circulation of both androgyny and femininity produced through such orientalisms.[58] But in this next set of paintings, Nugent moves away from Salomé as an increasingly commonplace signifier for queer identification—for instance, Oscar Wilde was photographed in drag as Salomé—to explore other forms of queer identification through orientalist signifiers. Perhaps because Salomé was so embedded within modernist queer male iconography, even as it explored cross-gendered representation, it was necessary for Nugent to move to other Arab characters in order to imagine modes of queer female (and cross-gendered) identification. In a series of nudes, Nugent explores the queer potential of other orientalized feminine figures—in which all the veils are dropped. In *Untitled [Two Women]* (fig. 3.3) and *Naomi and Ruth* (fig. 3.4), Nugent ex-

Figure 3.3 Richard Bruce Nugent, *Untitled [Two Women]* (1930).
© 2002 Thomas H. Wirth.

plores the homoeroticism of a biblical tale set in an ancient Palestine. In *Untitled*, the physical intimacy of the bodies appear in stark contrast to the solo nature of Salomé's "Dance of the Seven Veils." This painting recalls more closely the twining (or twinning) of two bodies on the dance floor at, for instance, a spot for queer nightlife like Harlem's Lenox Avenue Club. The painting's indistinct lines fail to demarcate where one body begins and the other ends, marking sensuality and the intimacy of broken boundaries. The women's almond-shaped eyes are emphasized by theatrical makeup, while the ambiguous drawing of the genitals again questions the boundaries of gender and sex, even as the painting's subtitle repositions

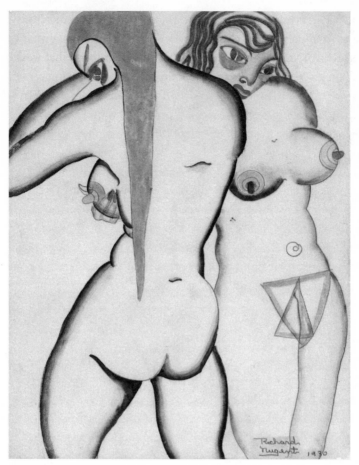

Figure 3.4 Richard Bruce Nugent, *Naomi and Ruth* (1930).
© 2002 Thomas H. Wirth.

the bodies as "Two Women." Rather than insisting on an affirmative reclamation of race and gender (relied on by racial uplift discourse), this painting references notions of sexual excess so often connected to the Orient in order to celebrate the transgressive possibility of queer desire without recourse to bourgeois respectability. Likewise, in *Naomi and Ruth*, the two bodies are shown in intimate relation to one another, body contours overlapping, hand to breast. Drawing again on the gendered play that exotic, erotic visions of the Orient offered Western audiences, Nugent offered another sort of cross-gender identification, a type of queer color line.

Nugent's artworks call into question the completeness and fastness of the orientalist archive as something that can be collected and then called on. Whereas the performers of the previous sections derived authority from this archive, Nugent's drawings suggest objects or forms that would complicate the archive's genealogy, that undo its structuralist signification. Nugent's works call to mind Derrida's pronouncement that "anarchivizing destruction belongs to the process of archivization."[59] By rendering the archive itself as an assemblage marked by race, gender, the foreign, the strange, and the mysteries of the harem and its attendant sexualities, Nugent introduced a queer chaos into the meaning-making schema of the archive, but it is a chaos that does not foreclose the possibility of the archive itself. Rather, his drawings make visible the contradictory structure of the archival project, and thus of imperial logic. For Nugent, the potential to manipulate and transform the meanings and forces found in the imperial archive can make possible the creation of queer of color subjectivities at exactly the point where they are to be controlled: a vexed, yet productive, archival project.

SEX AND THE SHEIK

A similarly complex knot of space and race, gender and sexuality, can be seen in performances of Jazz Age masculinities through the use of the word *sheik* in songs, films, and literature. In this section, I focus on manifestations of Arab masculinities and the movements of Arab masculinity across heterogeneous bodies. As with performances of Salomé, the work of marking people with the name *sheik* could be mobilized for distinct signifying purposes, though each relied on the imperial logic of distance and intimacy. Reproducing the imperial logic of British orientalism (interestingly, sometimes British imaginings were of French colonial Algeria, so the layers of colonialism and imperialism are manifold here) the mania for sheiks in U.S. popular culture of the early 1920s produced a variety of domestic masculinities marked through empire and orientalism. Perhaps the most popular rendering of the term came with the 1921 release of Rudolph Valentino's famous film *The Sheik*, based on the novel of the same name by the British writer E. M. Hull.[60] Numerous lyricists and composers responded to the film's tremendous appeal with songs such as "Burning Sands: An Answer to 'The Sheik'" (1922) and perhaps the most popular and enduring Tin Pan Alley "sheik" song of the period, "The Sheik of Araby" (1921).[61] The term was also used in newspaper reporting (as discussed in chapter 1) and novels such as Carl Van Vechten's popular and controversial novel *Nigger Heaven*.[62] The kinds of masculinities represented through images and narratives of sheiks, like those of the femininities connected to Salomé, worked across diverse bodies and for various purposes. Once again, the meanings ascribed to orientalisms resisted stasis both in terms of referents, signifiers, and implications.

Although these references to sheiks were based on an imperial logic of racialized gender and sexual difference, in popular usage *sheik* produced heterogeneous masculinities in its interaction with domestic discourses of race and gender. Sheik masculinities were infused with a strange desirability, but such allure carried positive and negative significations contingent on a racial order. For instance, white men reorienting themselves toward imagined Arabians might simultaneously claim and conquer the oriental other's erotic powers.[63] For them, to be named a sheik did not necessarily imply the forfeiture of imperial personhood, though the name could, at times, be used to censure aberrational sexual practices like queerness. For men of color (and masculine women), however, sheik pejoratively modified, or reoriented, masculinities perceived to be in need of disciplining because of racialization. Though the name might also impart erotic power to these bodies of color, such doubled racialization meant that the imprint of Arab masculinities would cohere distinctly from black masculinities. Orientations toward the Arab other thus circumscribed racialized masculinities; representations that named men of color sheik did so through the lens of distance, making them once again national strangers. Finally, like orientalist femininities, orientalist masculinities facilitated queer identification. In all these instances, orientations toward the Arab other are fraught with affiliation and subjugation, desire and domination. Furthermore, the distinctions redrawn through naming people sheiks helped reinforce the tremendous distance between empire's subjects, at home.

Popular songs often presented Arab men as sexually voracious and especially coveting white women. The men's appetites could be figured both as highly attractive, and as sexually overaggressive. Following elements of *The Sheik*'s plot, the Tin Pan Alley ditties "The Sheik of Araby" and "Burning Sands: An Answer to 'The Sheik'" tell of a fantastic seduction of a white woman by a mysterious Arab man. Both songs tell the story of a dashing Arabian who kidnaps and seduces a white woman against the alluring backdrop of the desert, palm trees, and the open sky. The cover of the sheet music for "The Sheik of Araby" directly reflects the film's influence, showing a racially ambiguous "Arab" man scowling over a supine blonde, who gazes adoringly at him. The combination of the lyrics and music conjure an aura of strangeness that here played out a peculiar form of sexual seduction, wherein the sheik captures his bride by singing to her and instilling in her both fear and longing. Presumably, as in *The Sheik* and E. M. Hull's novel, the woman is a stranger to the desert lands over which the sheik rules, but as his consort, she will join him in governing it. In his rendition of the song, the Harlem pianist Fats Waller intones in the chorus: "You'll rule this land with me, 'cause I'm the shook, the shake, the Sheik of Ar-a-by."[64] Although "Burning Sands" is written as a feminine fantasy (though with queer potential) — "Across the burning sands, there waits my Arab man / Beyond the coral strands, I'll share his caravan" — "The Sheik of Araby" is written from a first-person perspective, in which the singer adopts the voice of the sheik himself. The song thus proffers to the non-Arab man a fantasy of an uncivilized Orient, where he might exercise unrestrained power as a conqueror of exotic lands and an irresistible ruler of all women. Similarly in Andy Razaf's lyrics for "He Wasn't Born in Araby, but He's a Sheikin' Fool," the song's main character, "Sam of Birmingham," is described as being a sheik so sexually attractive that he has "more work than he can do," and the song explains that though "he don't know what a harem is, . . . every lover [says] he knows his biz."[65] Here, the sheik is reimagined in the U.S. context, with the South taking the place of the exotic. Such double entendres as "he never rode a camel, but he sure can ride a mule" place this hypersexualized sheik within a firm geographic and racial imaginary particular to the United States and its recent history of black migration from South to North. The sheik, then, remains a stranger come to town, and one with magnetic sexual power. Black and white men may have employed similar strategies for producing their subjectivity through this imperial logic, but their outcomes varied because of domestic histories of racialization. Indeed, references to the film strengthen just such a fantasy of imperial conquest. Near the end of the film, the sheik is revealed to be European by birth, an origin story that functions not only as a soothing disclosure of his essential civilizational being (through whiteness) but also as the natural justification for his rightful place as conqueror. The songs' themes thus bring the conquest of territory together with sexual conquest as the core of imperial governance.[66]

If imperial thinking produced the Orient as both morally aberrant and erotically alluring, it also informed the uses of *sheik* as a mobile signifier for sexual pathology in the United States and in contexts of racialization. It is for this reason that the term *sheik* was often attached to men known for their womanizing. When used to describe desirable white men such as Valentino, the name became a declaration of his virility, the bare traces of the term's racialization only occasionally spilling over into public displays of sexual excess. Attached to the bodies of black men, however, the name could tap into and reinforce existing U.S. discourses about race and aberrant masculinity through comparisons with pathologies ascribed to empire's racial degenerates. In the prologue of Van Vechten's *Nigger Heaven*, for example, Anatole Longfellow, a regular participant in Harlem's nightlife who is also known as the Scarlet Creeper, is referred to as a sheik. Marked as a narcissistic dandy through his elaborate dress, the Creeper also falls outside the bounds of bourgeois respectability. "Was there another sheik in Harlem who possessed one-tenth his attraction for the female sex? Was there another of whose muscles the brick-pressers, ordinarily quite free with their audible, unflattering comments about passers-by, were more afraid?" the Creeper muses.[67] These rhetorical questions point to both his threatening virility and his awesome manliness, channeled through his proud and supposedly perverse claim to the orientalist signifier. But the Creeper appears in the prologue of the book because of a suggestion made by the Harlem Renaissance novelist and physician Rudolph Fisher to Van Vechten, a white man: Fisher told the author that his original opening painted too idyllic a view of Harlem, that it was "too pro-Negro."[68] As a consequence, Van Vechten changed the novel's beginning to feature more prominently his black villain, the Creeper, who is demonstrably abhorrent and aberrant, in part through his extravagant modes of dress and orientalist self-naming.

Thus established in the opening scenes as a no-good Lothario, the Creeper operates as a foil to the middle-class aspirations of his opposite, the writer Byron Kason. Interestingly, Kason is also referred to as a sheik by his romantic interest, Mary Love, but the term has a different meaning in his case. For the Creeper, *sheik* points to excess and aberration; for Byron, it initially signifies his attractiveness, though by the end of the novel he is also criminalized. The shared name sets these characters up as foils for one another, as two examples of doomed African American masculinity.

At the end of the novel, both are involved in a nightclub gunfight that culminates with Byron being arrested for shooting a man who, unbeknown to the police, had already been shot by the Creeper—who escapes into the night. The Creeper is both more terrible and more successful than Byron. Although his aberrant masculinity is not to be celebrated within the novel's arc, his version of sheikhood is more threatening, and more trenchant, than Byron's. As illustrated so well in the final scene of a life-and-death struggle in a Harlem nightclub, the multiple meanings of the name point to tense negotiations over the ways in which African American sexuality and masculinity were being produced, controlled, and fetishized through discourses activated by their particular intimacies with empire.

Like Salomé, the naming of sheiks might be used to signal queer identities and sexual and sexed practices, particularly through the use of dress. Knadler connects the figure of the "sweetback" with that of the "sheik dandy," arguing that "constitutive of the sheik's performance in 1920s Harlem was already an inner division, one that manifested itself in both a gay permissiveness and virulent homophobia."[69] Like other attempts at creating modern subjecthood through imperial logic, these performances were vexed, and their outcomes mixed. The imperial logic that guides the multiple formulations of sheik also helps forge the indeterminacy of the Creeper's dandified dress. As dandies, men sporting carefully chosen outfits could drift into a manner of "'feminine' social performance," existing "in the space between masculine and feminine, homosexual and heterosexual, seeming and being."[70] The liminality of this figure also offers a commentary on the "politics and aesthetics of racialization and identity formation."[71] The orientalist aesthetic performance or narrative of being a sheik pointed to subject formations that were filled with multiple arrangements of identification. Loosening the predetermined nature of orientalist performance—those readings that imagine the relationship between the Occident and the Orient as stable and hegemonic, and the appropriative performance of the Orient as tied to specific bodies, meanings, and outcomes—opens the range of possibilities, even those queer ones, to the staging of orientalist discourses.

In this figuration of the sheik dandy, the play between femininity, as marked through race and nation, and masculinity, also as marked through race and nation, provides an example of when and where the inhabitants of the modern city might enter into an imperial discourse to fashion new possibilities for domestic queer identification. As Knadler shows, Thurman's, Nugent's, and even Wilde's performances were not the only queer or gender-queer performances to borrow the vestimentary vocabulary of the Orient to explore the boundaries of racialized genders. These performances popped up around the city at balls and nightclub shows and on city streets. Another example can be found in Julian Costello's snake dance in drag, as part of a performance suggestively called "The Valley of the Nile," reported in the pages of *Variety*. The article mentions that Costello appeared "very feminine" in his costuming, but that his arms were "quite muscular,"[72] disturbing his seamless transition into the oriental feminine and producing an oscillating order of gender presentation. Costello's performance thus produced another iteration of queer masculinity, though one that was still dependent on oriental signifiers to carry out the difficult labor of disturbing gendered and racial norms. His body—marked simultaneously as masculine, through primary and secondary sex characteristics and musculature, and as feminine, through movement and orientalism—disrupted dimorphic sex presentation. Furthermore, his body—marked simultaneously as black, through bodily characteristics, and as Asian through orientalist movement and, presumably, dress—confused the racial order of things by making the boundaries of race indeterminate. In these ways, the Orient was used to navigate gender, racial, and sexual prejudices by calling into question the solidity of the categories on which the wielding of power rests.

Such uses of an oriental aesthetic demonstrate that the imperial logic of distance and intimacy could be marshaled for competing interests. The sexual excess of the Orient was often mobilized to signal moral decay, or at least a very different moral order than that of the civilized, bourgeois West, but of course this decay could be interpreted differently by dissimilar groups and for numerous purposes. For nightclub owners, performers, and patrons, as well as for some artists and writers, the loosening of gendered and sexual strictures as signified by allusions to the sensual Orient was immensely profitable, sexually liberating, voyeuristically pleasurable, and a political project of critique, respectively; but, for reformers, vice investigators, and politicians, such claims of affinities with the Orient signaled a degradation that was moral and social, even physical in terms of the body as well as the neighborhood or community, and it urgently required policing. All these positions afforded figurations of modern personhood through imperial registers, if even some were more fleeting than others, and even if they revealed different and unequal forms of such personhood for various groups of New Yorkers.

The orientalist archive described by the types of performances and artworks found in this chapter is an archive existing without stable referents. This simulacral archive refers not to the bodies of people of the Orient—which are disappeared, re-placed, and replaced—but, rather, to fantasies of the Orient that prompt viewers to rethink colonial and imperial inventions for a multitude of purposes. The rendering of these orientalist fantasies does not act simply as appropriations of Asian culture, aesthetics, or performance; instead, these simulacral depictions destabilize referential apparatuses and the meanings produced through them, demonstrating that there was nothing fixed to appropriate in the first place. The meanings of the Orient are always already constructed, and the meanings attached to the Orient are also mobile. Involved in this reformulation of the power inherent in representation are two notions: first, that racial, national, and sexual representation is always already a fantasy; and second, as a result the appropriation of such representations does not constitute simply power over them. As seen in this chapter, the appropriation could be about creating power for white people over people of color in domestic space or over racialized bodies abroad, but it could also mean the reracialization of bodies at home, the power of subjectification for bodies of color and queer bodies, or the application of queer meanings to the gendered, raced, and sexual body. The many meanings ascribed—sometimes simultaneously—to these performances may rely on an imperial logic of otherness, exoticism, and spatialization, but the significance of the performances shows the contradictions inherent both in aesthetic production and the making of empire.

....

CHAPTER FOUR

DREAMING OF ARABY

In Irving Berlin's Tin Pan Alley song "Araby," the singer croons about "dreaming of Araby," where the narrator, presumably male, proclaims, "everything is oriental" and where he might meet a fair maiden beneath a palm tree. The second verse concludes: "Oh, how I wish I was there!"[1] The structure of the dream is instructive in thinking about orientalist discourses. The narrator of a dream is present in two worlds, here both fictional ones, but of varying fictional orders. The first world takes place in the present, perhaps on a stage in the setting of a nightclub, or in a modern city apartment, for those playing the song on a piano at home. A dreamed-up Araby constitutes the second world. Here unfurls an Araby concocted and mastered by journalistic accounts, movies, songs, and other figurations of a mysterious East, and the song moves seamlessly between the reality of New York and speculations regarding an Orient outside the bounds of the city and nation. Though the United States did not have a direct colonial relationship to these regions in the 1920s and 1930s, its geopolitical interest and imperial influence were nonetheless expanding into West and Central Asia and North Africa. Perhaps not coincidentally, and as seen in the previous chapter, lavish Hollywood studio productions such as *The Sheik* and *The*

Thief of Baghdad featured exotic settings, erotic costuming, and fantastical tales populated by enslaved princesses, kidnapped aristocrats, irresistible princes, and rapacious sultans.[2] Meanwhile, thrilling stories about intrepid Western explorers and scholars, including the British archaeologist and Egyptologist Howard Carter, circulated in popular U.S. magazines like *National Geographic*, informing scientific knowledge production and racial thinking about West and Central Asia and North Africa.[3] Berlin's "Araby" breaks down the distinctions between these fictional, studied registers and New York, where the song was performed. In so doing, it collapses the space between this imagined Orient and places like a Manhattan nightclub. Despite a lack of direct rule, then, imperial discourses about this Orient "over there" were nonetheless transported "home" in endless ways—in popular and educational literature, newspaper accounts, exhibitions, films, and, as we shall see, more songs, performances, and dreams.

Even as the spatial logic of empire describes these places as separate, at a great remove from center and civilization, these cultural artifacts point to intense connections between the places. As demonstrated by the scholarship of Lisa Lowe and Ann Laura Stoler and the artwork of Yinka Shonibare, imperialism creates connections—or what Lowe calls intimacies—between continents, thus obscuring the boundaries between geographic designations and social groups, between colonial histories and civilizational imaginaries.[4] Stoler eloquently argues that such connections were purposefully elastic, creating similarities and triggering complicities: "Colonial officials both created and called up a set of transnational equivalences between 'their' indigent Europeans and those elsewhere. What was produced was less often viable social policy than anxious efforts to identify an elusive social category available for cross-colonial comparison. Not least, these administrative recitations bear witness to how analogies were fashioned, and how the casual narratives that tied racial membership, class belonging, and impoverishment accumulated, gained, lost, and regained credibility when they were cross-referenced and (re)stored."[5] The kinds of references across various colonial spaces that are described by Stoler played a part in generating images of the Orient for New Yorkers. This chapter draws connections between empires, or would-be empires, to show how imperial logic travels across constructions of space and distance that are meant to divide some groups and to bring others into proximity in order to make sense of, implicate, or reinforce relations of power through reference, metaphor, and analogy. At the same time, these stories and their effects produced more than what was intended—often, clearer divisions between rulers and subjects—generating anxious slippages between spatial and social categories of nationality, race, and sexuality.[6]

Where the previous chapter brought peripatetic orientalisms visited on domestic subject formations into focus, this chapter considers the mobility of place markers across geographies of scale as a way to both regulate racialized sexualities in Harlem and expand colonial projects in western North America. Working from the international scale to the most intimate scales of sexualized bodies in Harlem and then back out to new U.S. colonial projects, the chapter explores space's collapse, in which imperial logic could be used to control racialized populations and their sexual practices and to lend credence to New Yorkers' roles in furthering contemporary colonial forays into the California desert.

The scope of people identifying and identified through or against orientalisms was large: white men and women regularly consumed exotic accouterment, décor, and performance as part of nightlife; black men and women reimagined their place in a domestic racial order by mobilizing stories and signs of places beyond the U.S. border, though not the U.S. reach; and indigenous peoples of Western North America were imagined through peripatetic orientalist rubrics that justified the acquisition of territory and resources by the U.S. state. Thus the reordering of racialized knowledge that was produced in art and entertainment had effects well outside of cabarets, nightclubs, and art galleries; and the stakes were high in these racial reorderings, including the right to inhabit space within the city, the rights of citizenship, and the rights to nationhood. These imperial imaginaries were made manifest in the cabarets and nightclubs of New York City as promises of exoticism and in the stated reasons for the surveillance of those places, as sites of criminality and pathology. As seen in the previous chapters, because orientalisms and their signifiers are dynamic and mobile—attached to particular bodies but also detached from them because they are so often imaginary—the music, movements, and accouterment of West Asia could easily be reproduced by and importantly on the bodies of cabaret and nightclub performers, as well as the material spaces of New York. Trappings alluding to the mystique of the Orient, borrowing from West, Central, and East Asian and North African themes, enticed customers with their creation of distant lands for closer inspection. The Hotel

Martinique, for example, had a room downstairs called the Omar Khyyam Room, after the author of the *Rubaiyat*. A Turkish restaurant at 146 Rivington Street held cabaret shows, the Egyptian Garden at 105 Second Avenue catered to a Slavic and Polish clientele, and Harlem boasted the Old Lybia on 139th Street.[7] Indeed, spatial discourses inspired by empire building and circulating through music, art, and performance produced a sense of civilizational entitlement to enter and conquer—both abroad and at home.

The narration of space as something that could be collapsed made for a variety of juxtapositions in popular discourses of Araby in New York. Harlem, for example, might become Araby (for better or worse), New Negroes might nationally identify with Egypt and resituate it in nightclub settings, and the elsewhere that Araby represents for New Yorkers might be displaced onto the U.S. West. Across diverse cultural sites, the aesthetic of the Orient interpolated both subjects and objects through changing narratives of space, fabricating imperial and sexual divisions such as seer and seen, explorer and explored, with the promise of travel and the observation of others' bodies. Concurrently, those divisions and the meanings inherent in their creation might be tried out, broken, or reiterated. Whether an article describing the intimate interior of a speakeasy, or a recording of Sophie Tucker singing "In Old King Tutankhamen's Day," each representation demonstrates how the signs and symbols of empire circulated within domestic cultures of travel (to a Harlem nightclub, for example) to produce imperial subjecthood—though that was differentially distributed, as observed above—and create complexly racialized contexts for conquest.[8] Furthermore, these representations did not just legitimate existing social hierarchies, though they often did this, too. They also concretized new divisions as well as what Grace Kyungwon Hong and Roderick A. Ferguson call "heterotopic" through stories and analogies of racial or sexual deviance that were used for various purposes.[9] In examining the language of travel and conquest from these entries into and replacements of an imagined Orient, I focus first on how imperialist fantasies provided a racial vocabulary for domestic colonialism. That is, the mutability of signs and symbols of the Orient provided references for containing and displacing racialized populations imagined to be unruly, sexually deviant, and dangerously uncivilized. Second, I explore how narratives of racial affinity across disintegrating geographic boundaries could produce a variety of meanings for black subjecthood within jazz cultures. Last, this chapter moves out into new imperial spaces, where the imperial logic of nightlife itself traveled, as New Yorkers toured beyond the city and into the West, catalyzing the forcible acquisition of new territory. These various uses of spatial narrative were related to a multiplicity of strategies to defy control, police populations inside the city and out in the empire of the West, and imagine new visions of sexual intimacy and alterity.

"AIN'T NOTHING LIKE THE ORIENT IN HARLEM'S ARABY"

Joyce Carrington's September 1928 illustration on the cover of the *Crisis*— the official magazine of the NAACP, founded and published by W. E. B. Du Bois—features a New Woman, a New Negro (fig. 4.1). Posed before a pyramid, a palm tree, and sand dunes, a light-skinned black woman sports a flapper's bob and wears modernist jewelry meant to evoke an African past. This image taps into the complicated territory of Africa as a symbol, at once primitive and civilized, that circulated to various effects during the Jazz Age. The image of foreign lands here operated as a marker of an imperial self-possession. The art historian Caroline Goeser, for instance, argues that Carrington's illustration provides a way for African American women to participate as modern subjects: "Circumventing the stereotypes of the mammy or the tragic mulatta, women illustrators often created images of sophisticated brown-skinned African American women, whose fashionable clothing and hairstyles marked them as fully engaged with modern consumerism and beauty culture."[10] The art historian Amy Helene Kirschke furthers this reading of the image, calling the figure in the illustration a symbol of "a universal woman of the diaspora."[11] Indeed, the figure's cosmopolitanism is recognizable not only through her primitivist jewelry and modernist look, but also through her ability to tour Arab lands. Such tourism, though, is suspect in some respects and in need of further questioning. This woman, dressed as though to head out to a Harlem nightclub rather than to visit the Egyptian pyramids, is thereby rendered out of place. The illustration may leave the viewer wondering how this woman has transported herself to Egypt, or even if she has done so. A third possibility might be to think of the woman as belonging to an Egyptian modernity, where she inhabits the space of her nation while wearing the hairstyle and jewelry of an international jazz culture. Because jazz is a contact zone, and because intimacies between continents might be found there, this image might also figure a collapse of distance: Harlem in Egypt,

Figure 4.1 Joyce Carrington, cover illustration for the *Crisis*,
September 1928. Courtesy of Crisis Publishing Co., Inc.,
the publisher of the magazine of the NAACP.

Egypt in Harlem. As one space and another are counterposed, juxtaposed,
and superimposed, the multiple readings of a drawing such as Carrington's
demonstrates the manifold methods of employing the spatial narratives of
an uncanny Orient to denote the character assigned to space itself, as well
as to signify subjectivity, the topic of the previous chapter.

This section focuses on the orientalization of the space of Harlem and
the variety of meanings and reactions engendered from the replacing of a
fantastic Orient into, onto, and in contrast to this Manhattan neighborhood. The orientalist signifiers that mapped moral perversion and sexual

freedom onto the bodies of cabaret and nightclub performers in New York also worked to remake the space of Harlem, whose vibrant and semilegal nightlife was sometimes imagined through an affinity with "Araby." The joining of polyphonous jazz, pleasure, and policing in spirited spaces of nightlife accommodated sexual exploration for residents and nonresidents alike, as well as internal colonialism in the form of increased scrutiny and moral outrage. With the entire neighborhood opened to intense surveillance from police, vice investigators, and journalists, traffic in orientalisms often came to emblematize fights over public space, both for those who sought to disrupt the social order and for those grimly dedicated to maintaining it. Making Harlem over as a colony through orientalist objects, narratives of space, and imperial logic helped justify the role of internal colonialism in a context of actual and metaphorical colonialism, where the usage of Arab signifiers augmented and activated domestic discourses of disorder and danger. Internal colonialism, in the form it took beginning in the 1960s, is often associated with racial repression in the form of economic injustice and political underrepresentation. In this section, I extend this kind of analysis to emphasize discourses of sexuality and connections between internal and external colonialism. The collocation of imperial space and New York City space frequently marked Harlem as foreign in a language that reflected the neighborhood's proximity to imperial space, and spatial discourses of aberrational race and sexuality further designated Harlem as a tourist destination, a place to have a good time, a space for creative endeavors, and a region requiring acute regulation.

The connections raised by renaming Harlem within a colonial context also tied the neighborhood to the need for policing. This is one important way the link to internal colonialism comes into play. Internal colonialism is often discussed as a metaphorical way of describing race and economic relations in the domestic sphere (often reiterating an imperial logic of domination, even as those making these assessments fought schemas of domination), but examples from the 1920s demonstrate how ties to colonial discourses produced reasons to control the population based on ideas of civility and incivility. The French writer Paul Morand, for instance, describes Harlem as "almost an outlying suburb, given over to Negroes and foreigners." [12] His comment creates both distance and distinction, resituating Harlem as a strange landscape at the edge of civilization proper. Writing of Harlem's precarious standing as close to, but irrevocably distant from, the imperial metropole, Morand suggests that this community teetered on a precipice: "Standing erect at the street-crossing, symbolic of white civilization, the policeman keeps his eye on this miniature Africa; if that policeman happened to disappear, Harlem would quickly revert to a Haiti, given over to voodoo and the rhetorical despotism of a plumed Soulouque."[13] This description of policing Harlem's inhabitants—inside the geographical boundaries of New York City, but outside its civilized society—is made sense of through colonial analogies, and here, notably, a French writer chronicles Harlem through the lens of French colonialism in Haiti. Through such analogies, Harlem became a strange land marked by imperial rule and also imperial travel, construed as an exotic destination outside of some denizens' everyday life that could be visited, consumed, and left behind, for Morand's text is a travelogue, and this description means to incite curiosity and draw readers into the space of Harlem. The appearance of the police protects these travels, both real and imagined, into darkest Harlem. Thus understood as an imperial outpost where visitors might meet natives, for the purposes of this book, it is a contact zone where copresence precipitates interactive and improvisational encounters. If Harlem was often already understood as belonging to a racial order beyond white Manhattan, this use of imperial aesthetics, with its metaphors and allusions, supplemented, enhanced, and reiterated Harlem as a locale for activities at the razor's edge of illegality and degeneracy.

I argue that internal colonialism is indeed a useful metaphor, especially with regard to black and, as we shall see by the end of the chapter, indigenous populations within and without the United States. I am interested in internal colonialism, but I want to be careful not to reproduce the imperial logic that often guides its usage as a hermeneutic device, assuming that the power of the colonists is predetermined as repressive rather than productive. To understand this, it is useful to turn to Linda Gordon's reading of internal colonialism. Gordon narrates the origins of the concept of "internal colonialism," which arose from the Marxist tradition and was used to describe the economic exploitation and political disenfranchisement of a racial population within a polity, rather than across its borders. "Internal colonialism," she argues, "was above all a metaphor, calling attention to similarities between classic colonialism—in which countries of the global north occupied and exploited 'Third World' developing regions and peoples—and intranational relations of domination in which exploitation coincided with racism and national chauvinism."[14] In the United States, civil rights activists and black nationalists (as well as Latino/a and indigenous nationalists) used the concept to claim affiliations between their movements and national liberation struggles around the world, and U.S. sociologists notably adopted the concept in the 1960s and 1970s to describe the continuing disenfranchisement of African Americans, especially in the inner city, to emphasize that U.S. racisms and "colonialism of the imperialist era" both "developed from the same historical situation and that racism and colonialism shared basic components."[15] As Gordon observes, the concept originally treated racism as an economic phenomenon, but its application can include cultural or ideological forms of dominance. In this regard, I follow Gordon's example to reclaim the term from Marxist economic determinism (and other analytic failures of its original conceptualization, which Gordon enumerates) through feminist and queer of color critique, and I use it to understand that the strength of racial discourses is their mutable and movable components, as well as to comprehend the concept's gendered and sexual imbrications, in contingent and contiguous intimacies with empires. I also use internal colonialism to understand comparative empire and to allow linkages within a single empire across oceans or borders, which may help us consider again the concept of jazz as a contact zone. Internal colonialism not only denaturalizes national boundaries as proper and inevitable, but it also allows us to recognize that some racialized others are already contradictorily considered enticing, decadent, undesirable, and immoral strangers to the national polity.

The image of Harlem as a domestic colony provided part of its appeal as a travel destination for those seeking entertainment, sex, and alcohol. Indeed, the entertainments sought by Harlem's visitors also reinforced notions of Harlem as colony. David Levering Lewis notes that Broadway musicals played a large part in producing Harlem as an exotic destination for cosmopolitan white audiences. Shows like *Dixie to Broadway* in 1924, with its interracial cast, and the interracial and blackface hit *Lulu Belle*, of 1926 "sent whites straight to Harlem in unprecedented numbers for a taste of the real thing."[16] Similarly, Irving Berlin's 1929 hit "Puttin' on the Ritz" remarked on the popularity of touring Harlem for white tourists, to see "the well-to-do up on Lenox Avenue . . . / On that famous thoroughfare with their noses in the air."[17] The lyrics prompt tourists from elsewhere to view Harlem through the lens of curiosity, describing the neighborhood as detached from the doldrums of ordinary city life and otherwise full of exotic entertainments: "If you're blue and you don't know where to go to, why don't you go where Harlem flits?"[18] The blackface character Lulu Belle, from the Broadway musical, also makes an appearance in the song: "That's where each and every Lulu Belle goes / Every Thursday evening with her swell beaus / Rubbin' elbows." If read intertexually, Lulu Belle is a white woman who wants to gallivant with the city's black population, and, being the subject of the song, she represents a break in both gender and sexual norms as a woman out on the town with men encountering interracial populations. Although performed in a playful tone, the lyrics also explore the possibility of going native as a part of the trip to Harlem—participating in a salaciously interracial and queer sexual culture spiked with alcohol, free love, and hot jazz—before a return to civilization south of 110th Street. Like other tourist sites, Harlem was noted for its cultural and social peculiarities, seen through a racialization that created an apparently delightful confusion around its particular versions of civilized norms of race, gender, and sexuality.

The remapping of orientalist space onto Harlem had many uses, and Harlemites themselves also participated in making Harlem strange, and a little queer, to establish Harlem both as a spot of pleasure and importance. "Harlem has been called the Mecca of the New Negro," remarks Wallace Thurman in one of the many essays he wrote in the persona of a native-informant tour guide, "Negro Life in New York's Harlem: A Lively Picture of a Popular and Interesting Section."[19] Likewise, Alain Locke's *The New Negro* anthology was originally published as a special issue of the *Survey Graphic* titled "Harlem: Mecca of the New Negro."[20] The fact that Mecca—the holiest site in the Islamic world as well as a bustling, exotic metropolis—might be used to make sense of Harlem suggests how such orientalist lenses activated and augmented domestic forms of spatial racialization. Renaming Harlem Mecca exhibits the neighborhood's cosmopolitanism, as a place from which important new arts movements might emanate. It also equates Harlem with an ancient and holy civilization, both as a marker of refinement and as an early connection between politically aware black activists and Islam. New Negro intellectuals, then, mobilized the idea of Mecca as a part of the project of racial uplift in the United States.

In a delightfully less dignified manner, Harlem's musicians and composers also took up the task of comparing and siting Orientalized space in the city. As an example, in May 1924, with Fats Waller in control at the piano, Porter Grainger recorded "In Harlem's Araby," leading the listener through various spaces in Harlem, rendered "mysterious" by its association with, and possession of key qualities of, "Araby." Grainger, in declaring, "Ain't nothing like the Orient in Harlem's Araby," marks a distance between Harlem and the Orient (where they are not alike), and simultaneously collapses the ideas around these two types of spaces by placing the Orient in Harlem. In considering this second meaning, the song thus transplants Araby into Harlem (though not necessarily all of Harlem). It accomplishes this through a narrative lens of travel in the first verse: "Oh New York is so mysterious / New York is so delirious / Just runnin' round to see the sites / But friends you ain't seen nothing yet / There ain't a place you can get a thrill like Harlem late at night."[21] As in "Puttin' on the Ritz," the song's narrator acts as a tour guide, introducing downtowners (or out-of-towners, or even other Harlemites) to the thrilling, titillating sights and sounds of Harlem. Making the space of Harlem strange and appealing, the song references the exotic Orient to describe Harlem's lively music culture and its denizens: "In Harlem's Araby / The funniest things you'll see / Yes, sheiks that do not live in tents / Jamming all night to pay their rent. . . . the dancers never move their feet / But shake from head to toe." "Harlem's Araby" is filled with orientalized characters familiar from floorshows and novels, the sheiks and belly dancers who inhabit the spaces of nightlife and lend an exotic flavor to its goings-on. It additionally presents such spirited music making and dancing as characteristic of the unrestrained, alien Orient, resignifying jazz life as belonging to a less civilized (Harlem's) Araby.

The theme of travel as well as an orientalized culture (albeit closer to home than Asia or Africa) fuel the popular reception of queer subcultures of Harlem, interpreting these through the strangeness of the Orient for the tourist in New York. Grainger sings: "Oh they've got women just like men. / Girls they acting like brothers. / It's hard to get along with them so I prefer the others." As in the drawings by Richard Bruce Nugent examined in previous chapters, the excessive, aberrant sexualities associated with the Orient make a queer turn. After Grainger notes the presence of female masculinities, he resolves this transgressive scene with the queerly ambiguous claim of preferring "the others." This stanza posits a tension between the trappings of tourism and the creation of a modern queer subjectivity. The stanza sets up queerness as a curiosity, available for viewing by folks interested in witnessing the unusual and exploring the wild life of Harlem, including bizarre displays of race, gender, and sexuality. Although actual queer acts that take place in Harlem may hold a different valence, because the song uses its narrative structure to introduce outsiders to a bizarre culture, the point of view expressed in the song resembles that of a tourist tract promoting the space of Harlem in parallel to an exotic Orient. At the same time, the song's narrator is a kind of native informant, establishing a particular racial and sexual identity through the metaphors of space; his participation in the life of Harlem is presented matter-of-factly, even if it is aberrational. The guide's knowledge and experience in this form of sporting life collocates orientalist ontologies and epistemologies with those of the racialized populations of Harlem in a manner that speaks to the joy and pleasure to be found in an imagined Orient as well as that in Harlem, and to the place of the black population of the United States in an international cosmopolitanism.

This displacement of boundaries and proprieties did not go unnoticed by police, vice investigators, and journalists—those interested in securing their careers through the naming of moral and legal curiosities. To explore negative reactions to these forms of sexual expression, I turn now to an article by Edgar M. Grey from 1927 titled "White Cabaret Keepers Conduct Dives," which argues that the white invasion of Harlem brought with it a decadent and orientalized immorality to the neighborhood. Grey worked variously as a journalist, an editor, and briefly as the general secretary of the Universal Negro Improvement Association.[22] In these roles, he often espoused the rhetoric of black respectability, and the article on cabarets was no different, recounting a journey into the recesses of Harlem, moving readers first into a racialized section of the city and then into the close, fantastic, and orientalized space of a cabaret interior. The description of this journey is rendered in terms of imperial power, remapping colonial discourse onto the city as a means of disciplining the local black urban population. Grey vividly maps this imperial logic onto the space of Harlem to restructure a racial order within the United States:

> A visit to the raided flat, then under police guard, disclosed a palace indeed. Here was a single room, large enough to be comfortable, decorated with the pictures of naked women and men in poses which smelt of the horrible stench of sex perversion; there, in another corner of the

room were couches of varying sizes, covered with the most costly silks, of varying hues; in the centre of the lay-out, rose as from a fairy background, a fountain plant, from which sprang, as if by magic, a flow of perfume over the nude body of a woman. Around this fountain were strewn costly and imported rugs, of every pattern and description, and on these the dope addicts gathered to revel in the dreams of unrealities.

In still another room, were couches decorated with multi-colored lights and a large colonial bed-stead, with a large covering canopy, with electric lights at each corner, flaring forth as at a grand bazar [*sic*]. At the one side of this bedstead was a step-platform, garnished with silk ribbons of all colors and on each step a dimmed electric light, covered with tissue paper. In addition to these were drinking outfits of various sorts and the police say that when the raid was made these were the hard and fresh smell of liquors. At the door, of the palace, one was met by a flunky in Oriental garb who, questioned one as to one's business and directed one to a reception room where the "Sultan" soon arrived to make arrangements.

The patrons of this dive were white men, and rich, who sought the great fire-eating gift of black folk to the American scene: Sex served scientifically, garnished with Jazz, and washed down by poisonous liquors and more poisonous drugs. These are numerous in Harlem. They are run in conjunction with cabarets; they are part and parcel of the general business ventures of the white invaders of the community who come not to raise the moral standard of the community, but to destroy it. Not that they are charged with any duty to raise morals of the colored youth, or even keep it at its original level; but surely a community so helpless as not to have the ability to drive these immoral kings and dukes from its confines, is surely weak indeed.[23]

Writing from a liberal reactionary impulse, the author re-creates colonial structures within cabaret space, disempowering, disappearing, and disapproving of black urban populations, even when advocating for their protection and uplift. As Stoler argues, such racializing discourses "may serve a reactionary political agenda or a reformist one."[24] Extending Stoler's assertion that racializing discourse is polyvalent in its mobility, I explore here an example of a politically reactionary article. It makes use of many imperial tropes to prove its point: colonial power relations, orientalist objects to signify sexuality, and the relocation of jazz as an orientalized discourse that supports exotic eroticism. Although the article avails itself of these imperial themes to make its argument, the presentation of evidence also speaks to the fun and allure of these types of spaces. I argue, then, that although the article has a politically reactionary agenda, its reactionary discourse produces the acts that the author claims to want to curtail. In this way, the work of political discourse is not an either-or proposition, either reactionary or reformist; rather, the article produces a multiplicity of meanings simultaneously by playing with the impulse to dichotomize political discourse.

As a proliferating metaphor and a profound analogy for making sense of a complex array of racial interactions occurring in Harlem, colonialism provides a civilizationist logic for the control of racialized populations in the United States and offers new ways to look at people of color as outside the flow of Americanness proper.[25] The taxonomy of giving characters in the Harlem scene names from orientalist imaginations—white tourists as "immoral kings and dukes," there to visit "the 'Sultan'" and "a flunky in Oriental garb"—remaps Harlem as a colonial landscape and thereby restructures race relations in the city. Through this colonial metaphor, Harlem's community is positioned as weak, helpless, and in need of control; and though the kings and dukes may be immoral, they nonetheless are of the ruling class, able to choose their own course. The white visitors from outside Harlem, however, are neglecting their duty of civilizing and uplifting—the "white man's burden" of Rudyard Kipling's famous colonialist poem transplanted to a "heart of darkness" different from Joseph Conrad's. Though the article states that it is not the visitors' "duty to raise morals of the colored youth," it is still clear that the author expects them to do so to some degree. As part of the rewriting of race relations in the city through colonial metaphors, the article reinforces a blend of domestic and imperial logics of white governance over bodies of color. This other form of colonization—not as civilizing mission but as destructive tourism, encouraging and exploiting the worst elements of human society—is demonized in this article, which castigates "the general business ventures of the white invaders of the community who come not to raise the moral standard of the community, but to destroy it." Instead, in this denunciation, the colony of Harlem becomes the outlandish playground of the colonizers, a place where they can shed the trappings of civilization and vest themselves in an exotic, fantasy underworld, as described later in the article. For its author, this is unacceptable.

Imperial logic also underpins assumptions about sexuality and power, inherent in the article's description of the "palace," built through the inclusion of orientalist objects that mark the space as sexually immoderate. The metaphorical Orient is at once manageable and unmanageable, able to be consumed but overflowing with the ever-present threat of uncontrollable sexuality. The author describes an excessive collection of oriental objects such as perfumes, "costly and imported rugs," and "costly silks" that transform the cabaret space and evoke sensual experience in what the article calls "palatial dope dens, harems of prostitution, [and] gin-palaces."[26] These catalogued items demonstrated the commodification of the Orient, with luxurious accouterment that could be traded, possessed, and controlled spread over floors, couches, and walls. Through this itemizing, the article makes visible that which is usually constructed as invisible, echoing descriptions in article after article, vice report after vice report, and police statement after police statement. These spaces are public but narrated as invisible, hidden, and off the beaten path. This constructed invisibility lends the space the mysterious air of exoticism, making it a foreign and enticing territory. But although the space of the cabaret is contained by both city regulations and physical walls, its foreign nature threatens to break through these bounds. The article itself is a performance of the tension between allure and repulsion, as the voyeuristic description betrays the author's desire to consume the Orient, a desire momentarily resolved in the language of management. Seductive but also overstimulating, this space is imagined as being on the verge of breaking free of its bounds and overpowering its visitors' rational faculties with an orientalist contagion.

The orientalist objects present at the scene of the cabaret speak both to the sexual variety available to the Harlem community and to the author's desire to enforce strictures on this community. Again, the author uses the logic of imperialism to prove that the sexuality afforded by this orientalized space is aberrational and in need of censure. To complement the "pictures of naked women and men in poses which smelt of the horrible stench of sex perversion," the author mentions the presence of couches and, more vividly, a "large colonial bed-stead." Although beds and couches might have been seen as sexual in any club, the special context of orientalism added to both the allure and the danger of the furnishings. Describing the bed "as at a grand bazar" betrays the sexual economy at work in the article. The imperial logic used to describe the club's interior also transmits particular sexual fantasies about the consumable bodies of women of color for the white kings and dukes who frequented the club. Even if the actual bodies offering sexual pleasures at the scene were not women of color, the use of colonial metaphors nonetheless makes it possible to play out this colonial fantasy, assigning to the club, the people in it, and the people in the neighborhood surrounding it a place on this imperial map. The orientalist trope of incivility—here imagined through sexual excess—is used to demonstrate the inappropriateness of certain intimate relationships on the domestic frontier. Simultaneously, the loving details and attention paid to these sexualized objects demonstrate the power they have to attract visitors and even the author, exerting a possibly irresistible compulsion.

The construction of space is more than just the built environment and decorative furnishings. Music also fills and shapes space, speaking its own language of signification, hailing bodies into its own moral order. Interestingly, the music that signals the Orient is jazz; here, modes of Orientalism merge with existing racial discourses to inform musical meanings. That is, the connection between illicit sexuality and the Orient is congruent with existing ideologies that link black sexuality and jazz. The article reports that the clients "sought the great fire-eating gift of black folk to the American scene: Sex served scientifically, garnished with Jazz, and washed down by poisonous liquors and more poisonous drugs." The elements placed in relation to one another in this passage make the assigned character of Harlem residents visible through a series of mixed—and mixing—metaphors. The sexual energies assigned to "fire-eating . . . black folk" constitute an irresistible threat to white patrons, and the colonial vernacular of going native warns of the danger. ("Sex served scientifically" also recalls sexological hypotheses imputing to blackness a deviant, and unsentimental, sexuality.) Black Harlemites, according to this view, inhabit a space of moral depravity and sexual and consumptive overindulgence doubly marked through blackness and orientalism, race and imperialism. Like the illegal drugs and alcohol flowing freely there, which are imagined to be critical to the orientalist sensibility cultivated through the décor and the costumes, the music of jazz filtering through the club suggests the aberrant sexuality of strange, uncivilized others. This linking of the orientalisms to blackness directs us again to the doubled labor the article accomplishes, naturalizing sexual and social chaos through colonial metaphors to demand the control and necessary civilizing of orientalized black bodies in Harlem.

Although the article's express intent is to point out the depravity of the white invaders of Harlem, the author's reliance on imperial metaphors places the white interlopers and black residents in a tension-filled relationship of internal colonialism, replete with hierarchical power differences. This narration of power in Harlem's clubs constitutes white subjects as often amoral, but also as powerful and charged with moral obligations, while black Harlemites are seen as acquiescent, easily corruptible, and uncivilized—not unlike empire's others. The rewriting of black space through colonial signs and symbols positions Harlem as empire's outpost, needing surveillance and control, justifying intervention and racialized management. Thus imperial logic collapses the distance between internally and externally colonized peoples. Jazz cultures, as contact zones, lead some people to enjoy their entertainments and others to decry the interracial, sexualized mixing that is inherent in these aesthetic and spatial constructions of modernity. Those discourses and practices that structured ventures in West Asia and elsewhere, here move along geographies of scale to enforce civilizing narratives of surveillance and control over the neighborhood of Harlem and its wayward populations.

EGYPTOMANIA

In "Jazzonia," Langston Hughes connects the participants in a cabaret scene—a jazz combo and a dancer—to characters from West Asian and North African history: Eve and Cleopatra. As "six long-headed jazzers play," a "dancing girl whose eyes are bold / Lifts high a dress of silken gold," writes Hughes.[27] Hinting at Egyptian connections in describing the musicians as "long-headed," a reference to visual representations of ancient Egyptians, he begins to spin associations between domestic modernity and a distant African past. The dancing girl, imagined at once as sexual (lifting her dress) and majestic, has inherited a great transnational history that lives on in her body, clothes, and movements. Hughes compares her bold eyes to those of Eve, and her gold dress and beauty to those of Cleopatra. In doing so, he retells the narrative of forced diaspora that marks the present state of African Americans as less a pathology than the result of others' assumption of the role of rulers, including primogeniture, that creates juridical rights and, ultimately, a historical context for black subjectivity that reaches across centuries and continents. The site of jazz, then, becomes a place for understanding the intimacies of continents and, as we shall see in this section, for negotiating black subjecthood.

In this section, then, I investigate the purposeful collapsing of time and space as a way to both promote and deny black subjectivity through the circulation of ideas about Egypt. If Harlem was often made legible through the colonial metaphor and imperial analogy brought home, then domesticated colonialisms also circulated throughout empires' intimacies. The previous section focused on orientalist fantasies that collocated the space of Harlem with the space of an imagined Orient, and this section takes up a slightly different register of contact: the interaction between domestic jazz cultures as an ideological contact zone and the contemporaneous archaeological exploration of Egypt. In the 1920s Egypt rose to prominence in the international imaginary, as Britain's colonial properties struck out for national independence around the globe and new scientific discoveries of ancient advances in the region attracted the world's fascinated attention. A particularly contested site because of its historical role as an alternate seat of civilization and progress to ancient Greece and Rome, Egypt became a vehicle for constructing modern selfhood for African Americans through a claim to an enlightened past. As Kirschke notes, the New Negro movements of the early twentieth century turned to Africa to excavate old connections and forge new affinities: "Although Africa encompassed many different cultures, W. E. B. Du Bois, for example, wanted to connect readers to the entire continent. This included North African and Islamic regions which also suffered under colonialism and foreign rule."[28] Pan-Africanism as a strategy depended on building affiliations with all the colonized peoples of Africa, including its Arab populations. Sometimes these affiliations included insistent claims that Africa was the seat of the modern;[29] other, equally invested arguments described Africa as an archaeological wonder firmly located in antiquity. These latter discourses about Egypt were often composed in and circulated from the privileged perspective of explorers, imperial travelers who considered themselves masters of the lands and cultures of the past. In some cases, this ostensibly scientific perspective, forged in the crucible of imperial conquest, lent powerful support to a logic of control over black (and indigenous) populations at home.

Although the preceding section considered the usage of orientalist signifiers and colonial analogies about a distant "there" to demarcate and control urban space and racialized bodies "here," this section moves with the back-and-forth circulation of Egypt in the U.S. imagination. Stories and fantasies about Egypt were important for assembling a wide range of spatial relations between populations in the United States, on the one hand, and populations past and present in North Africa, on the other hand. Works like Hughes's "Jazzonia" made direct links through the collapse of time and space between Egypt's ancient high culture and Harlem's contemporary jazz urbanity. In other cases, Egypt denoted the historic reach and power of the British, who had thoroughly trumped these ancient empire builders, and discourses and images of their reach and power could be mobilized to shore up racial hierarchies in the United States. In this section, I compare the visual works of the African American painter Aaron Douglas with "In Old King Tutankhamen's Day," a song recorded by Sophie Tucker, a popular Russian-born American singer and actress. Both artists produce figurations of Egypt, but each embody distinct psychic and political economies of identification. The former pursues racial affinity, while the latter seeks to conjure up a racial distance. But this difference takes another turn: even as these distinct figurations betray different intentions and identifications, together they reference and rely on an imperial logic that informs the relationship of the United States to Africa, its peoples, and its resources. As Ella Shohat has argued, Egypt and its figures, notably Cleopatra and the pyramids, have provided a testing ground for racial and national pride.[30] Ultimately, these works create different places for race in the U.S. context, yet together they provide an imperial logic for the appropriation of other lands and other peoples, for other purposes.

Like Hughes, Douglas made a concerted effort to link Harlem's burgeoning jazz scene with Egypt's ancient high culture. These connections moved along the orientalist history of art movements like Art Deco, the histories of heterogeneous African populations (both orientalized and tribalized), and African American modernity. In a 1926 series, Douglas illustrates a black genealogy that creates a path from Egyptian elegance to the grace notes of jazz and the blues. In the first image I consider, the *Krigwa Players Poster* printed in the *Crisis* in May 1926, the orientalism of Art Deco style is reinterpreted as what the art historian Richard Powell dubs "Afro-Deco."[31] This subtle shifting of Art Deco from its orientalist origins into an aesthetic form describing a racial project of black uplift capably demonstrates the ability of orientalist signifiers to reattach themselves to other bodies and modern political movements. Douglas's poster certainly encapsulates a pan-African sensibility, featuring instantly recognizable Egyptian icons such as a sphinx and pyramids flanking a central figure with a masklike face and hoop earrings, and a river running along the bottom of the poster. Brought together, these iconic images present what Goeser calls "a pastiche of visual symbols that tells the reader to see black American origins quickly as both tribal African and Egyptian."[32] Thus, the drawing illustrates multiple layers of colonial and imperial discourses, here repurposed to illuminate the power of U.S. jazz cultures vis-à-vis a proud African past.

This poster also works as a referential key to the symbols that Douglas mobilized in many of his other illustrations in the rest of 1926. For example, the sphinx and the masklike face are repeated in the cover art he drew for *FIRE!!*.[33] Here, in the words of Goeser, "Douglas visually conveyed the integral linkage between the 'tribal' and the 'civilized' faces of Africa."[34] Douglas's work in both the *Krigwa Players Poster* and the cover of *FIRE!!* demonstrates a refusal to choose a singular origin story for black populations in the United States. Instead, these illustrations depict heterogeneous connections to multiple African pasts and, via anticolonial struggles and archaeological excavations, to the present. At stake for Douglas in these images is the modernist vision of an ontological and epistemological sense of blackness as creative and majestic. The use of orientalisms to give additional significance to the work of the younger generation of Harlem's artists modifies the meanings of blackness at home through affiliation with, rather than distance from, "out there." Indeed, the Orient is again collapsed into Harlem.

Another of Douglas's illustrations to use an Egyptian visual vocabulary is *Play de Blues* (fig. 4.2), which accompanied Langston Hughes's "Misery" in *Weary Blues*, his 1926 book of poems. As in the cover of *FIRE!!*, Douglas uses some of the graphic icons in the *Krigwa Players Poster*. Here, the wavy river lines from the bottom of the *Krigwa Players Poster* are transformed into the reverberations of blues music emanating from the piano. The singer reaches up, entering the musical stream. Douglas creates a heterologic relationship between blues musicians and Africa: the heads of the performers here are inspired by Dan masks from the Ivory Coast,[35] and through the river as a trope connecting continents and eras, he links Egypt and New York. These illustrations depict a deep and profound exchange across the black Atlantic—in which U.S. black artists are influenced by an African and Egyptian past—and demonstrate that these same artists are

Figure 4.2 Detail of Aaron Douglas, *Play de Blues* (December 1926). Spencer Museum of Art, the University of Kansas, Museum purchase: Helen Foresman Spencer Art Acquisition Fund, Lucy Shaw Schultz, 2003.0012.05.

the ones rendering this Egyptian past. Thus Douglas relies on a particularly modernist formulation, one that determines that Egypt can be known but that is also aware that the Egypt being presented is a creation of the modern artist. Indeed, the stakes of black internationalism and black cosmopolitanism, as represented by Douglas, depend on this connection to Africa and deliberately erode the distinctions between multiple pasts and multiple presents. The collapse of time and space occurring in Douglas's illustrations comes from a cosmopolitan aesthetic—though it is one whose restrictions racialized peoples in the United States could not outrun—and that ambivalence creates a visual language describing a heterogeneous, creative, and modern black subject in the United States.

The construction of black subjectivity was policed by other interests, which mobilized the language of an orientalized Egypt in order to make their case. News of explorers' findings in Egypt influenced aesthetic production in the United States by people like Hughes and Douglas, and it also made a splash in the world of popular music. In November 1922 Howard Carter uncovered the tomb of Tutankhamen, the boy pharaoh. The archaeological find caused waves of excitement around the world, including New York City, whose Metropolitan Museum of Art partially funded the expedition and provided logistical support during the excavation. Therefore, though Egypt had most recently fallen under British influence, U.S. citizens also participated in colonial fantasies about Eastern ancient cultures and Western scientific expertise. The following year, Sophie Tucker recorded "In Old King Tutankhamen's Day," a Tin Pan Alley song that took Carter's dig as a starting point for a fantasy about the psychological and sexual life of an Egyptian pharaoh.[36] In this popular ditty, the same symbols that could be so powerfully mobilized by Douglas to produce a majestic black genealogy are used for very different purposes. Although the song included some of the familiar oriental signifiers that had appeared in nightclubs and cabarets, it also drew on newspaper reports of the tomb's unearthing to create an affinity between the singer and the archaeologist, both figures who might be understood as collectors of artifacts and, in this case, as shapers of international and domestic relations. To do this, "In Old King Tutankhamen's Day" demarcates at least three lines of distinction between the United States (and, by logical extension, Europe) and Egypt: first, the music itself makes an aural difference between continents; second, the lyrics reify oriental sexual difference; and third, the song invites its listeners to mimic the archaeologist, to unearth the past's curiosities and catalogue Tutankhamen's possessions. Although it is this third line of distinction that I focus on in this reading of Tucker, it is important to note that taken together, the music and lyrics weave a tale of the ancient roots of the Orient's aberrant sexualities together with an imperial justification for control of its land, resources, and bodies. Here another past intrudes on the present: it is significant that Sophie Tucker made her name at the end of the nineteenth century as a "coon shouter," performing in blackface.[37] Jayna Brown observes that Tucker "shaped her stage persona against and through versions of racialized femininity," even after leaving her blackface performances behind.[38] It is in this way that her performance of "In Old

King Tutankhamen's Day" bound together colonial fantasy and racial minstrelsy, oriental signifiers and U.S. domestic cultures, in new configurations of mimicry and scorn.

The musical modes in the song tell a story of contact, where Western might is naturalized and orientalization marks the collapse of space and historical time. In untangling the song's condensed themes of racial hierarchies and imperial logic, I discuss first the demarcation of this civilizational distance through Tucker's juxtaposition of musical modes: a dominant mode that is meant to represent the West, and a minor mode that is meant to represent the East. As in "Palesteena," Tucker's tune relied heavily on a flatted minor third in order to demarcate the Orient and highlight its difference from the Occident. The song opens with a variation on the refrain along the major scale and then sinks into its first orientalized measures, repeating a sequence of B, D flat, and D in the key of B major, the D being the third. The use of this half step between D flat and D builds both anxiety and anticipation—anxiety at the coming of the unknown, and anticipation at the prospect of finally seeing and knowing. This sequence is repeated throughout the song, usually at vocal breaks. As a marker of contact, the use of the minor third is juxtaposed with a straight major scale, which signifies for the listener the difference between the Orient and the West. The vocal melody relies solely on the major scale, denoting the crucial difference between the surveyor and the surveyed, between Tucker's world and King Tutankhamen's. The major scale is standard and a relatively strong mode, but the excessive use of the flatted third, because it mimics the minor scale, gives the Egyptian other a sense of weakness and exoticism. As described in the musical relationship of the major and minor orientalized modes, the West is "knowing," with a colonial eye, and the Orient is set up to be seen.

Following these musical impressions of contact, the song's lyrics rely on a sexual exoticism, previously instantiated through the recollection of tropes already familiar to nightclub and cabaret audiences. So, as with the music, the lyrics confound the time and distance between contemporary audiences and ancient Egypt, just as archaeological digs are contemporary, political, and embedded in the past. The song, for instance, mentions "1,000 dancing girls" who, with "lots of hip hip hooray," would "move and move and move, but never move their feet." The listener is put into the position of viewing Tutankhamen viewing these ancient belly dancers, a doubled position of lascivious voyeurism (because such words conjure up Salomé, Hawaiian dancing, the hoochy coochy, and other exoticized performers who could be experienced more immediately) as well as one that claims a distant, historical remove and a way to enter the world through its doubling of the style of modern cabaret, nightclub, and Broadway performances.

This collocation of ancient Egypt with New York's sexualized nightlife in the song emphasizes an identification with the whiteness of the West and its ability to collect and know the Orient, even as it indicates the pleasures of nightlife. What is distinct about Tucker's tune is its affinity for the archaeologist as an arbiter and producer of imperial taxonomies—the song directly references Carter's discovery: "They opened up his tomb the other day, and just with glee, / they learned a lot of ancient history"—and how this affinity is brought to bear on racial hierarchies at home. The fight to control the past was being waged not just in Egypt, over the tomb's contents and significance, but also in newspaper accounts, popular songs, and everyday debates. Recorded within a year of Carter's discovery in Luxor, Tucker's song relied on the same narrative devices that filled newspapers reporting on the shared U.S.-British discovery and the subsequent fight to remove the tomb's carefully itemized contents from Egypt. This removal was intensely contested in diplomatic skirmishes between Egypt, Great Britain, and the United States. According to Timothy Mitchell, "the discovery coincided with Egypt's winning partial independence from the British military occupation established in 1882, and provided the new nationalist government with a powerful expression of the nation's identity."[39] As an expression of its new semi-autonomy under indirect British rule, the Egyptian government retained control of 50 percent of the discovered items. The United States inserted itself into this tug-of-war under the auspices of the Metropolitan Museum of Art. The *New York Times*, using the accumulative logic of Western expertise, argued: "The Metropolitan Museum authorities owe it not only to themselves but to science to use every endeavor to secure the intervention of the American government with the Egyptian Government with the object of preventing abolition of the present law under which such excellent research organization has developed in Egypt."[40] It is within the context of these debates that the song emerges and becomes part of the conversation. The premise of the song, then, was based in part on the control of national resources in and expertise about Egypt, and thus the song reflects ideas that depend on the glorification of Western civilization and the naturalization of the rule of whiteness over the racialized populations of the world.

It is through these Western epistemologies that the song forwards archaeological, archival, and public display projects. It mimicked the newspapers' narrative revelation of artifacts emerging from the tomb with its own inventory of the goods and possessions that one might find in the royal tomb of King Tutankhamen. Just as Carter stunned the crowds gathered around the archaeological dig by bringing out objects like vases filled with perfume, Tucker sings about "gold and silverware / From big hotels of every land and clime," robes, and "the first fig leaf that Adam gave to Eve." This list, though comical, invites the listener to share in the cultivation of expertise through the discoveries made in the excavation. The unveiling of these artifacts also provides an entry point for understanding the stakes involved in producing a story of these objects. (For example, a *New York Times* article, arguing for the release of artifacts to the United States, notes that the finds "confound many former beliefs" about the history of Egypt's rise and fall.[41]) The song, then, describes a contest for ownership not only of artifacts but also of history, its meanings, and knowledge of how it might apply to contemporary populations.

As demonstrated to radically different effect in Douglas's artwork, Tucker's song also suggests that high stakes were involved in the control of Egypt's history for African Americans. The connection between control of Egypt's legacy and America's "Africans" is made clear in the final verse of the song. Here, assumed affinities between black people in the United States and the people of West Asia and North Africa are mobilized to imagine a disciplinary racial regime informed by imperial logic for domestic affairs. This logic dictated an "imposed relationship to empire, an imposition that persists even as the categories and relationships themselves shift."[42] Though originally released on Okeh Records, a label known for its "race records," the song asserts particular restraints on modern black subjectivity, wrought through orientalisms. Turning sharply away from Egypt and Tut's tomb, the lyrics move to the relation of blacks in the United States to this tale of Egyptian pharaohs. "Why Sam from Alabam'," sings Tucker, "would not run one, two, three / or what a mark he'd be for old Mark Anthony." This couplet references another popular song of the time, "Lovin' Sam." "Lovin' Sam" describes a ladies' man, more effective than even Rudolph Valentino's sheik: "Lovin' Sam, he's the sheik of Ala-bam / He's a mean love makin', a heartbreakin' man!"[43] But the swagger and virility afforded to black masculinity via orientalisms in this earlier tune (pathological and dangerous as it is) is trumped in Tucker's song. "Sam from Alabam'" is a second-rate lover in comparison to Mark Antony, the Roman general. Bridging the centuries to imagine Sam from Alabam' and Mark Antony as contemporaries, the song finally cautions African Americans not to make too much of their Egyptian roots, since Egypt had been defeated by Europe's military, masculine prowess in the ancient past. Even as the treasures and marvels of early African civilizations were being uncovered, the song reminds the descendants of Africans to "know their place" on the civilizational pecking order: they had been conquered in the past and remain conquered in the present. The promise of this distant land, these ancient wonders, should not be interpreted, the song warns, as an opportunity for black people in the United States to claim power and pres-tige for themselves.

The collapse of time and space set the scene for racial affiliation across continents and eras. Affiliation, however, also could be read through mul-tiple valences. The work of Hughes and Douglas used connections to Egypt as a way to mark an honored past that lived on in the present, in scenes of jazz cultures inflected by the importance and majesty of past civilizations. As such, these affiliations promote associations with the wondrous ancient societies of West Asia and North Africa that carry over into the present day, are embodied by musicians and dancers, and ring out through the sound of jazz horns. Understanding this as a rhetorical technique, other people made the same connections, but mobilized them in entirely different ways. This song resituates the contemporary African American population at the mercy of the white conqueror Mark Anthony to reinstate a racialized social order in the United States. The song, then, falls into line with the forms of internal colonization that were discussed in the first section of this chapter, though in this section, I have tried to show that modes of power were not absolute, but that imperial logic provided sometimes competing narratives of subjectivity that appear to go unresolved. These examples demonstrate how the collocation of space and time could be used to contest black sub-jectivity, and that the mobilization of orientalist narratives neither guar-anteed nor automatically denied these modes of subjectivity; rather, these discourses occurred concurrently as a way to map contemporary debates about and instantiations of subject making.

NEW CONQUESTS

Whereas the first section of this chapter considered the touristic fantasy of Araby in Harlem to produce modes of both pleasure and regulation, and the second section explored the mobilization of orientalist figurations of ancient Egypt as appearing contemporaneous with modern domestic jazz cultures as a way to contest black subjectivity, this final section takes up the task of thinking through how the kinds of narratives that appeared in the first two sections might be mobilized to justify and naturalize continuing imperial projects for New Yorkers. This approach, I believe, illuminates a different set of stakes in the circulation of colonialist discourses and imperial logic, where the colonial common sense suggested by aesthetic production can be seen to move from the metropolis into the western geographies of North America. Jodi A. Byrd presciently reminds us, "As metropolitan multiculturalism and dominant postcolonialism promise the United States as postracial asylum for the world, the diminishing returns of that asylum meet exactly at the point where diaspora collides with settler colonialism."[44] In order to take seriously the claims that imperialism has affected the inhabitants of New York, I think that it is necessary to understand how imperial logic might then circulate outside the bounds of the metropolis. Throughout the 1920s, cosmopolitan New Yorkers were being hailed as world travelers, whether closer to home in Harlem or abroad in farther-flung territories. The figure of the tourist, like that of the archaeologist, was central to the modern management of "foreign" lands, bodies, and resources. But the orientalisms that rendered Harlem's nightclubs and cabarets exotic destinations could also be deployed in other struggles to civilize primitive regions of the United States in its avid expansion. As an example of these ways of enticing New Yorkers to visit different destinations, I turn now to a 1923 booster tract for the "sophisticated tourist of the nineteen-twenties" authored by J. Smeaton Chase and provocatively titled *Our Araby: Palm Springs and the Garden of the Sun*.[45] Published in New York, the volume sought to lure the discriminating traveler to the California desert.[46] The tract appealed specifically to East Coast adventurers, pointing out that "connecting closely with Palm Springs is the main stage-road across the desert, by which you may go down the valley as far as you like—or on to New York, for that matter."[47] In doing its part for California boosterism, the publication adapted some orientalist tropes familiar to New Yorkers. The reference to the desert as "our Araby" explicitly recalls cinematic images of West Asia, but in doing so it also creates a containment imperative for the indigenous populations of western North America. Like the doctrine of Manifest Destiny, the idea of "our Araby" thus clarifies for us the fact that the distance between the domestic and the foreign is ideological. Weaving these two narratives together, the tract drew on the imperial logic of orientalized signs and symbols to further entrench U.S. empire in the country's western territories. If the first two sections of this chapter speak to the complex productions of orientalisms in the city and the price and limitations of internal colonialism, this final section reminds us that these colonial fantasies compelled the continuation of the violence of conquest.

Considering the instructive details of Chase's volume on Palm Springs reveals how imperial logic is mobilized and furthered in ways that resonate with the circulation of orientalist parables in New York. *Our Araby* dreams of the California desert through orientalist signifiers conjuring up both a paradisiacal Holy Land and a nationless, and thus premodern, "Araby," contrived through the popular cultural imagination by purposefully calling on orientalist films and religious texts. The tract thus intersperses biblical language with more secular visions of West Asia throughout its pages. In a chapter on amusements, Chase lures his readers with breathless reports of the film shoots around Palm Springs. He notes that this little village, with its exciting promise of pristine sands and green hills, has been "headquarters, so to speak, for Algeria, Egypt, Arabia, Palestine, India, Mexico, a good deal of Turkey, Australia, South America, and sundry other parts of the globe."[48] In a clever sleight of hand, Chase blurs the line between an original and its copy, substituting the former for the latter in frank admiration of its staged authenticity, writing that being in Palm Springs provides the "more exciting firsthand experience of seeing [the films] made, the thrill of the real thing."[49] The California desert, then, stands in for the imagined Orient of the films, a doubled geographical destination for those who loved watching Valentino in *The Sheik* and who might picture themselves in his place, or in his arms, in the same simulacral landscape. Because Hollywood imagery reduces "Araby" to the desert, and the desert is "presented as the essential unchanging décor of the history of the Orient," an Arabic desert is essentially interchangeable with one in California.[50] This U.S. desert provides additional scenery as the untamed site of the wild West and is thus "associated with productive, creative pioneering, a masculine redeemer of the wilderness."[51] Here the romantic and religious lure of the desert is mobilized to entice settlers to uncivilized regions of the U.S. imperial expansion. The text, then, acts in an imperialist manner to justify the repopulation of the area with tourists who might be willing to stay on in town through the fantasies created in films, novels, and floor shows.

Echoing concerns over the management of neighborhoods like Harlem and multiracial spaces like dance halls that are focused on sexuality, race, and gender transgression, the booster tract employs other narratives of spatial regulation that also result in the circumscription of racialized populations. Our Araby appeals to scientific curiosity and exploration, as well as land management and the new conservation movement, as a way to justify conquest. Chase notes that "the American tourist expects to have Nature served up in up-to-date fashion, and Uncle Sam may be trusted to comply, in due time,"[52] connecting the desires of the tourist-explorer to the responsibilities of the nation-state. Chase muses about trips to canyons and other points of natural interest, spending a considerable amount of space detailing the novel flora and fauna of the desert landscape, even as he assures readers they will be able to survive both the rugged terrain and its inhabitants.[53] Operating in this manner not unlike an imperial archive, the publication thus functions as a Baedeker for budding experts on the region. Thus do "colonial narratives," as Shohat notes, "legitimize the embarking upon treasure hunts by lending a scientific aura."[54] Here the scientific authority of the tract attests to the civilizing powers of potential tourists as a form of anticonquest—a supposedly innocent, bloodless conquest done in the name of science, not greed.[55] But as many scholars have shown, land management and conservation were not distinct from, but vital to, the mission of empire and its coercive bids for control of lands and resources. Here the management of space, even at the level of the desert environment, can thus be manipulated to justify a civilizing mission with the result of controlling and displacing indigenous populations.

The racial logic of Our Araby is a complicated one, for Chase not only refers to the Orient but also plays on existing U.S. racial mythologies of the country's westward expansion, referencing—while also absenting—

indigenous cultures and the Mexican *ranchera* population in order to make his pitch. This was not an unusual spatial juxtaposition of the deserts of North America and those of the Maghreb. As Brian Edwards notes, regarding later incursions into North Africa, observers identified "a frontier aspect to the desert landscape and sometimes elaborate comparisons of the Maghreb to the American Southwest."[56] For Edwards, this means that the renarration of space could be mobilized to make African conquest seem more palatable.[57] Interestingly, this juxtaposition could work in reverse as well. The conquest implied in Chase's section on the scientific management of land becomes explicit when he suggests the replacement of indigenous bodies with those of tourists. Furthermore, he examines current legislation that would enable the appropriation of native lands. In regard to going native, here seen as a way to replace one population with another, Chase carefully notes that "our village is bisected by the Reservation line, which thus makes a geographical division of the population,"[58] but he later disallows this national and racial border. The methods that Chase employs are related to those discussed by Shari Huhndorf in *Going Native*. Writing about the changing American mythos in the late nineteenth century, Huhndorf argues: "Mounting social change caused many European Americans to 'remember' Native American life with nostalgia. Indians, now safely 'vanishing,' began to provide the myths upon which white Americans created a sense of historical authenticity, a 'real' national identity which had been lacking in the adolescent colonial culture."[59] Huhndorf describes an imperial ambivalence, one that simultaneously embraces and seeks to conquer the natives of America. A similar management of race and imperialism is exhibited in Chase's tract. What might appear at first glance to be a narrative tension between happy division and productive intermingling does not, after all, negate the potential of white mastery in the region; rather, it strengthens the claim for that mastery. On the one hand, the volume invites readers to the hot springs "as bygone generations of Cahuillas have enjoyed" them, an enticement to live like the natives once did (notably, the natives that the tourist might emulate are imagined to be long dead).[60] This rhetorical move replaces indigenous bodies with those of New Yorkers through a narrative of affiliation, in a way similar to the kinds of racialized entertainments that had women dancing in orientalist costumes on urban stages. On the other hand, Chase assumes that the land needs to be settled—attracting settlers is the purpose of the tract, after all. Rather than affiliation, this argument depends on the production of difference between the indigenous population and the would-be tourist. Additionally, Chase pointedly links the settlement of the land with the conservation of nature, a move that can happen only through the removal of existing populations, an argument that makes sense particularly in light of legislative moves that had recently occurred. To reassure potential tourists and settlers of the inevitability of settlement, the tract moves to a discussion of a bill in Congress to preserve tracts of land in the area around Palm Springs. However, the bill's authors had not yet accounted for the fact that the land was not controlled by the U.S. government, but was part of the Agua Caliente Reservation.[61] Though the bill did not directly provide for appropriation of the land, Chase was hopeful that some sort of appropriation would eventually occur, even if it were left up to "citizens in general to provide the money, in an amount to be determined by the Secretary of the Interior, for purchase of the Indians' rights. This, it may be hoped, will not long delay the bill's coming into operation."[62] The tourist-explorer, then, was invited to both enjoy the peaceful California community and help settle the region, wresting the land from the care of its indigenous populations.

The vision of Araby floating through the dreams of would-be tourists and patrons of nightclubs produced unique intimacies and recalibrated distances between bodies, as well as producing modern mythologies and allegorical translations between continents. The colonial racial classifications that circulated in song, dance, and tourist tract also created connections and comparisons between imperial enterprises abroad and race relations at home, allowing Harlem to be described as a lawless colony and *Our Araby* to imagine California as both foreign territory and a site for natural domestic expansion. But the hegemony of an imperial imaginary in U.S. popular culture nonetheless produced differential access to imperial selfhood. Moving along geographies of scale, the terms *natives* and *sheiks, invaders* and *civilizers, slaves* and *explorers* were transactional and mobile. Depending on the array of discourses brought together, they acted as terms of endearment, warnings of danger, and modes of access to modern subjectivity, resources, and land.

This chapter has taken up the collapse of colonial space, domestic space, and space marked as ripe for annexation, using texts as diverse as Tin Pan Alley songs, widely published drawings and poems, newspaper debates over the ethics of archaeology, and J. Smeaton Chase's *Our Araby*. The intertextuality of these cultural artifacts demonstrates that the logic that guided aesthetic production not only emanated from imperial modes but also lent itself to furthering and continuing the violence of imperialism. In this way, imperial logic and its effects reached through these texts, tying them together to be used for a common purpose. That is, that rather than, say, culture shaping and reflecting contemporary ideologies, imperial logic pervaded meanings of power; negotiations over identities; and fights over land, space, and place, from the large to the small across these kinds of discursive productions. Because of its antithetical modes, imperial logic could be mobilized as a way to discover personhood, rationalize the policing of racialized populations, or naturalize the further expansion of empire. As a result, imperial logic created, through these contradictory means, the grounds for understanding geographies of race and sex and, thus, the turbulent construction and variable meanings of subjectivity across bodies, neighborhoods, and nations.

CONCLUSION

ACADEMIC INDISCRETIONS

In *Imperial Blues*, I fixate on unfixing boundaries that divide fields and objects of study and on configurations of space and identity. In short, my project continues with and alongside scholarship that rethinks the epistemological and ontological grounds for American studies, shifting the conversation across disciplines, archives, and geographies. The joining of interests and objects across disciplines, I argue, forces a certain academic indiscretion, a productive faux pas performed along the grain of institutionally discrete disciplines. Part of what disciplinary indiscretion has granted me is a way of thinking about how colonial desire travels back home in the form of migrating bodies—material but also ideological bodies, in which imperial logic helps determine sexual, gender, and racial formations in a place like New York City.[1] Because ideas and objects travel back and forth across the presumed lines of cities and nations, metropoles and colonies, the other of the U.S. nation-state might be found at home, in your neighborhood, or in your bed. These thoughts can be dangerous if we imagine that the people we willfully refuse to acknowledge abroad, the people on whom our countries visit violence, might have an effect on us here. Our continued imperial work abroad might in fact be connected to social inequalities at home because of the ideologies we embed ourselves in to wage war, because of our wartime economy, because of the austerity measures we pursue in the name of security and freedom. In these ways, visiting theories of how sexual conquest in the colonies might predicate sexualized power relations in New York's Jazz Age can become dangerous even in the present. At stake in my conceptualization are the ways we imagine power in the formation of subjectivity, and how we might then proceed in our scholarship to examine the history of sexuality, national belonging, ideas that separate home and abroad, and the violence of imperial action.

One of the devices I have found useful in pondering these questions is imperial logic, which also orients contemporary political schemas of empire. In thinking through the unfixing of boundaries, interdisciplinary scholarship has begun to ask a different set of questions about the discreteness of boundaries. The idea of imperial logic is indebted to Kandice Chuh, who frames her scholarship as contending with the "nature of language and knowledge" and as "investigating the structures of power and meaning that give rise to identity and difference as national and racial epistemes."[2] Keeping this in mind, the relationship between racial (as well as sexual and gendered) epistemologies are indelibly linked to national ones. The construction of these categories domestically is linked to how the nation as image and apparatus travels abroad in its shows of economic and military might, and how those imagined as outside of the nation-state are imagined at home. In thinking through the stakes of these types of connections, Grace Kyungwon Hong and Roderick A. Ferguson, in their introduction to *Strange Affinities*, argue for a comparative analytics to examine the "changing configurations of power in the era after the decolonizing movements and new social movements of the mid-twentieth century demand that we understand how particular populations are rendered vulnerable to processes of death and devaluation over and against other populations, in ways that palimpsestically register modalities of racialized death but also exceed them."[3] I appreciate here the idea of the palimpsest, as it speaks to how histories of racialization can become apparent, erased, or even both simultaneously. In imagining a comparative analytics, then, we must grapple with questions about the meanings and context of racial discourse. And, although Hong and Ferguson seem to often equate racialization with "death and devaluation," I believe their collection of essays, taken as a whole, demonstrates that racial discourse as indiscrete, as promiscuously emanating from particular bodies, has its own histories that may be drawn on, ignored, or exaggerated for a multiplicity of purposes.

This conjunction of interests has not only produced a way to think through the situating of sexuality in the United States, say, through the lens of queer of color critique, aesthetic production, and postcolonial studies, but it also reminds us that we write these texts in a moment of danger. A field such as postcolonial studies itself was formed at the intersections of many disciplines (and those many disciplines were formed at the intersections of many other disciplines), including anthropology, literature, international studies, cultural studies, and feminist studies. These academic indiscretions even drew the ire of the U.S. government: suspicious of this field formation, the House of Representatives proposed in October 2003 to regulate the "anti-American" field.[4] This suspicion also reared its head in the legislation proposed in Georgia in 2009 to eliminate courses in queer theory and gender and women's studies at state institutions. As George Lipsitz notes, American studies as a discipline is at a "dangerous crossroad," and as a field it needs to reimagine its political import in the twenty-first century by drawing on "the organic grassroots theorizing about culture and power that has informed cultural practice, social movements, and academic work for many years."[5] His suggestions remind us that the work of the academy and the work of social justice organizing need not be separated, and therefore the ways we orient our fields can be not just acts of indiscretion but also acts of organizing for social change, depending on what questions we ask across the borders of knowledge construction and circulation. This kind of thinking is what produces eye-opening ideas like Kevin Gaines's understanding of the "transnational dimensions of American citizenship,"[6] which becomes particularly prescient when, in 2011 and 2012, lawmakers in Arizona worked to ban ethnic studies material from classrooms because of tensions presumably caused by the state's proximity to national borders, and to contentious struggles about the scope of national security and the rights of citizenship.

Understanding the structure of imperial logic exposes the justifications for continuing wars, social policies that devalue citizens and non-citizens alike, and wartime actions that ignore legal protections and rights, often through creating affiliations with national others, peoples whose allegiances, cultures, and ethnicities mark them as non-normative both within designated national spaces and abroad. In this way, the geographic and the ideological mingle in our thinking through tried and true categories of race, class, gender, and sexuality, categories that still bear the burdens of representation in the realms of aesthetics, ethics, law, and politics. Ferguson's reading of Weberian rationality gives us a clue as to why and how these categories manage so much. "As social order achieves normativity by suppressing intersections of race, class, gender, and sexuality," Ferguson argues, "rationality must thus conceal the ways in which it is particularized by those differences."[7] The seeds of this kind of rationality blow across our fields of inquiry in palimpsestic gusts that sometimes expose and at other times hide how these categories interact, shape, and undo one another. For example, as Ferguson observes of postnationalist American studies, "as it arises out of cultural and revolutionary nationalisms, this version of history suppresses knowledge of the gender and sexual heterogeneity that composes social formations."[8] My work interrupts this discrete thinking to extract knowledge about the complexities of power's machinations across the categories through which it defines itself: the "multiple axes of power," in the words of Lisa Lowe.[9] For example, I have been interested in how knowledge of these categories is affected by space and spatialization—how they travel across borders and use spatial reasoning—which has led to my current understanding of how epistemologies and ontologies are grounded in imperial logic. Just as Jazz Age New Yorkers emerged from behind city lines to populate the California desert, using knowledge gained in nightclubs and cabarets to make sense of this both strange and yet hauntingly familiar landscape and its inhabitants, my methodologies expand beyond discrete categories to recontextualize the way in which ideas about space, subjectivity, and power also travel across borders, even as they are formed by those borders. In this way, my work lingers between the solidity and instability of the formation of identity categories. Rather than view this solidity and instability as contradictory states, I understand their relation as a way to apprehend the palimpsest of identity formation that precedes and exceeds discourses of regulation, violence, liberation, resistance, citation, and reiteration.

The kinds of contradictions that guide my methodology have helped me ask a different set of questions about the circulation of imperial signifiers. Not content with a model of power that simply exposes imperialism as producing repression, I have sought the variety of meanings available to those signifiers in order to understand the range of meaning-making practices produced by imperialism. This methodology springs in part from the work of Foucault in critiquing the repressive hypothesis and in part from Derrida's notion of différance. From Foucault I have learned that, even in situations of violence, more is produced than simply repressive force.[10] So, in instances of imperial violence, or in the use of imperial logic to justify violence at home, more must be produced than a quieting of a population, the regulation of race and sex, or nation building. The palimpsestic excess of these moments might instead be resistance, a reconfiguration of subjectivity, or the unearthing of creative impulse. Furthermore, in mobilizing Derrida's concerns about the concomitant deferral and granting of meaning, a model that also guides my reading of the palimpsest here, I have analyzed the circulation of imperial logic through received and productive meanings, drawing on the sometimes contradictory histories of words, movements, objects, and spaces that are both known and manipulated, solidified and creative.[11] Imperial logic, as it feeds on these contradictory modes of meaning making, thus becomes a useful heuristic device for examining identity formation at home, the political power of imperialism as it relates to urban environments, and the creation of subjectivity on and off the stages of New York. In short, this work demonstrates that the meanings attached to cultural production, more than simply shaping and reflecting the larger political landscape, are already inherently part of the societal systems of logic that traffic in older and continuing forms of national conquest.

NOTES

INTRODUCTION

1. For some of the canonical scholarship on the Harlem Renaissance that discusses the meanings of whites traveling into Harlem, see David Levering Lewis, *When Harlem Was in Vogue* (New York: Vintage, 1982); Nathan Irvin Huggins, *Harlem Renaissance* (New York: Oxford University Press, 1971).

2. "The Vogue," report, 25 January 1917, Box 31, Committee of Fourteen Records, 1905–32, Rare Books and Manuscripts Division, New York Public Library, New York (hereafter cited as C14, NYPL).

3. See, for example, Huggins, *Harlem Renaissance*; Lewis, *When Harlem Was in Vogue*; Lewis A. Erenberg, *Steppin' Out: New York Nightlife and the Transformation of American Culture, 1890–1930* (Westport, CT: Greenwood, 1981); Ann Douglas, *Terrible Honesty: Mongrel Manhattan in the 1920s* (New York: Noonday, 1995); Mark Robert Schneider, *African Americans in the Jazz Age* (Lanham, MD: Rowman and Littlefield, 2006); Marlon B. Ross, *Manning the Race: Reforming Black Men in the Jim Crow Era* (New York: New York University Press, 2004). This is also evident in earlier work, such as James Johnson, *Black Manhattan* (New York: Knopf, 1930); and George S. Schuyler, *Black and Conservative* (New Rochelle, NY: Arlington House, 1966).

4. See Bill V. Mullen, *Afro-Orientalism* (Minneapolis: University of Minnesota Press, 2004); Daniel Kim, *Writing Manhood in Black and Yellow: Ralph Ellison, Frank Chin, and the Literary Politics of Identity* (Stanford, CA: Stanford University Press, 2005); Heike Raphael-Hernandez and Shannon Steen, *AfroAsian Encounters: Culture, History, Politics* (New York: New York University Press, 2006); Helen H. Jun, "Black Orientalism: Nineteenth-Century Narratives of Race and U.S. Citizenship," *American Quarterly* 58 (June 2006): 1047–66; Scott Kurashige, *The Shifting Grounds of Race: Black and Japanese Americans in the Making of Multiethnic Los Angeles* (Princeton, NJ: Princeton University Press, 2010). Vijay Prashad stands apart from this scholarship in that he does look beyond U.S. borders for racial meaning making. For instance, he examines connections be-

tween Bruce Lee's popularity and U.S. wars in Southeast Asia in *Everybody Was Kung Fu Fighting: Afro-Asian Connections and the Myth of Cultural Purity* (Boston: Beacon, 2001).

5. There is too much scholarship to name it all here, but see, for example, Winthrop Jordan, *White over Black: American Attitudes toward the Negro, 1550–1812* (Chapel Hill: University of North Carolina Press, 1968); Anne McClintock, *Imperial Leather: Race, Gender and Sexuality in the Colonial Contest* (New York: Routledge, 1995); Robert J. C. Young, *Colonial Desire: Hybridity in Theory, Culture, and Race* (New York: Routledge, 1995); Achille Mbembe, *On the Postcolony*, trans. A. M. Berrett, Janet Roitman, Murray Last, and Steven Rendall (Berkeley: University of California Press, 2001).

6. Lisa Lowe, "The Intimacies of Four Continents," in *Haunted by Empire: Geographies of Intimacy in North American History*, ed. Ann Laura Stoler (Durham, NC: Duke University Press, 2006), 193, 195, 202–3.

7. Douglas, *Terrible Honesty*, 73–74. The precise number cited by Douglas is 749,000. Also see Roland Marchand, *Advertising the American Dream: Making Way for Modernity, 1920–1940* (Berkeley: University of California Press, 1985). This vision of modernity also seems to be in accordance with that espoused by T. J. Jackson Lears in *No Place of Grace: Antimodernism and the Transformation of American Culture, 1880–1920* (New York: Pantheon, 1981).

8. U.S. Department of Commerce, Bureau of the Census, *Thirteenth Census of the United States Taken in the Year 1910*, vol. 3, *Population 1910: Reports by States, with Statistics for Counties, Cities and Other Civil Divisions, Nebraska-Wyoming, Alaska, Hawaii, and Porto Rico* (Washington: U.S. Government Printing Office, 1913), 240; U.S. Department of Commerce, Bureau of the Census, *Fifteenth Census of the United States: 1930*, vol. 3, part 2, *Population Reports by States, Showing the Composition and Characteristics of the Population for Counties, Cities, and Townships or Other Minor Civil Divisions, Montana-Wyoming* (Washington: U.S. Government Printing Office, 1932), 279.

9. Caren Kaplan, *Questions of Travel: Postmodern Discourses of Displacement* (Durham, NC: Duke University Press, 1996), 4–5.

10. See, for example, Bill Ashcroft, Gareth Griffiths, and Helen Tiffin, *The Empire Writes Back: Theory and Practice in Post-Colonial Literatures* (New York: Routledge, 1989); Edward Said, *Culture and Imperialism* (New York: Vintage, 1993); Inderpal Grewal and Caren Kaplan, introduction to *Scattered Hegemonies: Postmodernity and Transnational Feminist Practices*, ed. Inderpal Grewal and Caren Kaplan (Minneapolis: University of Minnesota Press, 1994), 1–33.

11. See Moon-Kie Jung, *Reworking Race: The Making of Hawaii's Interracial Labor Movement* (New York: Columbia University Press, 2006); Moon-Ho Jung, *Coolies and Cane: Race, Labor, and Sugar in the Age of Emancipation* (Baltimore: Johns Hopkins University Press, 2006); Mae M. Ngai, *Impossible Subjects: Illegal Aliens and the Making of Modern America* (Princeton, NJ: Princeton University Press, 2004).

12. Raymond Williams, *Politics of Modernism: Against the New Conformists* (London: Verso, 2007), 44.

13. "The Tokio" (27 September 1916), Box 31; "Night Clubs and Speakeasies Located on Numbered Streets" (1929), Box 37, Folder 8; "Speakeasy Clubs which Employ Hostesses" (1928), Box 51, C14, NYPL.

14. Carrie Tirado Bramen, "The Urban Picturesque and the Spectacle of Americanization," *American Quarterly* 52 (September 2000): 446.

15. The canonical historiographical texts for this time period portray race relations in the city as strictly between black and white. See Huggins, *The Harlem Renaissance*; Lewis, *When Harlem Was in Vogue*; Douglas, *Terrible Honesty*.

16. For more on *flâneurie*, see Walter Benjamin, *Reflections: Essays, Aphorisms, Autobiographical Writings*, ed. Peter Demetz, trans. Edmund Jephcott (New York: Harcourt Brace Jovanovich, 1978), 146–62. For the feminization of the *flâneur*, see Anne Friedberg, *Window Shopping: Cinema and the Postmodern* (Berkeley: University of California Press, 1993). Also see Leora Auslander, "The Gendering of Consumer Practices in Nineteenth-Century France," in *The Sex of Things: Gender and Consumption in Historical Perspective*, ed. Victoria De Grazia (Berkeley: University of California Press, 1996), 79–112, for a discussion of how *flâneurs* performed a type of failed masculinity by consuming women and products with their eyes, but—in failing to purchase them—failed to reproduce themselves or the state, the two mandates of masculine consumption. For more on the changing racial geography of New York, see Gilbert Osofsky, *Harlem: The Making of a Ghetto, Negro New York, 1890–1930*, 2nd ed. (1971; repr., Chicago: Ivan R. Dee, 1996), 82.

17. Wallace Thurman and William Jourdan Rapp, "Few Know Real Harlem, the City of Surprises: Quarter Million Negroes Form a Moving, Colorful Pageant of Life," in *The Collected Writings of Wallace Thurman: A Harlem Renaissance Reader*, ed. Amritjit Singh and Daniel M. Scott III (New Brunswick, NJ: Rutgers University Press, 2003), 67.

18. Wallace Thurman, *Negro Life in New York's Harlem: A Lively Picture of a Popular and Interesting Section* (Girard, KS: Haldeman-Julius, 1927), 64.

19. Thurman and Rapp, "Few Know Real Harlem," 67.

20. Minutes, 7 December 1926, 572, City Council, 1647–1977—Board of Aldermen, New York City Department of Records and Information Services, City Hall Library and Municipal Archives, New York. In 1926 the Board of Aldermen passed cabaret laws that were specifically aimed at clubs that featured jazz and dancing. For more on this, see chapter 1; Paul Chevigny, *Gigs: Jazz and the Cabaret Laws in New York City* (New York: Routledge, 1991).

21. Sara Ahmed, *Queer Phenomenology: Orientations, Objects, Others* (Durham, NC: Duke University Press, 2006), 121.

22. Langston Hughes, "When Harlem Was in Vogue," *Town and Country*, July 1940, 64. David Levering Lewis borrows the phrase from Hughes as well, discussing the ways in which Harlem became a popular destination for white people

who traveled uptown to sample cabarets, nightclubs, and even to rent parties. As noted by Lewis, this phenomenon became increasingly common after Carl Van Vechten published his famous and controversial work, *Nigger Heaven* (1926; repr., Urbana: University of Illinois Press, 2000). See Lewis, *When Harlem Was in Vogue*.

23. Andrew Jones, *Yellow Music: Media Culture and Colonial Modernity in the Chinese Jazz Age* (Durham, NC: Duke University Press, 2001), 1.

24. See, for instance, Pascal Blanchard, Eric Deroo, and Gilles Manceron, *Le Paris noir* (Paris: Hazan, 2001); Tyler Edward Stovall, *Paris Noir: African Americans in the City of Light* (Boston: Houghton Mifflin, 1996). On Josephine Baker, see, for example, Anne Anlin Cheng, "Skin Deep: Josephine Baker and the Colonial Fetish," *Camera Obscura* 69 (2008): 35–79; Daphne Ann Brooks, "The End of the Line: Josephine Baker and the Politics of Black Women's Corporeal Comedy," *S&F Online* 6, nos. 1–2 (2007–8), accessed 23 May 2013, http://sfonline.barnard .edu/baker/brooks_01.htm; Bennetta Jules-Rosette, *Josephine Baker in Art and Life: The Icon and the Image* (Urbana: University of Illinois Press, 2007); Jeanne Scheper, "'Of la Baker, I Am a Disciple': The Diva Politics of Reception," *Camera Obscura* 65 (2007): 73–101; Mae G. Henderson, "Josephine Baker and *La Revue Negre*: From Ethnography to Performance," *Text and Performance Quarterly* 23 (2003): 107–33.

25. Simon Gikandi, "Picasso, Africa, and the Schemata of Difference," in *Beautiful/Ugly: African and Diaspora Aesthetics*, ed. Sarah Nuttall (Durham, NC: Duke University Press, 2006), 35.

26. Konrad Bercovici, *Around the World in New York* (New York: Century, 1924), 211–48.

27. Thurman and Rapp, "Few Know Real Harlem," 67.

28. The musician Elton Fax recalled that "color wasn't the only problem. I remember a comedy routine that was popular at the Apollo as an outgrowth of the West Indian migration to Harlem. Two actors were onstage. Each was dressed as a woman, and each engaged in a heated exchange onstage about something minor. One would call the other 'monkeychaser.' The other would say, 'Don't call me nigger.' All this sort of thing. It laid the audience out in the aisles, because they did it in dialect of the Caribbean and the dialect of the South" (in *You Must Remember This: An Oral History of Manhattan from 1892 to World War II*, ed. Jeff Kisseloff [New York: Harcourt Brace Jovanovich, 1989], 294).

29. Michel Foucault, *The History of Sexuality*, vol. 1, *An Introduction*, trans. Robert Hurley (New York: Vintage, 1990), 103.

30. Fredric Jameson, "Modernism and Imperialism," in Terry Eagleton, Fredric Jameson, and Edward W. Said, *Nationalism, Colonialism, and Literature* (Minneapolis: University of Minnesota Press, 1990), 44.

31. I borrow these notions of power and fields from Michel Foucault, *The Birth of Biopolitics: Lectures at the Collège de France, 1978–1979*, ed. Michel Senellart, trans. Graham Burchell (New York: Palgrave Macmillan, 2008); Ruth Wilson

Gilmore, *Golden Gulag: Prisons, Surplus, Crisis, and Opposition in Globalizing California* (Berkeley: University of California Press, 2007); Jacques Rancière, *The Politics of Aesthetics: The Distribution of the Sensible*, trans. with an introduction by Gabriel Rockhill, afterword by Slavoj Žižek (London: Continuum, 2004).

32. Foucault, *The Birth of Biopolitics*, 186.

33. Charles W. Mills, "Racial Liberalism," PMLA 123 (October 2008): 1382.

34. Denise Ferreira da Silva, *Toward a Global Idea of Race* (Minneapolis: University of Minnesota Press, 2007), xxxvii.

35. Henri Lefebvre, *The Production of Space*, trans. Donald Nicholson-Smith (Oxford: Blackwell, 1991), 1.

36. Immanuel Kant, *Observations on the Feeling of the Beautiful and Sublime*, trans. John T. Goldthwait (Berkeley: University of California Press, 1960), 97–116.

37. Chandan Reddy, "Modern," in *Keywords for American Cultural Studies*, ed. Bruce Burgett and Glenn Hendler (New York: New York University Press, 2007), 161.

38. Sara Ahmed, *Strange Encounters: Embodied Others in Post-Coloniality* (New York: Routledge, 2000), 100.

39. Leti Volpp argues something similar in the post–9/11 context that begins to mark those that "appear to be 'Middle Eastern, Arab, or Muslim'" as not "represent[ing] the nation." Leti Volpp, "The Citizen and the Terrorist," in *September 11 in History: A Watershed Moment?*, ed. Mary L. Dudziak (Durham, NC: Duke University Press, 2003), 157.

40. See C. Kaplan, *Questions of Travel*; Inderpal Grewal, *Home and Harem: Nation, Gender, Empire, and the Cultures of Travel* (Durham, NC: Duke University Press, 1996).

41. Indeed, immigrants to the imperial city included many temporary laborers with no legal way to obtain permanent residency or citizenship. The Jazz Age also saw the passage of anti-immigration legislation that further curtailed the scope of their movements as well as where they could live.

42. C. Kaplan, *Questions of Travel*, 3.

43. Ibid., 110.

44. Linda Gordon, "Internal Colonialism and Gender," in *Haunted by Empire: Geographies of Intimacy in North American History*, ed. Ann Laura Stoler (Durham, NC: Duke University Press, 2006), 427–51, especially 428–30.

45. In his 1917 ditty "From Here to Shanghai," the Tin Pan Alley favorite Irving Berlin tells of a New Yorker who visits Chinatown, which fires his imagination of China beyond Chinatown.

46. Recent scholarship on New Orleans jazz also suggests that empire informs that musical scene. See Alecia P. Long, *The Great Southern Babylon: Sex, Race, and Respectability in New Orleans, 1865–1920* (Baton Rouge: Louisiana State University Press, 2004).

47. Helen H. Jun argues that African Americans and Asian Americans have long produced narratives of inclusion to achieve political, economic, and social incorporation into U.S. citizenry (*Race for Citizenship: Black Orientalism and Asian*

Uplift from Pre-Emancipation to Neoliberal America [New York: New York University Press, 2011]). Lisa Marie Cacho also argues for the use of a comparative lens in her brilliant analysis of the racializing discourse of the gang member (*Social Death: Racialized Rightlessness and the Criminalization of the Unprotected* [New York: New York University Press, 2012]).

48. Ann Laura Stoler, "Tense and Tender Ties: The Politics of Comparison in North American History and (Post) Colonial Studies," in *Haunted by Empire: Geographies of Intimacy in North American History*, ed. Ann Laura Stoler (Durham, NC: Duke University Press, 2006), 23–67. See also Stoler, *Along the Archival Grain: Epistemic and Colonial Common Sense* (Princeton, NJ: Princeton University Press, 2009).

49. Ahmed, *Queer Phenomenology*, 120–21.

50. Roderick A. Ferguson, *Aberrations in Black: Toward a Queer of Color Critique* (Minneapolis: University of Minnesota Press, 2004).

51. Charles Hiroshi Garrett, in his analysis of the Tin Pan Alley hit song "Chinatown, My Chinatown," argues that "musical fantasies bear important marks, however partial, of the lives, experiences, and treatment of the Chinese in America" (*Struggling to Define a Nation: American Music and the Twentieth Century* [Berkeley: University of California Press, 2008], 127). Calloway's "Minnie the Moocher" also shows the interaction of races within those fantasies of spaces not just as the denigration of Chinese subjectivities, but as a way to create diverse black ones.

52. Wallace Thurman, *The Blacker the Berry . . .* (1929; repr., New York: Collier, 1970).

53. Jennifer DeVere Brody, *Impossible Purities: Blackness, Femininity, and Victorian Culture* (Durham, NC: Duke University Press, 1998), 12.

54. Mary Louise Pratt, *Imperial Eyes: Travel Writing and Transculturation* (New York: Routledge, 1992), 6–7.

55. "Gigolo May Hold Key to Moth Murder," *New York Evening Journal*, 14 March 1931.

56. Jennifer A. González, *Subject to Display: Reframing Race in Contemporary Installation Art* (Cambridge, MA: MIT Press, 2008), 4.

57. Stuart Hall, "The After-Life of Frantz Fanon: Why Fanon? Why Now? Why Black Skins/White Masks?," in *The Fact of Blackness: Frantz Fanon and Visual Representation*, ed. Alan Read (London: Institute of Contemporary Art, 1996), 20.

58. Jacques Rancière, *The Politics of Aesthetics*, trans. Gabriel Rockhill (New York: Continuum, 2004), 40.

59. Wallace Thurman, *Infants of the Spring* (1932; repr., New York: Random House, 1999).

60. Richard Bruce Nugent, "Geisha Man (excerpt)," in *Gay Rebel of the Harlem Renaissance: Selctions from the Work of Richard Bruce Nugent*, ed. Thomas H. Wirth (Durham, NC: Duke University Press, 2002), 90–111; Richard Bruce Nugent, "The Geisha Man," unpublished manuscript, 1928.

61. Diana Taylor, *The Archive and the Repertoire* (Durham, NC: Duke University

Press, 2003); Jacques Derrida, *Archive Fever: A Freudian Impression*, trans. Eric Prenowitz (Chicago: University of Chicago Press, 1998).

62. Ahmed, *Queer Phenomenology*, 112–14.

63. Rancière, *The Politics of Aesthetics*, 39.

I. DESIRE AND DANGER IN JAZZ'S CONTACT ZONES

1. Marion Carter, "Fragile Blondes Float over Dance Floor in Arms of Filipino Partners," *New York Evening Journal*, 28 January 1930, clipping, Committee of Fourteen Records, 1905–32, Rare Books and Manuscripts Division, New York Public Library, New York, NY (hereafter cited as C14, NYPL).

2. Ibid.

3. Ibid.

4. Ibid.

5. Roderick A. Ferguson argues that in today's moment of globalization, "the regulation and transgression of gender and sexuality are the twin expressions of racial formation" (*Aberrations in Black: Toward a Queer of Color Critique* [Minneapolis: University of Minnesota Press, 2004], 145). Arguably, the same was true in the Jazz Age, even if the expression and structure were different.

6. For example, the Johnson-Reed Immigration Act of 1924 was passed in an attempt to shape the future population of the United States, favoring immigrants from Western Europe over those from imperial sites. For more on how legislation works to create national and racialized identities, see Lisa Lowe, *Immigrant Acts: On Asian American Cultural Politics* (Durham, NC: Duke University Press, 1996); Ian F. Haney-López, *White by Law: The Legal Construction of Race* (New York: New York University Press, 1996); Lisa Marie Cacho, "The People of California Are Suffering: The Ideology of White Injury in Discourses of Immigration," *Cultural Values* 4, no. 4 (2000): 389–418.

7. Caren Kaplan, *Questions of Travel: Postmodern Discourses of Displacement* (Durham, NC: Duke University Press, 1996), 31.

8. Mary Louise Pratt, *Imperial Eyes: Travel Writing and Transculturation* (New York: Routledge, 1992), 6–7.

9. Following the logic of Hazel V. Carby's arguments about the use of the figure of the mulatto as a "'narrative device of mediation'" (*Reconstructing Womanhood: The Emergence of the Afro-American Woman Novelist* [New York: Oxford University Press, 1987], 89), Siobhan B. Somerville argues that writings about interracial sexualities can function as "literary vehicles for exploring culturally specific structures of racialization, sexuality, and power" (*Queering the Color Line: Race and the Invention of Homosexuality in American Culture* [Durham, NC: Duke University Press, 2000], 80).

10. Scholars have explored the meanings of multiracial spaces as contact zones, or spaces of possibility and danger. For example, the critical geographer Edward W. Soja's notion of "thirdspace" (*Thirdspace: Journeys to Los Angeles and Other Real-and-Imagined Places* [Cambridge, MA: Blackwell, 1996]) and the historian

Kevin J. Mumford's notion of "interzones" (*Interzones: Black/White Sex Districts in Chicago and New York in the Early Twentieth Century* [New York: Columbia University Press, 1997]) both speak to how these spaces make it possible to cross racial and sexual boundaries and can then be turned into spaces of cross-racial allegiance. Scholars like the legal historian Ian Haney-López (*White by Law*) and the immigration historian Mae M. Ngai (*Impossible Subjects: Illegal Aliens and the Making of Modern America* [Princeton, NJ: Princeton University Press, 2004]) identify immigration legislation as a site of border control, but one that can be challenged and circumvented.

11. Wallace Thurman, *The Blacker the Berry . . .* (1929; repr., New York: Collier, 1970).

12. Asian/American masculinities, for example, were not constructed the same way in every time period; rather, they are time- as well as place-specific. For more on understanding histories of masculinities, see Gail Bederman, *Manliness and Civilization: A Cultural History of Gender and Race in the United States, 1880–1917* (Chicago: University of Chicago Press, 1995); Brian Klopotek, "'I Guess Your Warrior Look Doesn't Work Every Time': Challenging Indian Masculinity in the Cinema," in *Across the Great Divide: Cultures of Manhood in the American West*, ed. Matthew Basso, Laura McCall, and Dee Garceau (New York: Routledge, 2001), 251–74; Martin Summers, *Manliness and Its Discontents: The Black Middle Class and the Transformation of Masculinity, 1900–1930* (Chapel Hill: University of North Carolina Press, 2004).

13. For more on how legislation was aimed at guarding the whiteness of the state, see Haney-López, *White by Law*; Lowe, *Immigrant Acts*, 1–36.

14. One of Ferguson's main claims is that sociology as a discipline reproduced Enlightenment epistemology. I am attempting here to attach these epistemological concerns to imperialism and the entrance of immigrants into the city. See Ferguson, *Aberrations in Black*, especially the introduction and first chapter.

15. Henry Yu, *Thinking Orientals: Migration, Contact, and Exoticism in Modern America* (New York: Oxford University Press, 2001), 175.

16. Stephen Jay Gould writes about the fallacies in the logic of various eugenics tests and how the science was informed by social fears. He also makes the link with immigration legislation, noting that Robert M. Yerkes's tests for army recruits helped establish "the supposedly objective data that vindicated hereditarian claims and led to the Immigration Restriction Act of 1924, with its low ceilings for lands suffering the blight of poor genes" (*The Mismeasure of Man* [New York: Norton, 1981], 157). Nancy Ordover adds to this body of scholarship by making clear the effects of scientism in creating the national body in terms of race, sexuality, disability, and reproductive rights: "As national and ethnic and racial identities merged in public and political discourse, eugenic rhetoric acted as court empiricist, justifying, sustaining, and often initiating anti-immigrant attacks in the name of 'bettering and protecting' the white race" (*American Eugenics: Race, Queer Anatomy, and the Science of Nationalism* [Minneapolis: Minnesota University Press, 2003], 9).

17. Jennifer Terry makes clear the extreme attention to the body in trying to delineate the differences between heterosexual and homosexual in possible abnormalities ("Anxious Slippages between 'Us' and 'Them': A Brief History of the Scientific Search for Homosexual Bodies," in *Deviant Bodies: Critical Perspectives of Difference in Science and Popular Culture*, ed. Jennifer Terry and Jacqueline Urla [Bloomington: Indiana University Press, 1995], 129–69).

18. Somerville makes the important connection between the racial science of eugenics and the sexual science of sexology from the end of the nineteenth century to the beginning of the twentieth (*Queering the Color Line*, 15–38). Ordover connects sexological science in the early part of the twentieth century to immigration legislation and congressional debates (*American Eugenics*, 81–82).

19. Chad Heap writes about sociologists' interest in the racialization and sexuality of city space and how spaces of nightlife were often singled out as possibly queer ("The City as a Sexual Laboratory: The Queer Heritage of the Chicago School," *Qualitative Sociology* 26, no. 4 [2003]: 457–87). Heap's work focuses on Chicago, but in other cities social workers, vice investigators, policemen, tourists, and even Harlem Renaissance writers drew meanings from city space through race and sex.

20. Other scholars who have consulted the Committee of Fourteen reports at the New York Public Library include George Chauncey (*Gay New York: Gender, Urban Culture, and the Making of the Gay Male World, 1890–1940* [New York: Basic, 1994]) and Mumford (*Interzones*).

21. The details are from an investigative report form used in 1928 (C14, NYPL).

22. Susan McClary, "Same as It Ever Was: Youth Culture and Music," in *Microphone Fiends: Youth Music and Youth Culture*, ed. Andrew Ross and Tricia Rose (New York: Routledge, 1994), 32.

23. Ibid., 33. McClary has, in effect, taken notions of illocutionary force from the literary field and transposed them to music. In the process, she makes it clear that music is a more powerful force than are texts because of the direct relation of music with the body. Still, it may be useful to briefly return to the word-centered writings of Luce Irigaray in order to further illuminate the gendered meanings of performance. Irigaray has noted that the female body could be a means of disruption if the limiting discourses that are enforced on the body could be illuminated and therefore made transparent. In this way, Irigaray suggests that women could rewrite themselves more accurately; as it is, woman "resists all adequate definition" (*This Sex Which Is Not One*, trans. Catherine Porter [Ithaca, NY: Cornell University Press, 1985], 26). As women performing woman, artists can attempt to define themselves against a cultural current. In the case of the 1920s, female artists were able to begin to define themselves in resistance to popular cultural images by singing the blues. Indeed, the Harlem Renaissance was very much interested in self-definition.

24. For information on who was playing where, see *Roseland News*, October 1923, C14, NYPL; "Roseland Offers a New Band," *New York Evening Graphic*, 21 June

1932; "Cab Calloway at Roseland," *New York Evening Graphic*, 13 April 1932; James Gavin, *Intimate Nights: The Golden Age of New York Cabaret* (New York: Grove Weidenfeld, 1991).

25. Chick Webb, "Swinging on the Reservation," recorded 29 October 1936, *Stomping at the Savoy*, with vocals by Ella Fitzgerald, Proper B000DNVRZ6, 2006, compact disc; Fletcher Henderson with Ethel Finnie, "He Wasn't Born in Araby, but He's a Sheikin' Fool," composed by Edgar Dowell and lyrics by Andy Razaf, recorded April 1924, on *Fletcher Henderson & the Blues Singers, Volume 2*, Document Records DOCD-5343, 1995, compact disc; Duke Ellington, "Swingtime in Honolulu," recorded 11 April 1938, *Cotton Club: A Nostalgia Collection*, Gallerie GALE 455, 2000, compact discs; Porter Grainger, "Hula Blues," recorded April 1924, *Porter Grainger in Chronological Order, 1923–1929*, RST Records JPCD-1521–2, 1995, compact disc.

26. Anonymous report dated 9 May 1923, Box 35, C14, NYPL.

27. Philippe Zani, liner notes, trans. Charlemagne, *Hawaii's Popular Songs: "Unforgettables," 1920–1930*, EPM Musique 995842, 1997, compact disc.

28. Quoted in Alan P. Merriam and Fradley H. Garner, "Jazz—the Word," in *The Jazz Cadence of American Culture*, ed. Robert G. O'Meally (1960; repr., New York: Columbia University Press, 1998), 21.

29. Ibid.

30. Kathy Ogren, *The Jazz Revolution: Twenties America and the Meaning of Jazz* (New York: Oxford University Press, 1989), 146.

31. "Dreamland Dancing," report, 3 January 1931, Box 35, C14, NYPL.

32. I choose these words specifically for their intimations of racial and sexual danger.

33. "'Sax' Tooter's Bigamy Tunes Lead to Jail: Modern Pied Piper, Wed to 7 Wives, Gets 2½ to 5 Years in Sing Sing," *New York Evening Journal*, 9 April 1931.

34. I am thinking here of Michel Foucault's critique of the repressive hypothesis that forms of sexuality are created through the language that is meant to prohibit them (*The History of Sexuality*, vol. 1, *An Introduction*, trans. Robert Hurley [New York: Vintage, 1990], 17–49).

35. Minutes, 7 December 1926, 573, City Council, 1647–1977—Board of Aldermen, New York City Department of Records and Information Services, City Hall Library and Municipal Archives, New York, NY.

36. According to the ordinance, places that allowed music did not need a special permit if there was no dancing and if there were no more than three musicians who played only piano, organ, accordion, guitar, or other stringed instruments. A singer could be present, but only if the singer accompanied herself on one of the aforementioned instruments. As Paul Chevigny has noted, the ordinance "forbade percussion as well as typical jazz frontline instruments such as horns" (*Gigs: Jazz and the Cabaret Laws in New York City* [New York: Routledge, 1991], 15).

37. Nathan Irvin Huggins notes that the white and black mixing that occurred in Harlem was a way for both groups to gain a foothold in the artistic world, though there were incredible racial disparities in how whites and blacks gained

those footholds (*The Harlem Renaissance* [New York: Oxford University Press, 1971]).

38. "Roseland Dance Hall," report dated 27 January 1920, box 34; "Moon Dancing Studio," report dated 19 November 1920, box 35; "St. Nicholas Rink," report dated 7 and 8 December 1920, box 34; "Yeaples," report dated 7 August 1922, box 37; "Sunbeam Dance Palace," report dated 18 October 1923, box 37; "Yeaple's Dancing," report dated 19 October 1923, box 37; "Happyland," report dated 17 November 1924, box 37; "St. Nicholas Rink," report dated 3 April 1926, box 37; "Mayflower Dancing Academy," report dated 29 September 1927, box 37; "Cathedral Ballroom," report dated 2 December 1927, box 37; "Rose Danceland," report dated 7 December 1927, box 37; "Romey Dancing School," report dated 20 February 1928, box 36; "Lincoln Square Dancing," report dated 18 April 1928, box 37; "Bamboo Inn," report dated 17 May 1928, box 37; "Roma Danceland," report dated 7 February 1930, box 37; and "Lincoln Square Dancing," report dated 27 February 1931, box 35, C14, NYPL. Romey Dancing School may be the same as Remey Dancing School, given the various spellings of names in these reports.

39. "Spanish" may have referred to Cubans, Puerto Ricans, Filipinos, and other Latino patrons or to men from Spain. For descriptions of dancing at Yeaple's, see "Yeaples," report dated 7 August 1922, box 37; "Yeaple's Dancing," report dated 19 October 1923, box 37; "Yeaple's Dancing School," report dated 8 March 1928, box 37 (which noted the presence of "Japs, Chinese, Philipinos and Argentines"), and "Yeaple's Dancing Academy," report dated 11 April 1930, box 37; ibid.

40. Dreamland Dancing," report dated, 6 and 7 November 1930, box 35; and "Dreamland," report dated 5 October 1931, box 35; ibid.

41. Doreen B. Massey, *Space, Place, Gender* (Minneapolis: University of Minnesota Press, 1994), 265.

42. Sherrie Tucker, "Together but Unequal: Dance Floor Democracy at the Hollywood Canteen," paper presented at the Annual Conference of the American Studies Association, Washington, DC, 5–8 November 2009.

43. Bruno Lasker, *Filipino Immigration to Continental United States and to Hawaii* (1931; repr., New York: Arno, 1969), 99. For Filipino participation in dance hall culture, also see ibid., 120, 139; Carlos Bulosan, *America Is in the Heart: A Personal History* (1946; repr., Seattle: University of Washington Press, 1973). Lasker, a German immigrant, was an interesting character in his own right. A social worker associated with the Henry Street Settlement, he traveled to U.S. imperial sites like the Philippines and Hawaii to write sociological reports for the Institute of Pacific Relations.

44. Lasker, *Filipino Immigration to Continental United States and to Hawaii*, 99.

45. Rhacel Salazar Parreñas argues that the points of difference used to marginalize these two groups were race for the Filipino men and class for the white women ("'White Trash' Meets the 'Little Brown Monkeys': The Taxi Dance Hall as a Site of Interracial and Gender Alliances between White Working Class Women and Filipino Immigrant Men in the 1920s and 30s," *Amerasia Journal* 24, no. 2 [1998]:

115–34). Mumford calls the dance halls the "quintessential border institution" be-
cause they hosted a heterogeneous group of racialized men, including Chinese,
Japanese, Filipinos, blacks, and whites (*Interzones*, 53–71). Ronald Takaki also
writes about this type of marginalization, particularly in his recounting of Carlos
Bulosan's days in the dance halls on the West Coast (*Strangers from a Different
Shore: A History of Asian Americans* [New York: Penguin, 1989], 339–40, 347–48).

46. For a much more hopeful reading of racial mixing in dance halls, see Matt
Garcia, *A World of Its Own: Race, Labor, and Citrus in the Making of Greater Los
Angeles, 1900–1970* (Chapel Hill: University of North Carolina Press, 2001).

47. "Cathedral Ballroom," report dated 2 December 1927, box 37, C14, NYPL.

48. For more on white women entering the workforce and spaces of public amusement see Kathy Peiss, *Cheap Amusements: Working Women and Leisure in Turn-
of-the-Century New York* (Philadelphia: Temple University Press, 1986); for more
on men of color and white women in dance halls see Parreñas, "'White Trash'
Meets the 'Little Brown Monkeys.'"

49. Though Filipinos were sometimes considered Asian, at other times they were
considered black, or white, or Spanish, depending on who was viewing them. As
an illustration of the confusion over racial categories at the time, Lasker noted
in 1931: "Until lately, there has been much uncertainty concerning the Filipino's
'official' race in states that impose restrictions upon marriages between Mongo-
lians and white. Marriages between Filipinos and white women were frequent,
and it was left, apparently, to the discretion of county clerks in issuing licenses to
decide on the racial membership of applicants. . . . The majority of officials seem,
without any recourse to science at all, to have married Filipinos indiscriminately
with white and with Japanese and Chinese girls, thus exposing themselves to the
possible charge that if Filipinos should through some court decision be declared
to be white, then their marriages to the Asiatic girls would be illegal" (*Filipino
Immigration to Continental United States and to Hawaii*, 118).

50. Anonymous report, 2 December 1927, C14, NYPL.

51. "Cathedral Ballroom," report dated 2 December 1927, box 37, C14, NYPL.

52. Frank Dolan, "Spider Web Lures Old Harlem Fans," (clipping) *Saturday News*,
2 November 1929, C14, NYPL. Confirmation that the operator was a Chinese man
appears in a "Bamboo Inn," report dated 17 May 1928, box 37; ibid.

53. Dolan, "Spider Web Lures Old Harlem Fans."

54. Ibid.

55. See Yutian Wong's discussion about the orientalisms that informed the innovations of those white women named as founders of U.S. avant-garde dance movements (*Choreographing Asian America* [Middlebury, CT: Wesleyan University
Press, 2010]).

56. Peiss, *Cheap Amusements*, 6.

57. Ibid.; Ferguson, *Aberrations in Black*, 17.

58. According to Burton W. Peretti, McLaughlin was later suspended for being part
of an operation that framed young women as prostitutes (*Nightclub City: Politics

and Amusement in Manhattan [Philadelphia: University of Pennsylvania Press, 2007], 139).

59. Judith Butler writes about the constitutive nature of juridical discourses, arguing that "the juridical formation of language and politics that represents women as 'the subject' of feminism is itself a discursive formation and effect of a given version of representational politics" (*Gender Trouble: Feminism and the Subversion of Identity* [New York: Routledge, 1990], 2). Vivian Gordon was produced both as a prostitute and an unfit mother by her husband, the police, and the court system. Produced as such, she lived a life of suspect sexuality.

60. Linda Mizejewski, *Ziegfeld Girl: Image and Icon in Culture and Cinema* (Durham, NC: Duke University Press, 1999), 71–72.

61. "Gigolo May Hold Key to Moth Murder," *New York Evening Journal*, 14 March 1931.

62. Gaylyn Studlar, "'Out-Salomeing Salome': Dance, the New Woman, and Fan Magazine Orientalism," in *Visions of the East: Orientalism in Film*, ed. Matthew Bernstein and Gaylyn Studlar (New Brunswick, NJ: Rutgers University Press, 1997), 116. Lea Jacobs describes the vamp as a common character in "fallen woman" films, a woman who "often got rich at the expense of her male victims" (*The Wages of Sin: Censorship and the Fallen Woman Film, 1928–1942* [Berkeley: University of California Press, 1995], 12).

63. Joanne J. Meyerowitz notes that a similar gold-digging phenomenon occurred in the lesbian community in Chicago, where women were paid to go out with wealthier women. The paid escorts would sometimes keep the names and addresses of these women and later borrow money from them. Meyerowitz also shows that there were kept women in wholly lesbian relationships (*Women Adrift: Independent Wage Earners in Chicago, 1880–1930* [Chicago: University of Chicago Press, 1988], 114). Brian Donovan also works on the figure of the 1920s gold digger ("The Peggy Joyce Scandals: Gold Diggers and Whiteness in Jazz-Age America," paper presented at the Race and Ethnic Studies Institute, Texas A & M University, 5 February 2010).

64. Harun al-Rashid was a caliph in the eighth and ninth centuries.

65. "Probe Suicide of Vivian's Daughter: Girl Faces Quiz on Vivian's 'Daddy,'" *New York Evening Journal*, 4 March 1931.

66. Quoted in "Vivian Raved at Daughter after Last Meeting," ibid., 6 March 1931.

67. "Trace Car in Vivian Gordon Murder: Slain Girl Is Linked to Dope Racket," ibid., 3 March 1931. The Cuban Mrs. Halsey, a maid, did not fare well in some reporters' estimation. Reporters pointed out her nationality and also noted that she was an unreliable witness because she changed her story. The *Evening Graphic* was somewhat understanding, since her story changed only after men came to her door to douse her with acid, but the *Evening Journal* seemed less inclined to be forgiving. The removal of this potential witness from the police investigations as well as from the court proceedings, first by the acid-throwing thugs and second by the newspapers, suggests that Mrs. Halsey's ability to be

considered a U.S. citizen was at stake as a result of her simultaneous gendering and racialization.

68. Paul Biese Trio with Frank Crumit, "Chile Bean," recorded in 1920, *1920: "Even Water's Getting Weaker,"* Archeophone 9001A, 2004, compact disc.

69. Winthrop Jordan writes about an "unthinking decision" in regard to why blacks were seen as automatic candidates for English slavery (*White over Black: American Attitudes toward the Negro, 1550–1812* [Chapel Hill: University of North Carolina Press, 1968], 44). In short, they fit Englishmen's notion of who was to be enslaved, and the English just happened on them and the Spanish and Portuguese slave traders. Likewise, stereotypes of Latino men fit many white people's imaginations of a sexual murderer. Because they were known as hot-tempered, but not too smart, Latino Americans could easily be pushed to the fore in cases involving sexual danger (ibid., 44–98). Feelings that Latinos were voracious, even dangerous, lovers were so prevalent that when Helen Brown Norden wrote "Latins Are Lousy Lovers" as an anonymous article for *Vanity Fair* in the 1930s, her words were shocking. She used the stereotypes of Latino, particularly Cuban, men's sensuality and willingness to discourse on sex to argue that these men were talkers rather than doers (*The Hussy's Handbook* [New York: Arden, 1942], 3–19). The stereotypes, however, had such a strong hold on the American imagination that the article was received with amazement.

70. Quoted in "Detective Burns Sees Diaries as Murder Key," *New York Evening Journal*, 5 March 1931.

71. "Dot King's Life Story Traced," *New York Evening Journal*, 5 March 1931.

72. Alex Feinberg, "Gigolo Angle in Vivian Death," *New York Evening Journal*, 18 March 1931.

73. "Gigolo May Hold Key to Moth Murder."

74. Feinberg, "Gigolo Angle in Vivian Death."

75. Michel Foucault describes the level of control that can instituted over another's body in his important study of space and the construction of identity in *Discipline and Punish: The Birth of the Prison* (trans. Alan Sheridan [New York: Vintage, 1979]). Sandra Lee Bartky argues that one of the purposes of disciplining a body is to "bring forth from this body a specific repertoire of gestures, postures, and movements" ("Foucault, Femininity, and the Modernization of Patriarchal Power," in *Feminism and Foucault: Reflections on Resistance*, ed. Irene Diamond and Lee Quinby [Boston: Northeastern University Press, 1988], 64). She also argues that a body can be disciplined specifically to be feminine. Her arguments point to a reading in which the dancing figures of the article by Feinberg are struggling against gendered norms at an intimate level. McClary makes the connection between discipline and music specific in "Same as It Ever Was."

76. *The Jazz Singer* used blackface in an obvious way. Sophie Tucker, discussed in chapter 3, was a huge vaudevillian star for decades. In the Gilded Age, she had been known as a "coon shouter," a woman performing songs in a black style. Her performances depended on these types of racial crossings. Of course, black-

face discourse continues throughout the twentieth century. In the documentary *Color Adjustment*, the cultural studies scholar Herman Gray argues that J. J. Walker's character in the television sitcom *Good Times* was also dependent on the figure of the "dandified" gentleman from the minstrel tradition. (Marlon Riggs, dir., *Color Adjustment* [San Francisco: California Newsreel, 2004, DVD]). Spike Lee's *Bamboozled* (Brooklyn, NY: Forty Acres and a Mule Filmworks/New Line Cinema, 2000, DVD) argues that blackface is still part of the entertainment industry.

77. See Monica Miller, *Slaves to Fashion: Black Dandyism and the Styling of Black Diasporic Identity* (Durham, NC: Duke University Press, 2009).

78. Sean Wilentz, *Chants Democratic: New York City and the Rise of the American Working Class, 1788–1850* (New York: Oxford University Press, 1984), 259. In Wilentz's account, the blacking up of the arriviste was a safe way to mock both white interlocutors and blacks, but the bulk of his argument centers on how the white working class disdained the presumably white upper class. Other works on minstrelsy also comment on the subversive potential that blacking up has for the white, male working class. David Roediger questions the oppositional nature of blackface, setting new limits for exploring the meanings of black representation (*The Wages of Whiteness: Race and the Making of the American Working Class* [New York: Verso, 1991], 116–27). George Lipsitz, in discussing the case of *Amos 'n' Andy*, explores the dialectical relationship of white and black culture in the production of blackface radio: "The desire to subjugate and degrade black people had political and economic imperatives of its own, but emotional and psychic reinforcement for that exploitation came from the ways in which racist stereotypes enabled whites to accept the suppression of their natural selves" (*Time Passages: Collective Memory and American Popular Culture* [Minneapolis: University of Minnesota Press, 1990], 64). Eric Lott has written a book-length study of the nuances of this same dialectical relationship (*Love and Theft: Blackface Minstrelsy and the American Working Class* [New York: Oxford University Press, 1993]). For the effects that blackface activities had on black communities specifically during the Jazz Age in New York, see Huggins, *The Harlem Renaissance*, 244–301. The character of the Duke also recalls the deceptive carpetbaggers in Mark Twain's *The Adventures of Huckleberry Finn*, the Duke and the Dauphin. The echoing of these well-known literary characters seems to equate Feinberg's Duke with a pretending white aristocracy à la Wilentz, but, again, the comedic value and the fun poked at this creation was limited in Feinberg's article; rather, the Duke's deception pointed to danger.

79. Feinberg, "Gigolo Angle in Vivian Death."

80. Monica Miller notes: "Black dandies may seem to mimic European dress styles in an effort to accrue power associated with whiteness. Such repetition, however, is never a strict copy of the original style" (*Slaves to Fashion*, 14). Miller sees this as a moment of liberatory potential, and the desire to deride and control behavior at the level of dress certainly speaks to the fear of this potential. She also de-

scribes black dandyism as "a knowingness, acknowledgement, and capitalization of the intersection of image and identity" (ibid., 41).

81. Feinberg, "Gigolo Angle in Vivian Death."

82. Ibid.

83. Anonymous report, 27 February 1928, box 36, C14, NYPL.

84. "Report on Cabaret Situation, 1917," December 1917, box 31; ibid.

85. In writing about the creation of lesbian communities around Greenwich Village and Harlem, Mizejewski argues: "Some feminists in the first two decades of the century, responding to [the sexologist Richard Freiherr von] Krafft-Ebing, deliberately took on male clothing as a political statement. On another level, available knowledge about a lesbian sexuality made it possible for individuals to name a desire" (*Ziegfeld Girl*, 86).

86. Summers, *Manliness and Its Discontents*, 152.

87. I have found no references to prove that Thurman had read sexological works, but it is probable that he had. According to Thomas H. Wirth, Thurman's roommate, Richard Bruce Nugent, read his father's copy of Krafft-Ebing's case studies at a young age (Thomas H. Wirth, "Introduction," in *Gay Rebel of the Harlem Renaissance: Selections from the Work of Richard Bruce Nugent*, ed. Thomas H. Wirth [Durham, NC: Duke University Press, 2002], 8).

88. Wallace Thurman, *Infants of the Spring* (1932; repr., New York: Random House, 1999).

89. For more readings of the "tragic mulatto" narrative, see Carby, *Reconstructing Womanhood*; Somerville, *Queering the Color Line*; Sterling A. Brown, "Negro Character as Seen by White Authors," *Journal of Negro Education* 2 (1933): 179–203.

90. Thurman also provides an exception in the African American literary canon by being explicit about his queer characters. Sharon Patricia Holland notes that African American literature and literary criticism often works through a disappearance of queer identities (*Raising the Dead: Readings of Death and [Black] Subjectivity* [Durham, NC: Duke University Press, 2000], 104).

91. Somerville, *Queering the Color Line*, 33.

92. Carby notes that the figure of the mulatto generally filled two roles—a way of understanding interracial contact and an expression of that contact (*Reconstructing Womanhood*, 89).

93. Gayatri Gopinath, *Impossible Desires: Queer Diasporas and South Asian Public Cultures* (Durham, NC: Duke University Press, 2005), 1–2.

94. Part of what is at stake in the policing of borders is the creation of safe spaces for people of color, queers, and queer people of color within the nation. Lisa Marie Cacho presciently argues that "imagined boundaries and arbitrary borders" can be used to legitimate violence in the creation of a national imaginary ("Disciplinary Fictions: The Sociality of Private Problems in Contemporary California," PhD diss., University of California, San Diego, 2002), 1–2.

95. Thurman, *The Blacker the Berry*, 106–7.

96. Ibid., 107.

97. For example, see, Sterling A. Brown, "The American Race Problem as Reflected in American Literature," *Journal of Negro Education* 8, no. 3 (1939): 286; Devon W. Carbado, Dwight A. McBride, and Donald Weise, "Wallace Thurman," in *Black Like Us: A Century of Lesbian, Gay, and Bisexual African American Fiction*, ed. Devon W. Carbado, Dwight A. McBride, and Donald Weise (San Francisco: Cleis, 2002), 63; Singh and Scott, "Excerpts from the Novels," 442–44.

98. Rudolph Fisher, "The City of Refuge," in *The New Negro: An Interpretation*, edited by Alain Locke (1925; repr., New York: Johnson Reprint, 1968), 57–74. The work includes black Caribbeaners.

99. For more on the logic of the construction of false categories, see Denise Riley, *"Am I That Name?" Feminism and the Category of "Women" in History* (Minneapolis: University of Minnesota Press, 1990). See also Butler's discussion of Riley (*Gender Trouble*, 3).

100. Thurman, *The Blacker the Berry*, 97.

101. Somerville, *Queering the Color Line*, 37. She further notes that at the end of the nineteenth century and the beginning of the twentieth, sexological texts often connected the figure of the mulatto with deviant sex categories: "The mixed-race body evoked the mixed-gender body" (80).

102. The historian Lillian Faderman rightly points out that Thurman displays a certain ambivalence in regard to discussions of homosexual writing because of the way he demonizes male homosexuality in particular, even though he was himself queer (*Odd Girls and Twilight Lovers: A History of Lesbian Life in Twentieth-Century America* [New York: Columbia University Press, 1991], 69–70). The similarities between characters in the novel and Thurman himself have also been pointed out by Mae G. Henderson ("Portrait of Wallace Thurman," in *The Harlem Renaissance Remembered*, ed. Arna Bontemps [New York: Dodd, Mead, 1972], 155–56) and Elenore van Notten ("Wallace Thurman's Harlem Renaissance," PhD diss., Leiden University, 1994, 223–40), who both note that, like Emma Lou, Thurman had moved from a western town to attend the University of Southern California, and later moved to Harlem. Van Notten also notes that Thurman shared biographical similarities with both Alva and Truman Walter, an intellectual doppelgänger.

103. Alva is misidentified by Faderman as "a black bisexual who is a scoundrel" (*Odd Girls and Twilight Lovers*, 69) and by the literary critic Marjorie Garber through a quotation of Faderman (*Vice Versa: Bisexuality and the Eroticism of Everyday Life* [New York: Touchstone, 1995], 124). This misidentification again points to both the powerful historical imagination of the Harlem Renaissance as solely characterized by blackness and to the seeming invisibility of Asians' contemporaneous presence. An exception to this type of misidentification is in Eugene Arden, "The Early Harlem Novel," *Phylon Quarterly* 20, no.1 (1959): 30.

104. Thurman, *The Blacker the Berry*, 128.

105. Even in contemporary scholarship, it is relatively new to speak about mixed-

race pairings beyond black and white. See Christina C. Iijima Hall and Trude I. Cooke Turner, "The Diversity of Biracial Individuals: Asian-White and Asian-Minority Biracial Identity," in *The Sum of Our Parts: Mixed Heritage Asian Americans*, ed. Teresa Williams-León and Cynthia L. Nakashima (Philadelphia: Temple University Press, 2001), 81.

106. I have written more on the connections between mixed-race embodiment, imperialism, and sexuality in Fiona I. B. Ngô, "A Chameleon's Fate: Transnational Mixed-Race Vietnamese Identities," *Amerasia Journal* 31, no. 2 (2005): 51–62. Kieu-Linh Caroline Valverde ("From Dust to Gold: The Vietnamese Amerasian American Experience," in *Racially Mixed People in America*, ed. Maria P. P. Root [Newbury Park, CA: Sage, 1992], 158) and Cynthia L. Nakashima ("An Invisible Monster: The Creation and Denial of Mixed-Race People in America," in *Racially Mixed People in America*, 168–69) have written more on the sexualization of mixed-race individuals, particularly women.

107. Somerville, *Queering the Color Line*, 17.

108. Thurman, *The Blacker the Berry*, 97.

109. My reading of Alva's body comes from the literature devoted to intersexuals, transgendered people, and transsexuals. Through the theories of sex and gender produced in these sites, it is possible to view Alva's body as sexually ambiguous at a physical level and to think through the meanings of that ambiguity and how they point to the possibility of many sexes. For more on intersexuals, see Anne Fausto-Sterling, "The Five Sexes: Why Male and Female Are Not Enough," *Sciences* (March–April 1993): 20–24; Fausto-Sterling "How to Build a Man," in *The Gender/Sexuality Reader: Culture, History, Political Economy*, ed. Roger N. Lancaster and Micaela di Leonardo (New York: Routledge, 1997), 244–48; Cheryl Chase, "Hermaphrodites with Attitude," GLQ 4, no. 2 (1998): 189–211. For more on transsexuals, see Kate Bornstein, *Gender Outlaw: On Men, Women, and the Rest of Us* (New York: Vintage, 1993); Bernice L. Hausman, *Changing Sex: Transsexualism, Technology, and the Idea of Gender* (Durham, NC: Duke University Press, 1995); Holly Devor, *FTM: Female-to-Male Transsexuals in Society* (Bloomington: Indiana University Press, 1997); Sandy Stone, "A Posttranssexual Manifesto," in *Body Guards: The Cultural Politics of Gender Ambiguity*, ed. Julia Epstein and Kristina Straub (New York: Routledge, 1991), 280–304. Related work on transgendered communities can be found in Judith Halberstam and Del LaGrace Volcano, *The Drag King Book* (London: Serpent's Tail, 1999); Halberstam, *Female Masculinity* (Durham, NC: Duke University Press, 1998); David Valentine, *Imagining Transgender: An Ethnography of a Category* (Durham, NC: Duke University Press, 2007).

110. Though Alva might be considered queer because his sex acts were non-normative, he may not have been considered homosexual because homosexual acts were not necessarily connected to homosexual identities. In other words, simply because Alva had sex with men did not mean that Alva was considered homosexual. As Chauncey notes, in early twentieth-century New York, effemi-

nate men may have been labeled "fairies" and deemed homosexual, but if men behaved in a masculine manner, they were not necessarily named as homosexual (*Gay New York*, 12–18).

111. See Frank Chin, "Come All Ye Asian American Writers of the Real and Fake," in *The Big Aiiieeeee! An Anthology of Chinese American and Japanese American Literature*, ed. Jeffery Paul Chan, Frank Chin, Lawson Fusao Inada, and Shawn Wong (New York: Meridian, 1991), 1–93; Elaine H. Kim, "Asian Americans and Popular Culture," in *Dictionary of Asian American History*, ed. Hyung-Chan Kim (New York: Greenwood, 1986), 99–114. For works on Asian American masculinities that critique these positions, particularly Chin's, see Richard Fung, "Looking for My Penis: The Eroticized Asian in Gay Video Porn," in *Q & A: Queer in Asian America*, ed. David L. Eng and Alice Y. Hom (Philadelphia: Temple University Press, 1998), 115–34; David L. Eng, *Racial Castration: Managing Masculinity in Asian America* (Durham, NC: Duke University Press, 2001); Daniel Kim, *Writing Manhood in Black and Yellow: Ralph Ellison, Frank Chin, and the Literary Politics of Identity* (Stanford, CA: Stanford University Press, 2005). For work on queer Filipino men in the later twentieth century, see Martin F. Manalansan IV, *Global Divas: Filipino Gay Men in the Diaspora* (Durham, NC: Duke University Press, 2003); Victor Bascara, "'A Vaudeville against Coconut Trees': Colonialism, Contradiction, and Coming Out in Michael Magnaye's *White Christmas*," in *Q & A*, 95–114; Gil Mangaoang, "From the 1970s to the 1990s," in *Asian American Sexualities: Dimensions of the Gay and Lesbian Experience*, ed. Russell Leong (New York: Routledge, 1996), 101–11.

112. Ann Laura Stoler, *Carnal Knowledge and Imperial Power: Race and the Intimate in Colonial Rule* (Berkeley: University of California Press, 2002), 144.

2. QUEER MODERNITIES

1. Thomas H. Wirth (editorial note) in Richard Bruce Nugent, "Early Works," in *Gay Rebel of the Harlem Renaissance: Selections from the Work of Richard Bruce Nugent*, ed. Thomas H. Wirth (Durham, NC: Duke University Press, 2002), 66.

2. In the language connecting the stranger and distance, I am drawing on Sara Ahmed's *Strange Encounters: Embodied Others in Post-Coloniality* (New York: Routledge, 2000) and *Queer Phenomenology: Orientations, Objects, Others* (Durham, NC: Duke University Press, 2006).

3. Flier for Un Bal Primitiv, Committee of Fourteen Records, 1905–32, Rare Books and Manuscripts Division, New York Public Library, New York, NY (hereafter cited as C14, NYPL).

4. Eric Garber, "A Spectacle in Color: The Lesbian and Gay Subculture of Jazz Age Harlem," in *Hidden from History: Reclaiming the Gay and Lesbian Past*, ed. Martin B. Duberman, Martha Vicinus, and George Chauncey Jr. (New York: New American Library, 1989), 324–25.

5. The racialized queering of words as they change meanings is also taken up by Tavia Nyong'o in "Punk'd Theory," *Social Text* 84–85, nos. 3–4 (2005): 19–34.

6. Roderick A. Ferguson, *Aberrations in Black: Toward a Queer of Color Critique* (Minneapolis: University of Minnesota Press, 2004), 139.

7. Gloria Anzaldúa, *Borderlands / La Frontera: The New Mestiza*, 2nd ed. (San Francisco: Aunt Lute, 1987). She does this throughout the book. For a discussion of imperialism, in particular, see 23–35. For her work on race, gender, and sexuality, see 37–45.

8. Helen H. Jun writes: "I refer to this contradictory process as *black Orientalism*, in order to name the paradoxical dilemma endemic to struggles for black citizenship. Nineteenth-century black Orientalism cannot be reductively understood as anti-Asian racism but is instead a concept that situates the contradictions of black citizenship in structural relation to American Orientalism and Chinese immigrant exclusion. My use of the term *black Orientalism* displaces the emphasis on group 'intentions' by highlighting how the institution of citizenship compelled narratives of black inclusion that converged with the rhetoric and logic of the anti-Chinese movement" (*Race for Citizenship: Black Orientalism and Asian Uplift from Pre-Emancipation to Neoliberal America* [New York: New York University Press, 2011], 6).

9. Jacques Rancière, *The Politics of Aesthetics: The Distribution of the Sensible*, trans. with an introduction by Gabriel Rockhill, afterword by Slavoj Žižek (London: Continuum, 2004), 39.

10. Gabriel Rockhill, the translator, provides a note about Rancière's use of *body* in ibid., 104, note 13.

11. Ibid., 39.

12. Richard Bruce Nugent, "Smoke, Lilies and Jade," in *FIRE!! Devoted to Younger Negro Artists*, ed. Wallace Thurman (1926; repr., Westport, CT: Negro Universities Press, 1970), 33–39.

13. Richard Bruce Nugent, "Geisha Man (excerpt)," in *Gay Rebel of the Harlem Renaissance: Selctions from the Work of Richard Bruce Nugent*, ed. Thomas H. Wirth (Durham, NC: Duke University Press, 2002), 90–111; Richard Bruce Nugent, "The Geisha Man," unpublished manuscript, 1928.

14. I am riffing here on Michel Foucault's notion of the "author-effect" in his classic work on subjectivity ("What Is an Author?," in *Critical Theory since 1965*, ed. Hazard Adams and Leroy Searle [Tallahassee: Florida State University Press, 1986], 138–48).

15. Nella Larsen, *Quicksand and Passing*, ed. Deborah E. McDowell (New Brunswick, NJ: Rutgers University Press, 1986), 171, 239. In addition, Clare Kendry's skin is described several times as ivory (157, 220, 221).

16. Ibid., 157, 220.

17. Deborah E. McDowell traces the language of queer desire in *Passing* (Introduction to Nella Larsen, *Quicksand and Passing*, ed. Deborah E. McDowell [New Brunswick, NJ: Rutgers University Press, 1986], xxvi–xxxi).

18. Zelda Fitzgerald, *Save Me the Waltz* (1932; repr., London: Arcturus, 1967), 51.

19. Ibid.

20. Thomas H. Wirth, introduction, in Richard Bruce Nugent, *Gay Rebel of the Harlem Renaissance: Selections from the Work of Richard Bruce Nugent*, ed. Thomas H. Wirth (Durham, NC: Duke University Press, 2002).

21. Ibid., 8. Nugent's older brother was a dancer on Broadway (see Richard Bruce Nugent quoted in *You Must Remember This: An Oral History of Manhattan from 1892 to World War II*, ed. Jeff Kisseloff [New York: Harcourt Brace Jovanovich, 1989], 283).

22. Wirth, introduction, 8. Richard von Krafft-Ebing, *Psychopathia Sexualis: With Especial Reference to the Antipathic Sexual Instinct*, trans. Franklin S. Klaf, 12th ed. New York: Stein and Day, 1965.

23. Nathan Irvin Huggins, Introduction to *Voices from the Harlem Renaissance*, ed. Nathan Irvin Huggins (New York: Oxford University Press, 1976), 7.

24. Marlon B. Ross, *Manning the Race: Reforming Black Men in the Jim Crow Era* (New York: New York University Press, 2004), 77–78.

25. In terms of mimesis, I am thinking primarily of Frantz Fanon, *A Dying Colonialism*, trans. Haaken Chevalier (New York: Grove, 1988); Homi Bhabha, *The Location of Culture* (New York: Routledge, 1994); Diana Fuss, *Identification Papers* (New York: Routledge, 1995).

26. Gilles Deleuze, *Difference and Repetition*, trans. Paul Patton (1968; repr., New York: Columbia University Press, 1994), 1.

27. Eve Kosofsky Sedgwick, *Epistemology of the Closet* (Berkeley: University of California Press, 1990), 175.

28. Elisa Glick writes: "Thurman uses the tropes of Orientalized decadence in order to construct queer identity as a secret, much in the way that Wilde does in *The Picture of Dorian Gray*, but he does not position the black dandy's rebellion as fundamentally murderous" ("Harlem's Queer Dandy: African-American Modernism and the Artifice of Blackness," MFS 49, no. 3 [2003]: 436).

29. Edward Said, *Orientalism* (1978; repr., New York: Vintage, 1994), 1–28. See also Joseph A. Massad, *Desiring Arabs* (Chicago: University of Chicago Press, 2007).

30. Daniel Kim presciently warns against viewing African and Asian American interracialisms as magical moments of manly homosocial alliance because interracialisms are "fractured by the asymmetry of African and Asian American concerns" (*Writing Manhood in Black and Yellow: Ralph Ellison, Frank Chin, and the Literary Politics of Identity* [Stanford, CA: Stanford University Press, 2005], xvii).

31. Curtis Marez argues that Wilde is racialized by his critics because of his use of orientalist objets d'art and the conflation of orientalist signs with queer signs ("The Other Addict: Reflections on Colonialism and Oscar Wilde's Opium Smoke Screen," ELH 64, no. 1 [1997]: 257–87). D. Kim repeats this reading in *Writing Manhood in Black and Yellow* (153–54).

32. For more on the "queer of color critique," see Ferguson, *Aberrations in Black*.

33. Ibid., 83.

34. Nyong'o, "Punk'd Theory," 20.

35. Judith Halberstam has also been exploring queer art practices that occur in the

absence of queer bodies in her recent work on failure (*The Queer Art of Failure* [Durham, NC: Duke University Press, 2011]).

36. Scott Herring, *Queering the Underworld: Slumming, Literature, and the Undoing of Lesbian and Gay History* (Chicago: University of Chicago Press, 2007), 23.

37. Sherrie Tucker, "When Did Jazz Go Straight? A Queer Question for Jazz Studies," *Critical Studies in Improvisation* 4, no. 2 (2008): 2.

38. Ferguson, *Aberrations in Black*, 55.

39. Roland Barthes, *Empire of Signs*, trans. Richard Howard (New York: Hill and Wang, 1982), 7. See also A. B. Christa Schwarz, *Gay Voices of the Harlem Renaissance* (Bloomington: Indiana University Press, 2003), 131–32.

40. D. Kim, *Writing Manhood in Black and Yellow*, 154 (emphasis added).

41. David Levering Lewis oral interview notes, Voices from the Renaissance Collection, Schomburg Center for Research in Black Culture, New York Public Library, New York, NY.

42. Nugent in Kisseloff, *You Must Remember This*, 288.

43. Chandan Reddy's reading of Du Bois and his talented tenth politics also points to its connection to European empire building. Reddy writes of the talented tenth ideology: "In focusing on spaces above and beyond the nation-state, and on cultures of supranational space formations, black cosmopolitanism must be distinguished from its European variant, even if it maintains an ambivalent relationship to that variant" (*Freedom with Violence: Race, Sexuality, and the US State* [Durham, NC: Duke University Press, 2012], 75). His reading coincides with my reading of a how even the production of a queer black aesthetic is still dependent on this kind of ambivalent relationship with European cosmopolitanism and its history in colonial contact.

44. Glick, "Harlem's Queer Dandy," 414–15.

45. Ibid., 415.

46. Henry Louis Gates Jr., "The Black Man's Burden," in *Fear of a Queer Planet: Queer Politics and Social Theory*, ed. Michael Warner (Minneapolis: University of Minnesota Press, 1993), 233. Scholars often repeat this claim as a way to point out the importance of studying black queer writers during the 1920s, but this formulation can also hide the fact that these queer writers were not well received when writing queer. See Siobhan B. Somerville, "Passing through the Closet in Pauline E. Hopkins's *Contending Forces*," *American Literature* 69, no. 1 (1997): 141; Michael L. Cobb, "Insolent Racing, Rough Narrative: The Harlem Renaissance's Impolite Queers," *Callaloo* 23, no. 1 (2000): 329; Schwarz, *Gay Voices of the Harlem Renaissance*, 1.

47. Rancière, *The Politics of Aesthetics*, 9.

48. I am drawing here on Voloshinov's reading of linguistic practice as dialogic but also on Bakhtin's later reformulation of dialogisms as heteroglossic. See V. N. Voloshinov, "Critique of Saussurian Linguistics," in *The Bakhtin Reader: Selected Writings of Bakhtin, Medvedev, Voloshinov*, ed. Pam Morris (London: Arnold, 1994), 25–37; Mikhail Bakhtin, "Social Heteroglossia," in *The Bakhtin Reader*, 73–81.

49. Caren Kaplan, *Questions of Travel: Postmodern Discourses of Displacement* (Durham, NC: Duke University Press, 1996), 1.

50. Schwarz, *Gay Voices of the Harlem Renaissance*, 120.

51. Cobb, "Insolent Racing, Rough Narrative," 347.

52. D. Kim, *Writing Manhood in Black and Yellow*, 154–55.

53. Nugent, "Smoke, Lilies and Jade," 36.

54. Rancière, *The Politics of Aesthetics*, 13.

55. Nugent, "Smoke, Lilies and Jade," 34–37.

56. Ibid., 36.

57. Subsequent Harlem Renaissance texts take up similar themes. For example, Wallace Thurman's *The Blacker the Berry* . . . (1929; repr., New York: Collier, 1970) explores interracial relationships, free love, and queer male characters who have sexual relationships with both men and women. For my purposes here, I focus on how queer aesthetics are introduced and brought into play, leaving the varieties of sexuality for future scholars to decode.

58. David Levering Lewis, *When Harlem Was in Vogue* (New York: Vintage, 1982), 76. These names come up repeatedly in scholarship of the Harlem Renaissance. See ibid., 197; Devon W. Carbado, Dwight A. McBride, and Donald Weise, "Richard Bruce Nugent," in *Black Like Us: A Century of Lesbian, Gay, and Bisexual African American Fiction*, edited by Devon W. Carbado, Dwight A. McBride, and Donald Weise (San Francisco: Cleis, 2002), 74; D. Kim, *Writing Manhood in Black and Yellow*, 155.

59. Wirth, introduction, in Nugent, *Gay Rebel of the Harlem Renaissance*, 11. Wirth notes that this was also where Nugent met Valentino (10).

60. Nugent also references Freud in regard to structures of desire ("Smoke, Lilies and Jade," 34).

61. Mimi Thi Nguyen, "The Biopower of Beauty: Humanitarian Imperialisms and Global Feminisms in an Age of Terror," *Signs* 36, no. 2 (2011): 364.

62. Nugent "Smoke, Lilies and Jade," 36. Nugent's use of the abbreviation "vd." in the first line of this quotation supports Wirth's idea that the character of Beauty must be based in part on the Panamanian Juan José Viana because this linguistic formulation (short for "vos otros") is common in Central America. Thanks to the historian Mireya Loza for calling this to my attention. In a reprint of the story the phrase is rewritten as "perdone me señor tiene usted fósforo." Richard Bruce Nugent, "Smoke, Lilies and Jade," in *Gay Rebel of the Harlem Renaissance: Selections from the Work of Richard Bruce Nugent*, ed. Thomas H. Wirth (Durham, NC: Duke University Press, 2002), 81.

63. Ibid.

64. Reddy, *Freedom with Violence*, 124.

65. Rancière, *The Politics of Aesthetics*, 19.

66. Ferguson has written about how the feminization of African American men relates to the formation of the sociology canon in "The Knee-pants of Servility: American Modernity, the Chicago School, and *Native Son*," in *Aberrations in*

Black: Toward a Queer of Color Critique (Minneapolis: University of Minnesota Press, 2004), 31–53.

67. On the aura, see Walter Benjamin, *Illuminations: Essays and Reflections*, ed. with an introduction by Hannah Arendt, trans. Harry Zohn (New York: Schocken, 1969), 217–52. On the aura and imperialism, see Rey Chow, *Writing Diaspora: Tactics of Intervention in Contemporary Cultural Studies* (Bloomington: Indiana University Press, 1993), 27–54.

68. Susan Gubar, *Racechanges: White Skins, Black Face in American Culture* (New York: Oxford University Press, 1997), 107, 111.

69. Sigmund Freud, *Three Essays on the Theory of Sexuality*, with a foreword by Nancy J. Chodorow and an introductory essay by Steven Marcus, ed. and trans. James Strachey (New York: Basic, 2000), 5.

70. The heads also make note of the racial trope of mixed raceness, but not just through the juxtaposition of black and white. Ella Shohat notes that mixed-race identity was a part of life in ancient Greece and Macedonia (*Taboo Memories, Diasporic Voices* [Durham, NC: Duke University Press, 2006]).

71. Ann Douglas, *Terrible Honesty: Mongrel Manhattan in the 1920s* (New York: Noonday, 1995). Douglas notes that skyscrapers became one of the distinguishing characteristics of the city in the 1920s.

72. "Report on Cabaret Situation, 1917"; anonymous reports, 11 February 1917, 23 March 1917, and 12 October 1917; Fredrick Whitin, letter to Adams Brown, 14 November 1917, C14, NYPL.

73. "Report on Cabaret Situation, 1917," early draft, ibid.

74. Irving Kolodin, *The Story of the Metropolitan Opera, 1883–1950: A Candid History* (New York: Knopf, 1953), 597–606.

75. Wallace Thurman, *Infants of the Spring* (1932; repr., New York: Random House, 1999).

76. Ibid.

77. Kolodin, *The Story of the Metropolitan Opera*, 605.

78. Thurman, *Infants of the Spring*, 24.

79. Ibid.

80. This scene also predicts a transformative passage in Ralph Ellison's *Invisible Man* ([New York: Vintage, 1947], 275–87), where the narrator gives a speech defending tenants' rights in Harlem and then is forced by a mob to run up the stairs of the building, cross several rooftops, and exit into the street as a transformed man, now a political activist. The narrator of Ellison's novel is also faced with a birth at the end of his transformative run: a woman is about to give birth in the building from which he exits. "What a hell of a time to be born," he thinks, as he bursts out onto the street a new man (287). Also, like Ellison's character and, by extension, his narrator, Paul later uses his own racial illegibility to become whatever he aspires to be.

81. Thurman, *Infants of the Spring*, 32–33.

82. Ibid., 25.

83. Ibid., 24–25.

84. Ibid., 174.

85. Rachel Kent, "Time and Transformation in the Art of Yinka Shonibare MBE," in *Yinka Shonibare, MBE*, edited by Rachel Kent, Robert Hobbs, and Anthony Downey (New York: Prestel, 2008), 12–13.

86. Anne Anlin Cheng, "Skin Deep: Josephine Baker and the Colonial Fetish," *Camera Obscura* 69 (2008): 67.

87. Reddy's reading of the character of Helga Crane in Nella Larsen's *Quicksand* complements my reading here. Reddy sees Crane as creating herself as part of a *tableau vivant* where she becomes an orientalized object rather than the subject she aspires to become (*Freedom with Violence*, 129–30).

88. Opera itself has been characterized as a queer male practice. In Wayne Koestenbaum's widely read autoethnography of queer operagoers, he connects his love of opera with his own coming of sexual age as a queer man: "[When] I began to listen, again and again, . . . to the four operas I owned, I had by that time acquired a boyfriend, a sexuality, and a hunger . . . to have opera take over my reason, as if opera were the antithesis of reason" (*The Queen's Throat: Opera, Homosexuality, and the Mystery of Desire* [New York: Vintage, 1994], 18). In Koestenbaum's thoughts the opera narrative produces illogic. By extension, then, he might imagine the queerness of opera as that which exceeds the logical. I imagine, however, that the recirculation of operatic signs in the Jazz Age used the contradictory modes of imperial logic that produced a queer black aesthetic and epistemology. Of course, the title of Thurman's novel is also a play on the title of Stravinsky's ballet *Le sacre du printemps* (The rite of spring), which— especially in performances with Vaslav Nijinsky—has been hailed as a benchmark of queer cultural identification. Through the circulation of some of the queer signs found in the genealogy of queer cultural production in Europe and the United States, Thurman and Nugent simultaneously reiterated the terms of empire and challenged its naturalization and stability.

89. For more on how sexuality, gender, and race can become illegible as part of that variety, see David Henry Hwang's reading of Puccini's *Madama Butterfly* (*M. Butterfly* [New York: Penguin, 1989]). See also David L. Eng, "In the Shadows of a Diva: Committing Homosexuality in David Henry Hwang's *M. Butterfly*," in *Asian American Sexualities: Dimensions of the Gay and Lesbian Experience*, ed. Russell Leong (New York: Routledge, 1996), 131–52.

90. Cobb, "Insolent Racing, Rough Narrative," 347–48.

91. Thurman, *Infants of the Spring*, 175.

92. Thomas H. Wirth, "Richard Bruce Nugent," *Black American Literature Forum* 19, no. 1 (1985): 16.

93. Though both Bhabha and Hall set up the possibility of multiple meanings, the importance of those meanings is quite different for the theorists: Bhabha sees ambivalence as creating a space of possible resistance to empire, while Hall views doubleness as the consolidation of racism. The possibility should be considered

that they are both right because both outcomes are potentials from moments of contact. See Bhabha, "Of Mimicry and Man: The Ambivalence of Colonial Discourse," in *The Location of Culture*, 85–92; Stuart Hall, "The Whites of Their Eyes," in *Gender, Race and Class in Media*, ed. Gail Dines and Jean M. Humez (Thousand Oaks, CA: Sage, 2010), 18–22.

94. Fiona I. B. Ngô, "The Anxiety over Borders," in *Embodiments of Asian Pacific Islander Sexuality*, ed. Gina Masequesmay and Sean Metzger (Lanham, MD: Lexington Press, 2008), 89–104.

95. Arguments of cultural appropriation also rely on notions of space as static, where groups can be defined and crossings between groups can contain only certain meanings.

96. Gilles Deleuze and Félix Guattari, *The Anti-Oedipus: Capitalism and Schizophrenia*, trans. Robert Hurley, Mark Seem, and Helen R. Lane (Minneapolis: University of Minnesota Press, 1983), 206–7.

97. C. Kaplan, *Questions of Travel*, 86.

98. Ibid., 70.

99. Victor Mendoza, "A Queer Nomadology of Jessica Hagedorn's *Dogeaters*," *American Literature* 77, no. 4 (2005): 816.

100. Nugent, "The Geisha Man," 34.

101. Ibid., 4.

102. Ibid., 50.

103. Schwarz, *Gay Voices of the Harlem Renaissance*, 140.

104. See Judith Halberstam, *Female Masculinity* (Durham, NC: Duke University Press, 1998).

105. Bessie Smith, "Foolish Man Blues," recorded 27 October 1927, *Bessie Smith: The Complete Recordings*, vol. 3, Columbia Records C2K47474, 1992, 2 compact discs.

106. Nugent, "The Geisha Man," 27.

107. Ibid., 50, 25.

108. Ibid., 15.

109. Ibid., 50.

110. C. Kaplan, *Questions of Travel*, 110.

111. Nugent, "The Geisha Man," 51.

112. Chandan Reddy, "Asian Diasporas, Neoliberalism, and Family: Reviewing the Case for Homosexual Asylum in the Context of Family Rights," *Social Text* 84–85, nos. 3–4 (2005): 101–3.

113. Catherine Clément, *Opera, or the Undoing of Women*, trans. Betsy Wing (Minneapolis: University of Minnesota Press, 1988), 45.

114. Cobb, "Insolent Racing, Rough Narrative," 347–48.

115. Nugent, "The Geisha Man," 65.

116. Ibid., 63–64.

117. Ibid., 66.

118. Ibid.

119. I am borrowing the idea of the queer aesthetic from Judith Halberstam, "Notes on Failure," lecture at the University of Illinois, Urbana-Champaign, 14 April 2006. I am inspired by her use of the visual, though her visual objects are much more abstract than mine, and mine mobilize racial tropes much more obviously than hers.

120. Rancière, *The Politics of Aesthetics*, 39.

3. ORIENTING SUBJECTIVITIES

1. Though their numbers were certainly quite low, some Arabs had already moved to New York. Susan A. Glenn notes that Syrians were living on the Lower East Side of Manhattan, working at home producing, interestingly enough, "kimonos, lace, crocheting, and embroidery" (*Daughters of the Shtetl: Life and Labor in the Immigrant Generation* [Ithaca, NY: Cornell University Press, 1990], 73; see also 56). It is important to note, however, that documents listing "Syrians" could be referring to many different Arabic-speaking national identities. In regard to another neighborhood in Manhattan, a vice report on the general conditions along Ninth Avenue between Thirty-seventh and Forty-third Streets in 1931 noted that the area was mostly populated by "Greeks, Turks, and Armenians" ("General Conditions," report, 29 December 1931, box 35, Committee of Fourteen Records, 1905–32, Rare Books and Manuscripts Division, New York Public Library, New York, NY [hereafter cited as C14, NYPL]).

2. Edward Said, *Orientalism* (1978; repr., New York: Vintage, 1994), 284.

3. Melani McAlister devotes a considerable portion of her introduction to *Epic Encounters: Culture, Media, and US Interests in the Middle East* ([Berkeley: University of California Press, 2001], 1–42) to thinking about late nineteenth-century and early twentieth-century representations of the Arab world.

4. See, for instance, Said, *Orientalism*; Rey Chow, *Writing Diaspora: Tactics of Intervention in Contemporary Cultural Studies* (Bloomington: Indiana University Press, 1993), 27–54; Deborah Gewertz and Frederick Errington, "We Think Therefore They Are?: On Occidentalizing the World," in *Cultures of United States Imperialism*, ed. Amy Kaplan and Donald E. Pease (Durham, NC: Duke University Press, 1993), 635–65; Sara Ahmed, *Queer Phenomenology: Orientations, Objects, Others* (Durham, NC: Duke University Press, 2006), 116.

5. See Ahmed, *Queer Phenomenology*; Joseph A. Massad, *Desiring Arabs* (Chicago: University of Chicago Press, 2007); Saba Mahmood, *Politics of Piety: The Islamic Revival and the Feminist Subject* (Princeton, NJ: Princeton University Press, 2012).

6. Timothy Mitchell, *Colonising Egypt* (Cambridge: Cambridge University Press, 1988), 12–13. Furthermore, Ahmed argues: "Objects become objects only as an effect of the repetition of this tending 'toward' them, which produces the subject as that which the world is 'around.' The orient is then 'orientated;' it is reachable

as an object given how the world takes shape 'around' certain bodies" (*Queer Phenomenology*, 120).

7. Lisa Lowe, "Intimacies of Four Continents," in *Haunted by Empire: Geographies of Intimacy in North American History*, ed. Ann Laura Stoler (Durham, NC: Duke University Press, 2006), 193.

8. Yutian Wong, *Choreographing Asian America* (Middletown, CT: Wesleyan University Press, 2010), 13.

9. Ahmed, *Queer Phenomenology*, 118.

10. Susan McClary, "Same as It Ever Was: Youth Culture and Music," in *Microphone Fiends: Youth Music and Youth Culture*, ed. Andrew Ross and Tricia Rose (New York: Routledge, 1994), 33.

11. Diana Taylor, *The Archive and the Repertoire* (Durham, NC: Duke University Press, 2003), 19; see also 1–52.

12. Ibid., 19–20.

13. Ibid., 20.

14. Jacques Derrida, *Archive Fever: A Freudian Impression*, trans. Eric Prenowitz (Chicago: University of Chicago Press, 1998), 1.

15. Ahmed, *Queer Phenomenology*, 116–17.

16. Frank Crumit, "Palesteena," recorded in 1920, *The Roaring Twenties*, Intersound 1401, 1997, 4 compact discs. All subsequent quotes from this song are from this recording.

17. Quotes from "Becky from Babylon" and "Rebecca (Came Back from Mecca)" are from Rebecca A. Bryant, "Shaking Big Shoulders: Music and Dance Culture in Chicago, 1910–1925," PhD diss., University of Illinois, Urbana-Champaign, 2003, 222.

18. Anna Lowenhaupt Tsing, *Friction: An Ethnography of Global Connection* (Princeton, NJ: Princeton University Press, 2005), 4. Though Tsing writes about the "transformation of tradition into modernity" (21) in terms of globalization as happening from the 1950s onward, her methodology is useful in examining how modernity and tradition were narrated in earlier moments of contact as well.

19. One account of this controversy appears in Theresa M. Collins, *Otto Kahn: Art, Money, and Modern Time* (Chapel Hill: University of North Carolina Press, 2002), 75–81. The figure of Salomé had also been circulated beyond the Bible in Gustave Flaubert's short story "Herodias" (1874), as well as in Oscar Wilde's play *Salomé* (1894, with illustrations by Aubrey Beardsley), on which Strauss's opera is based.

20. I am grateful to the dance scholar Yutian Wong for pointing out these continuities. For more scholarship on the shimmy, see Robert C. Allen, *Horrible Prettiness: Burlesque and American Culture* (Chapel Hill: University of North Carolina Press, 1991); Rebecca A. Bryant, "Shaking Things Up: Popularizing the Shimmy in America," *American Music* 20, no. 2 (2002): 168–87; Jayna Brown, *Babylon Girls: Black Women Performers and the Shaping of the Modern* (Durham, NC: Duke University Press, 2008).

21. For more on the specific orientalization of West Asia and North Africa, see Said's pathbreaking *Orientalism*.
22. Bryant, "Shaking Big Shoulders," 222.
23. Allen, *Horrible Prettiness*, 227.
24. Some scholars of orientalisms have noted that white women attempted to gain power through the use of such orientalisms. See, for example, Elaine Showalter, *Sexual Anarchy: Gender and Culture at the Fin de Siècle* (New York: Virago, 1989); Gaylyn Studlar, "'Out-Salomeing Salome': Dance, the New Woman, and Fan Magazine Orientalism," in *Visions of the East: Orientalism in Film*, ed. Matthew Bernstein and Gaylyn Studlar (New Brunswick, NJ: Rutgers University Press, 1997), 99–125; Miriam Hansen, *Babel and Babylon: Spectatorship in American Silent Film* (Cambridge, MA: Harvard University Press, 1991); Amy Koritz, "Dancing the Orient for England: Maud Allen's *The Vision of Salome*," in *Meaning in Motion: New Cultural Studies of Dance*, ed. Jane Desmond (Durham, NC: Duke University Press, 1997), 133–52; Toni Bentley, *Sisters of Salome* (New Haven, CT: Yale University Press, 2002); Mari Yoshihara, *Embracing the East: White Women and American Orientalism* (New York: Oxford University Press, 2003).
25. Studlar, "'Out-Salomeing Salome,'" 105–6.
26. Ella Shohat, "Gender and Culture of Empire: Toward a Feminist Ethnography of the Cinema," in *Visions of the East: Orientalism in Film*, ed. Matthew Bernstein and Gaylyn Studlar (New Brunswick, NJ: Rutgers University Press, 1997), 40.
27. "The Vampires" may have also been the name given to the musical number performed by this "bevy of exotic beauties" at the Coconut Grove ("Coconut Grove," report, 22 January 1919, box 33, C14, NYPL). Susan McClary notes the "radical interchangeability of exotic types for the cultural Orientalist: Persian, Greek, Jewish, Spanish, African—all wash together in an undifferentiated realm of Otherness," suggesting that the many guises these women took were important only in marking them all as exotic, not because the individual cultures that their garb was meant to invoke had special meaning in and of themselves (*Georges Bizet: Carmen* [Cambridge: Cambridge University Press, 1992], 30). Again, though, this interchangeability is contextually specific and may not have been true in other situations.
28. As mentioned in chapter 1, Bara's promoters released the story that her stage name had been chosen because it is an anagram for "Arab death"—a useful notion considering the range of orientalist roles that she played. Furthermore, according to David W. Menefee, the studio also promoted her as having been "born in Egypt in the shadow of the Sphinx, half-Arab and half-French" (*The First Female Stars: Women of the Silent Era* [Westport, CT: Praeger, 2004], 2).
29. See Irving Kolodin, *The Story of the Metropolitan Opera, 1883–1950: A Candid History* (New York: Knopf, 1953).
30. See Catherine Clément, *Opera, or the Undoing of Women*, trans. Betsy Wing (Minneapolis: University of Minnesota Press, 1988).
31. "Coconut Grove," report, 22 January 1919, box 33, C14, NYPL.

32. Lewis A. Erenberg also notes this collapse of space. He calls this an "action environment" because of the interaction between performers and clients (*Steppin' Out: New York Nightlife and the Transformation of American Culture, 1890–1930* [Westport, CT: Greenwood, 1981], 114–45).

33. "Coconut Grove," report, 22 January 1919, box 33, C14, NYPL.

34. For an excellent history of the change in Parisian audience participation from 1750 to 1850, see James H. Johnson, *Listening in Paris: A Cultural History* (Berkeley: University of California Press, 1995). Johnson tells how audiences went from being interactive to being silent and docile. For more on how danger was narrated for female performers, see the next chapter.

35. Quoted in Ella Shohat, *Taboo Memories, Diasporic Voices* (Durham, NC: Duke University Press, 2006), 41.

36. Gaylyn Studlar describes the doubleness of this kind of performative subjectivity and its limits in relationship to orientalist fantasy film of the time as allowing "women a fantasy release while they still (paradoxically) satisfied the regulatory demands of [bourgeois] morality" (*The Mad Masquerade: Stardom and Masculinity in the Jazz Age* [New York: Columbia University Press, 1996], 116).

37. Derrida, *Archive Fever*, 48.

38. Lisa Lowe, "Intimacies of Four Continents," in *Haunted by Empire*, ed. Ann Laura Stoler (Durham, NC: Duke University Press), 191–212.

39. Ahmed, *Queer Phenomenology*, 121.

40. Though respectability became a possibility for formal performances like those of Walker, vice investigators saw black women's belly dancing in the much less formal environment of cabaret dance floors as a cause for alarm. One report from 1929 noted the goings-on at the Lenox Avenue Club, a black and tan establishment in Harlem, where black and white patrons and performers could mix during times of legal racial segregation: "The dancing was not supervised in any manner as two couples were observed standing almost still in the center of the floor and doing sort of a hootchy-kootchy dance, in that they would rub their bodies together, without interference on the part of the management and in plain view of everyone" ("Lenox Avenue Club," report, 26–27 September 1929, box 36, folder 3, C14, NYPL). The vice investigator finds out from a waiter that this is normal for the club, and that the management does not like to interfere with anyone's "good time."

41. Daphne Ann Brooks, *Bodies in Dissent: Spectacular Performances of Race and Freedom, 1850–1910* (Durham, NC: Duke University Press, 2006), 328.

42. Ibid.

43. Ibid., 338.

44. Brooks notes that "by breaking the color line in modern dance and performing her own version of Salome, Walker staged her own coup of dominant cultural forms and recentered them in the context of all-black theatrical narrative" (ibid., 333).

45. J. Brown, *Babylon Girls*, 185.

46. Ibid., 182.

47. Hazel V. Carby, *Cultures in Babylon: Black Britain and African America* (New York: Verso, 1999), 23.

48. J. Brown, *Babylon Girls*, 158.

49. Sara Ahmed, *Strange Encounters: Embodied Others in Post-Coloniality* (New York: Routledge, 2000), 21–22.

50. For more on late twentieth-century queer tourism, see Jasbir Puar, ed., "Queer Tourism: Geographies of Globalization," special issue, GLQ 8, nos. 1–2 (2002); M. Jacqui Alexander, *Pedagogies of Crossing: Meditations on Feminism, Sexual Politics, Memory, and the Sacred* (Durham, NC: Duke University Press, 2006), 66–90; Massad, *Desiring Arabs*, 160–90.

51. Quoted in Massad, *Desiring Arabs*, 10.

52. Nina Miller, *Making Love Modern: The Intimate Public Worlds of New York's Literary Women* (New York: Oxford University Press, 1999), 175.

53. Edward Said, *Culture and Imperialism* (New York: Vintage, 1993), 5 (emphasis added).

54. N. Miller, *Making Love Modern*, 175.

55. Stephen Knadler, "Sweetback Style: Wallace Thurman and a Queer Harlem Renaissance," MFS 48, no. 4 (2002): 931.

56. For more on the Harlem ball scene, see Eric Garber, "A Spectacle in Color: The Lesbian and Gay Subculture of Jazz Age Harlem," in *Hidden from History: Reclaiming the Gay and Lesbian Past*, ed. Martin B. Duberman, Martha Vicinus, and George Chauncey Jr. (New York: New American Library, 1989), 324–25.

57. "Greenwich Village Affairs," undated subsequent draft of a report originally drafted in 1917, C14, NYPL.

58. Marjorie Garber, *Vested Interests: Cross-Dressing and Cultural Anxiety* (New York: Routledge, 1992), 304–52.

59. Derrida, *Archive Fever*, 94.

60. George Melford, dir., *The Sheik*, 1921, special ed., with *The Son of the Sheik*, 1926 (Chatsworth, CA: Paramount Pictures/Image Entertainment, 2002, DVD).

61. D. Onivas, "Burning Sands: An Answer to 'The Sheik,'" (New York: Richmond-Robbins, 1922); Harry B. Smith (lyricist), Francis Wheeler (lyricist), and Ted Snyder (composer), "The Sheik of Araby" (New York: Waterson, Berlin, and Snyder, 1921). "The Sheik of Araby" has become a jazz standard, recorded by artists such as Sidney Bechet, Eddie Condon, Duke Ellington, Louis Armstrong, Don Byas, Charlie Christian, Nat King Cole, Art Tatum, Jack Teagarden, and Albert Ammons, as well as by more modern performers like Arlo Guthrie and the Beatles.

62. Carl Van Vechten, *Nigger Heaven* (1926; repr., Urbana: University of Illinois Press, 2000).

63. There are exceptions, discussed in chapter 1. For instance, newspaper accounts

ascribed aberrational hypersexuality to Vivian Gordon's fictional affair with white lover Harry M. Joralman, described as "a Caliph of Bagdad." However, he also did not conquer this orientalization or orientation.

64. Fats Waller, "The Sheik of Araby," lyrics by Harry B. Smith, composed by Ted Snyder, recorded in 1939, *Very Best of Fats Waller*, RCA B000050G8C, 2000, compact disc.

65. Fletcher Henderson with Ethel Finnie, "He Wasn't Born in Araby, but He's a Sheikin' Fool," composed by Edgar Dowell and lyrics by Andy Razaf, recorded on April 1924, on *Fletcher Henderson & the Blues Singers, Volume 2*, Document Records DOCD-5343, 1995, compact disc. The lyrics in this version of the song seems to hold some specifically queer potential: "All the gals and yellas, too, follow him around the town the whole day through," with "yellas" possibly replacing "fellas" to clean up the song in the recording. The song originally appeared in Lew Leslie's *Plantation Revue* at the Winter Garden Theatre in 1923 and was first recorded by Lena Wilson with Porter Grainger in March 1924 (Barry Singer, *Black and Blue: The Life and Lyrics of Andy Razaf* [New York: Schirmer, 1992], 132–33).

66. In an instrumental version of "The Sheik of Araby," recorded by the band of the famous saxophone player Rudy Wiedoeft in 1921 (he also recorded "Karavan" in 1919, "When Buddha Smiles" in 1921, and "Suez" in 1922, all of which feature orientalist musical themes), the creation of an imperial masculine self through performance is more ambiguous (Rudy Wiedoeft's Californians, "The Sheik of Araby," recorded in 1921, *The Roaring Twenties*, Intersound 1401, 1997, 4 compact discs). Wiedoeft and his band performed orientalist music through the inclusion of a flatted minor third, similar to "Palesteena." In performance, Wiedoeft and his band might be said to inhabit the same position as Lena, inasmuch as they are American musicians performing songs meant to mimic the sounds of the Orient. However, Wiedoeft had a reputation as one of the best saxophone players around, and the recording also features an oboe, which takes the Orientalist lead. Here the orientalist signifiers are controlled through a musical language of virtuosity, especially in the absence of the first-person perspective given by the lyrics. Wiedoeft's performance could be read through his expertise, in contrast to that of an Arab musician for whom such sounds would come naturally, thus creating Wiedoeft's masterful subjecthood through imperial logic.

67. Van Vechten, *Nigger Heaven*, 6.

68. Kathleen Pfeiffer, introduction to ibid., xxv.

69. Knadler, "Sweetback Style," 900–901. Shane Vogel also lists "sheik" among terms like "fairies," "pansies," "sweetmen," "bull dikes," and "bulldaggers" that signify queerness, though I think the example from Van Vechten tells us that this was not an overdetermined meaning at the time (*The Scene of Harlem Cabaret: Race, Sexuality, Performance* [Chicago: University of Chicago Press, 2009], 20, 135).

70. Knadler, "Sweetback Style," 900; Monica Miller, *Slaves to Fashion: Black Dandy-*

ism and the Styling of Black Diasporic Identity (Durham, NC: Duke University Press, 2009), 5.

71. Miller, *Slaves to Fashion*, 5.

72. Quoted in J. Brown, *Babylon Girls*, 210. Although Brown marks this as a moment that possibly dissolves heterosexism, I am viewing it here more as a particular gendered performance.

4. DREAMING OF ARABY

1. Irving Berlin, "Araby" (New York: Waterson, Berlin, and Snyder, 1915).

2. George Melford, dir., *The Sheik*, 1921, special ed., with *The Son of the Sheik*, 1926 (Chatsworth, CA: Paramount Pictures/Image Entertainment, 2002, DVD); Raoul Walsh, dir., *The Thief of Baghdad: An Arabian Nights Fantasy*, 1924, deluxe ed. (Douglas Fairbanks Pictures/Kino Video, 2004, DVD). *The Thief of Baghdad* took place in settings similar to those of the uptown nightclubs and cabarets, settings where the East is manufactured and then populated by Americans looking for exotic adventure. Though there were no Salomé dances in the film, the viewer was treated to exotic sets, props, and revealing costumes inhabited, manipulated, and worn mostly by white actors and actresses. For discussions of images of the Orient in film, see Gina Marchetti, *Romance and the "Yellow Peril": Race, Sex, and Discursive Strategies in Hollywood Fiction* (Berkeley: University of California Press, 1993); Robert Lee, *Orientals: Asian Americans in Popular Culture* (Philadelphia: Temple University Press, 1999).

3. Beginning in the late nineteenth century, composers and lyricists of popular music began using West Asian and North African themes. Orientalisms were already "well established in fashion, design, and the arts" prior to the advent of the 1920s, though the 1920s and 1930s arguably saw their escalation (Gaylyn Studlar, "'Out-Salomeing Salome': Dance, the New Woman, and Fan Magazine Orientalism," in *Visions of the East: Orientalism in Film*, ed. Matthew Bernstein and Gaylyn Studlar [New Brunswick, NJ: Rutgers University Press, 1997], 103).

4. Lisa Lowe, "The Intimacies of Four Continents," in *Haunted by Empire: Geographies of Intimacy in North American History*, ed. Ann Laura Stoler (Durham, NC: Duke University Press, 2006), 191–212; Ann Laura Stoler, "Tense and Tender Ties: The Politics of Comparison in North American History and (Post) Colonial Studies," in *Haunted by Empire*, 23–67. I am thinking of Yinka Shonibare's sculptural pieces that feature often headless mannequins in Victorian-style clothing made from batik cloth, such as *The Swing (after Fragonard)* (2001) and *How to Blow Up Two Heads at Once (Ladies)* (2006). The cloth, which has become synonymous with Africa, originated in Indonesia, which became a Dutch colony. The cloth was copied in European factories and distributed in colonial Africa. Shonibare's art demonstrates how multiple spaces of imperialism can come together both ideologically and materially (in this case, in both senses of the word). For more on Shonibare's use of cloth see Rachel Kent, "Time and Trans-

formation in the Art of Yinka Shonibare MBE," in *Yinka Shonibare, MBE*, ed. Rachel Kent, Robert Hobbs, and Anthony Downey (New York: Prestel, 2008), 12–23.

5. Ann Laura Stoler, *Along the Archival Grain: Epistemic and Colonial Common Sense* (Princeton, NJ: Princeton University Press, 2009), 107.

6. Though not the only sexual imperial discourses that existed during the Jazz Age, the orientalist discourses explored in this chapter are also important for what they foreshadow during the next century. Although scholars have followed the U.S. imagination of these geographical areas and their inhabitants after World War II, when the United States had a more direct imperial interest in the regions, the early part of the twentieth century from the 1900s to 1930s has not been fully explored, and my work here only adds to the conversation that has begun about this time period. The images, performances, and sounds explored here anticipate the Islamophobia that reached fever pitch at the end of the twentieth century and beginning of the twenty-first. Whereas the affiliations between black communities in the United States and the peoples of West Asia and North Africa anticipate the spread of Islam across black communities at home. For more on Islamophobia, see Junaid Rana, "The Story of Islamophobia," *Souls* 9, no. 2 (2007): 148–61.

7. Report, 8 February 1918, box 33; "Hotel Martinique," report, 9 March 1918, box 33; "Egyptian Garden," report, 21 February 1929, box 36; "The Old Lybia," report, 3 November 1921, box 34, Committee of Fourteen Records, 1905–32, Rare Books and Manuscripts Division, New York Public Library, New York, NY (hereafter cited as C14, NYPL).

8. Sophie Tucker, "In Old King Tutankhamen's Day," recorded in 1923, *The Roaring Twenties*, Waves 1400, 1997, 4 compact discs.

9. Building on Michel Foucault's definition, they describe a method as being heterotopic as "it refuses to maintain that objects of comparison [such as races, genders, and sexualities] are static, unchanging, and empirically observable, and refuses to render illegible the shifting configurations of power that define stuck objects in the first place," Grace Kyungwon Hong and Roderick A. Ferguson, introduction to *Strange Affinities: The Gender and Sexual Politics of Comparative Racialization* (Durham, NC: Duke University Press), 9.

10. Caroline Goeser, *Picturing the New Negro: Harlem Renaissance Print Culture and Modern Black Identity* (Lawrence: University Press of Kansas, 2007), 6.

11. Amy Helene Kirschke, *Art in Crisis: W. E. B. Du Bois and the Struggle for African American Identity and Memory* (Bloomington: Indiana University Press, 2007), 144.

12. Paul Morand, *New York*, trans. Hamish Miles (1929; repr., New York: Henry Holt, 1930), 239.

13. Ibid., 270. Faustin Soulouque was president and emperor of Haiti in the middle of the nineteenth century.

14. Linda Gordon, "Internal Colonialism and Gender," in *Haunted by Empire*, 428.
15. Ibid., 431.
16. David Levering Lewis, *When Harlem Was in Vogue* (New York: Vintage, 1982), 164.
17. Irving Berlin, "Puttin' on the Ritz" (New York: Waterson, Berlin, and Snyder, 1929). All references to this song are from the recording by Fred Astaire, "Puttin' on the Ritz," recorded in 1930, *The Roaring Twenties*, Intersound, 1401, 1997, 4 compact discs. Berlin rewrote the lyrics for the film *Blue Skies*, changing the location of the song's action to Park Avenue (Stuart Heisler and Mark Sandrich, dirs., *Blue Skies*, 1946, special ed., with *Birth of the Blues*, 1941 [Universal City, CA: Paramount/Universal Studios, 2003, DVD]).
18. In the sheet music from 1929, the wording is "why don't you go where Harlem sits?" (Berlin, "Puttin' on the Ritz"), but both Harry Richman, who originally recorded the song for the Broadway show *Puttin' on the Ritz*, and Fred Astaire, who popularized it, sang "flits."
19. Wallace Thurman, *The Collected Writings of Wallace Thurman: A Harlem Renaissance Reader*, ed. Amritjit Singh and Daniel M. Scott III (New Brunswick, NJ: Rutgers University Press, 2003), 39. His essays on touring Harlem also include "Harlem: A Vivid Word Picture of the World's Greatest Negro City" (1927); "Harlem Facets" (1927); "Harlem Directory: Where to Go and What to Do When in Harlem" (1928); "Harlemese" (1929); "Few Know Real Harlem, the City of Surprises: Quarter Million Negroes Form a Moving, Colorful Pageant of Life" (1929); and "Harlem House Rent Parties" (unpublished). See ibid., 32–39, 63–71, and 73–74.
20. Alain Locke, ed., *The New Negro: An Interpretation* (1925; repr., New York: Johnson Reprint, 1968).
21. Fats Waller, "In Harlem's Araby," recorded May 1924, *The Complete Recorded Works, Volume 1*, JSP Records, JSP927A, 2007, 4 compact discs.
22. According to Marcus Garvey, Grey was a "scoundrel" because he embezzled monies from both the Black Star Line and the UNIA. Marcus Garvey, *The Philosophy and Opinions of Marcus Garvey*, ed. Amy Jacques Garvey (Dover, MA: Majority Press, 1986), 188.
23. Edgar M. Grey, "White Cabaret Keepers Conduct Dives," 10 December 1926, *New York News*, newspaper clipping, Box 82, C14, NYPL.
24. Ann Laura Stoler, *Carnal Knowledge and Imperial Power: Race and the Intimate in Colonial Rule* (Berkeley: University of California Press, 2002), 160.
25. Grey wrote other articles expressing his suspicion of the interracial and international character of Harlem and how it affected the economic prospects of the black residents. For instance, in his "Intimate Glimpses of Harlem," he notes that Harlem's "population is not made up of Negroes alone, but of mixed bloods generally—Mexicans, Porto Ricans, Cubans, East Indians, Chinese, Japanese, half-Jews, Jews, Filipinos and a few Negroes" (4). This multiculturalism, though is a threat according to Grey, where Jewish people squeeze black residents for

rent, and Asian American restauranteurs have taken the clientele from "so-called Negro food houses" (4). Edgar M. Grey, "Intimate Glimpses of Harlem," *New York Amsterdam News*, 27 August 1927, 4.

26. Grey, "White Cabaret Keepers Conduct Dives." This string of associations occurs earlier in the article than the part quoted above.

27. Langston Hughes, "Jazzonia," in Locke, *The New Negro*, 226.

28. Kirschke, *Art in Crisis*, 147.

29. Kirschke argues that "Du Bois also promoted African art as an inspiration for the 'high culture' of modern art" (ibid., 153).

30. Ella Shohat, *Taboo Memories, Diasporic Voices* (Durham, NC: Duke University Press, 2006), 166–200.

31. Richard J. Powell, *Black Art: A Cultural History*, 2nd ed. (London: Thames and Hudson, 2002), 44. Goeser also uses this terminology (*Picturing the New Negro*, 34).

32. Goeser, *Picturing the New Negro*, 29.

33. Wallace Thurman, ed. FIRE!! *Devoted to Younger Negro Artists* (1926; repr., Westport, CT: Negro Universities Press, 1970).

34. Goeser, *Picturing the New Negro*, 30. Troublingly, Goeser sees Egypt is linked to "civilization" while the rest of Africa is implicitly "tribal."

35. Kirschke also notes that Douglas used this in his 1927 illustration *The Burden of Black Womanhood*, a technique influenced by his relationship with the artist Winold Reiss (Amy Helene Kirschke, *Aaron Douglas: Art, Race, and the Harlem Renaissance* [Jackson: University Press of Mississippi, 1995], 30, 83).

36. Tucker, "In Old King Tutankhamen's Day." All subsequent references to this song are from this recording.

37. "Coon shouter" was a name for white singers who built a repertoire of songs associated with the African American tradition. For more on coon shouters, see Nicholas E. Tawa, *The Way to Tin Pan Alley: American Popular Song, 1866–1910* (New York: Schirmer, 1990), 65, 185.

38. Jayna Brown, *Babylon Girls: Black Women Performers and the Shaping of the Modern* (Durham, NC: Duke University Press, 2008), 214.

39. Timothy Mitchell, *Rule of Experts: Egypt, Techno-Politics, Modernity* (Berkeley: University of California Press, 2002), 181–82.

40. "Americans Saved Tutankhamen Treasures, Halting Their Own Work to Serve Science," *New York Times*, 28 January 1923.

41. "Tutankhamen's Tomb Is Revising History; It Reveals That Egypt Reached the Zenith in Power and Arts in His Period," *New York Times*, 27 December 1922.

42. Ann Laura Stoler and Carole McGranahan, "Introduction: Refiguring Imperial Terrains," in *Imperial Formations*, ed. Ann Laura Stoler, Carole McGranahan, and Peter Perdue (Santa Fe, NM: School for Advanced Research Press, 2007), 26.

43. Jack Yellen (lyricist) and Milton Ager (composer), "Lovin' Sam (The Sheik of Alabam)" (New York: Ager, Yellen, Bornstein, 1922).

44. Jodi A. Byrd, *The Transit of Empire: Indigenous Critiques of Colonialism* (Minneapolis: University of Minnesota Press, 2011), xix.

45. J. Smeaton Chase, *Our Araby: Palm Springs and the Garden of the Sun* (New York: J. Smeaton Chase, 1923), 16.

46. Ibid., 42.

47. Ibid., 47–48.

48. Ibid., 48.

49. Ibid.

50. Shohat, *Taboo Memories*, 32.

51. Ibid.

52. Chase, *Our Araby*, 48–49.

53. Shohat notes that this desire to master land is written through a language of "masculinist desire" to conquer the feminine: "The masculinist desire of mastering a new land is deeply linked to colonial history and even to its contemporary companion, philosophy, in which epistemology partially modeled itself on geography. The traditional discourse on nature as feminine—for example, Francis Bacon's idea that insofar as we learn the laws of nature through science, we become her master, as we are now in ignorance, 'her thralls'—gains, within the colonial context, clear geopolitical implications" ("Gender and Culture of Empire: Toward a Feminist Ethnography of the Cinema," in *Visions of the East: Orientalism in Film*, ed. Matthew Bernstein and Gaylyn Studlar [New Brunswick, NJ: Rutgers University Press, 1997], 27).

54. Ibid., 28.

55. I borrow this notion of "anti-conquest" from Mary Louise Pratt, *Imperial Eyes: Travel Writing and Transculturation* (New York: Routledge, 1992), 7.

56. Brian T. Edwards, *Morocco Bound: Disorienting America's Maghreb, from Casablanca to the Marrakech Express* (Durham, NC: Duke University Press, 2005), 32.

57. Ibid.

58. Chase, *Our Araby*, 19.

59. Shari M. Huhndorf, *Going Native: Indians in the American Cultural Imagination* (Ithaca, NY: Cornell University Press, 2001), 22.

60. Chase, *Our Araby*, 18.

61. Ibid., 42.

62. Ibid., 42–43.

CONCLUSION: ACADEMIC INDISCRETIONS

1. Robert J. C. Young's *Colonial Desire: Hybridity in Theory, Culture, and Race* (New York: Routledge, 1995) is one of the classic postcolonial texts that brings the race and sexuality of empire home, in his case to London. See especially 1–2.

2. Kandice Chuh, *Imagine Otherwise: On Asian American Critique* (Durham, NC: Duke University Press, 2003), x.

3. Grace Kyungwon Hong and Roderick A. Ferguson, introduction to *Strange Af-*

finities: *The Gender and Sexual Politics of Comparative Racialization*, ed. Grace Kyungwon Hong and Roderick A. Ferguson (Durham, NC: Duke University Press, 2011), 1–2.

4. Cynthia G. Franklin, *Academic Lives: Memoir, Cultural Theory, and the University Today* (Athens: University of Georgia Press, 2009), 136–37.

5. George Lipsitz, *American Studies in a Moment of Danger* (Minneapolis: University of Minnesota Press, 2011), 27, 315.

6. Kevin K. Gaines, *American Africans in Ghana: Black Expatriates and the Civil Rights Era* (Chapel Hill: University of North Carolina Press, 2006), 277.

7. Ferguson, *Aberrations in Black*, 83.

8. Ibid., 139.

9. Lisa Lowe, *Immigrant Acts: On Asian American Cultural Politics* (Durham, NC: Duke University Press, 1996), 67.

10. Michel Foucault, *The History of Sexuality*, vol. 1, *An Introduction*, trans. Robert Hurley (New York: Vintage, 1990), 17–35.

11. I have drawn my reading of Jacques Derrida's différance from his "Différance," trans. Alan Bass, in *Critical Theory since 1965*, ed. Hazard Adams and Leroy Searle (Tallahassee: Florida State University Press, 1986), 120–36. The work also appears in Jacques Derrida, *A Derrida Reader: Between the Blinds*, ed. Peggy Kamuf, trans. Alan Bass (New York: Columbia University Press, 1991), 61–79.

BIBLIOGRAPHY

....

LIBRARIES AND ARCHIVES

Beinecke Rare Book and Manuscript Library, Yale University, New Haven, CT
    The James Weldon Johnson Collection

Columbia University, New York, NY
    Alfred A. Knopf Oral History Interview
    August Mencken Oral History Interview
    Carl Van Vechten Oral History Interview
    George Samuel Schuyler Oral History Interview
    Jazz Project Oral History Collection
    Jimmy Walker Oral History Interview
    Popular Arts Oral History Collection
    Richard Rodgers Oral History Interview

Lesbian Herstory Archives, Brooklyn, NY

New York City Department of Records and Information Services, City Hall Library
and Municipal Archives, New York, NY (NYC)
    City Council, 1647–1977—Board of Aldermen (Minutes from the Board of
    Aldermen)
    Minutes from the Board of Estimate and Apportionment

New York City Department of Records and Information Services, Municipal
Archives, New York, NY
    John F. Hylan, Mayor's Papers
    James Walker, Mayor's Papers

New York Public Library, Special Collections, Stephen A. Schwarzman Building,
New York, NY (NYPL)
    Carl Van Vechten Papers
    Committee of Fifteen Records, 1900–1901
    Committee of Fourteen Records, 1905–32 (C14)

New York Public Library for the Performing Arts
Eva Gautier Letters

New York Public Library Schomburg Center for Research in Black Culture, New York, NY (SC)
Aaron Douglas Papers
Alberta Hunter Papers
Arthur Alonso Schomburg Papers
Bert Williams Portrait Collection
Bill Robinson Portrait Collection
Charles Gilpin Photograph Collection
Claude McKay Letters and Manuscripts
David Levering Lewis, "Voices from the Renaissance" Collection
Ethel Waters Portrait Collection
Eubie Blake Interviews
Fletcher Henderson Portrait Collection
George Walker Portrait Collection
George Washington Glover Papers
Glenn Carrington Papers
Gwendolyn Bennett Papers
J. Rosamond Johnson Portrait Collection
Josephine Baker Portrait Collection
Jules Bledsoe Papers
Katherine Handy Lewis Papers
Langston Hughes Vertical Files
Lawrence Brown Papers
Louis Armstrong Jazz Oral History Project
Louis Armstrong Portrait Collection
Ma Rainey Portrait Collection
Mamie Smith Portrait Collection
Marcus Garvey Portrait Collection
Negro Labor Committee Records
Paul Robeson Collection
Ralph J. Bunche Papers
Regina Andrews Photograph Collection
Samuel Edwin Heyward Papers
Victoria Spivey Photograph Collection
Voices from the Renaissance Collection
Wilhelmina Adams Papers and Photograph Collection
William Pickens Papers

NEWSPAPERS AND PERIODICALS

New York Amsterdam News
New York Evening Graphic
New York Evening Journal
New York Times
Saturday News

PUBLISHED PRIMARY SOURCES

Bercovici, Konrad. *Around the World in New York*. New York: Century, 1924.

Bulosan, Carlos. *America Is in the Heart: A Personal History*. 1946. Reprint, Seattle: University of Washington Press, 1973.

Chase, J. Smeaton. *Our Araby: Palm Springs and the Garden of the Sun*. New York: J. Smeaton Chase, 1923.

Ellison, Ralph. *Invisible Man*. New York: Vintage, 1947.

Fisher, Rudolph. "The City of Refuge." In *The New Negro: An Interpretation*. Edited by Alain Locke, 57–74. 1925. Reprint, New York: Johnson Reprint, 1968.

Fitzgerald, Zelda. *Save Me the Waltz*. 1932. Reprint, London: Arcturus, 1967.

Hughes, Langston. "Jazzonia." In *The New Negro: An Interpretation*. Edited by Alain Locke, 226. 1925. Reprint, New York: Johnson Reprint, 1968.

———. "When Harlem Was in Vogue." *Town and Country*, July 1940, 64.

Johnson, James Weldon. *Black Manhattan*. New York: Knopf, 1930.

Kisseloff, Jeff, ed. *You Must Remember This: An Oral History of Manhattan from 1892 to World War II*. New York: Harcourt Brace Jovanovich, 1989.

Krafft-Ebing, Richard von. *Psychopathia Sexualis: With Especial Reference to the Antipathic Sexual Instinct*. 12th ed. Translated by Franklin S. Klaf. New York: Stein and Day, 1965.

Larsen, Nella. *Quicksand and Passing*. Edited by Deborah E. McDowell. New Brunswick, NJ: Rutgers University Press, 1986.

Lasker, Bruno. *Filipino Immigration to the Continental United States and to Hawaii*. 1931. Reprint, New York: Arno, 1969.

Locke, Alain, ed. *The New Negro: An Interpretation*. 1925. Reprint, New York: Johnson Reprint, 1968.

Morand, Paul. *New York*. Translated by Hamish Miles. 1929. Reprint, New York: Henry Holt, 1930.

Norden, Helen Brown. *The Hussy's Handbook*. New York: Arden, 1942.

Nugent, Richard Bruce. *Gay Rebel of the Harlem Renaissance: Selections from the Work of Richard Bruce Nugent*. Edited by Thomas H. Wirth. Durham, NC: Duke University Press, 2002.

———. "The Geisha Man." Unpublished manuscript, 1928. (The second part of this manuscript was published in 2002 in *Gay Rebel of the Harlem Renaissance: Selections from the Work of Richard Bruce Nugent*.) Copyright 2002, 2012 Thomas H. Wirth.

———. "Smoke, Lilies and Jade." In *FIRE!! Devoted to Younger Negro Artists*. Edited by Wallace Thurman, 33–39. 1926. Reprint, Westport, CT: Negro Universities Press, 1970.

Thurman, Wallace. *The Blacker the Berry. . . .* 1929. Reprint, New York: Collier, 1970.

———. *The Collected Writings of Wallace Thurman: A Harlem Renaissance Reader.* Edited by Amritjit Singh and Daniel M. Scott III. New Brunswick, NJ: Rutgers University Press, 2003.

———, ed. *FIRE!! Devoted to Younger Negro Artists.* 1926. Reprint, Westport, CT: Negro Universities Press, 1970.

———. *Infants of the Spring.* 1932. Reprint, New York: Random House, 1999.

———. *Negro Life in New York's Harlem: A Lively Picture of a Popular and Interesting Section.* Girard, KS: Haldeman-Julius, 1927.

Thurman, Wallace, and William Jourdan Rapp. "Few Know Real Harlem, the City of Surprises: Quarter Million Negroes Form a Moving, Colorful Pageant of Life." In *The Collected Writings of Wallace Thurman: A Harlem Renaissance Reader.* Edited by Amritjit Singh and Daniel M. Scott III, 66–71. New Brunswick, NJ: Rutgers University Press, 2003.

Van Vechten, Carl. *Nigger Heaven.* 1926. Reprint, Urbana: University of Illinois Press, 2000.

SECONDARY SOURCES

Ahmed, Sara. *Queer Phenomenology: Orientations, Objects, Others.* Durham, NC: Duke University Press, 2006.

———. *Strange Encounters: Embodied Others in Post-Coloniality.* New York: Routledge, 2000.

Alexander, M. Jacqui. *Pedagogies of Crossing: Meditations on Feminism, Sexual Politics, Memory, and the Sacred.* Durham, NC: Duke University Press, 2006.

Allen, Robert C. *Horrible Prettiness: Burlesque and American Culture.* Chapel Hill: University of North Carolina Press, 1991.

Anzaldúa, Gloria. *Borderlands / La Frontera: The New Mestiza.* 2nd ed. San Francisco: Aunt Lute, 1987.

Arden, Eugene. "The Early Harlem Novel." *Phylon Quarterly* 20, no. 1 (1959): 25–31.

Ashcroft, Bill, Gareth Griffiths, and Helen Tiffin. *The Empire Writes Back: Theory and Practice in Post-Colonial Literatures.* New York: Routledge, 1989.

Auslander, Leora. "The Gendering of Consumer Practices in Nineteenth-Century France." In *The Sex of Things: Gender and Consumption in Historical Perspective.* Edited by Victoria De Grazia, 79–112. Berkeley: University of California Press, 1996.

Bakhtin, Mikhail. "Social Heteroglossia." In *The Bakhtin Reader: Selected Writings of Bakhtin, Medvedev, Voloshinov.* Edited by Pam Morris, 73–81. London: Arnold, 1994.

Barthes, Roland. *Empire of Signs.* Translated by Richard Howard. New York: Hill and Wang, 1982.

Bartky, Sandra Lee. "Foucault, Femininity, and the Modernization of Patriarchal Power." In *Feminism and Foucault: Reflections on Resistance*. Edited by Irene Diamond and Lee Quinby, 61–86. Boston: Northeastern University Press, 1988.

Bascara, Victor. "'A Vaudeville against Coconut Trees': Colonialism, Contradiction, and Coming Out in Michael Magnaye's *White Christmas*." In *Q & A: Queer in Asian America*. Edited by David L. Eng and Alice Y. Hom, 95–114. Philadelphia: Temple University Press, 1998.

Bederman, Gail. *Manliness and Civilization: A Cultural History of Gender and Race in the United States, 1880–1917*. Chicago: University of Chicago Press, 1995.

Benjamin, Walter. *Illuminations: Essays and Reflections*. Edited with an introduction by Hannah Arendt. Translated by Harry Zohn. New York: Schocken, 1969.

———. *Reflections: Essays, Aphorisms, Autobiographical Writings*. Edited by Peter Demetz. Translated by Edmund Jephcott. New York: Harcourt Brace Jovanovich, 1978.

Bentley, Toni. *Sisters of Salome*. New Haven, CT: Yale University Press, 2002.

Bhabha, Homi K. *The Location of Culture*. New York: Routledge, 1994.

Blanchard, Pascal, Eric Deroo, and Gilles Manceron. *Le Paris noir*. Paris: Hazan, 2001.

Bontemps, Arna, ed. *The Harlem Renaissance Remembered*. New York: Dodd, Mead, 1972.

Bornstein, Kate. *Gender Outlaw: On Men, Women, and the Rest of Us*. New York: Vintage, 1993.

Bramen, Carrie Tirado. "The Urban Picturesque and the Spectacle of Americanization." *American Quarterly* 52 (September 2000): 444–77.

Brody, Jennifer DeVere. *Impossible Purities: Blackness, Femininity, and Victorian Culture*. Durham, NC: Duke University Press, 1998.

Brooks, Daphne Ann. *Bodies in Dissent: Spectacular Performances of Race and Freedom, 1850–1910*. Durham, NC: Duke University Press, 2006.

———. "The End of the Line: Josephine Baker and the Politics of Black Women's Corporeal Comedy." *s&F Online* 6, nos. 1–2 (2007–8). Accessed 23 May 2013, http://sfonline.barnard.edu/baker/brooks_01.htm.

Brown, Jayna. *Babylon Girls: Black Women Performers and the Shaping of the Modern*. Durham, NC: Duke University Press, 2008.

Brown, Sterling A. "The American Race Problem as Reflected in American Literature." *Journal of Negro Education* 8, no. 3 (1939): 275–90.

———. "Negro Character as Seen by White Authors." *Journal of Negro Education* 2 (1933): 179–203.

Bryant, Rebecca A. "Shaking Big Shoulders: Music and Dance Culture in Chicago, 1910–1925." PhD diss., University of Illinois, Urbana-Champaign, 2003.

———. "Shaking Things Up: Popularizing the Shimmy in America." *American Music* 20, no. 2 (2002): 168–87.

Butler, Judith. *Gender Trouble: Feminism and the Subversion of Identity*. New York: Routledge, 1990.

Byrd, Jodie A. *The Transit of Empire: Indigenous Critiques of Colonialism*. Minneapolis: University of Minnesota Press, 2011.

Cacho, Lisa Marie. "Disciplinary Fictions: The Sociality of Private Problems in Contemporary California." PhD diss., University of California, San Diego, 2002.

———. "The People of California Are Suffering: The Ideology of White Injury in Discourses of Immigration." *Cultural Values* 4, no. 4 (2000): 389–418.

———. *Social Death: Racialized Rightlessness and the Criminalization of the Unprotected*. New York: New York University Press, 2012.

Carbado, Devon W., Dwight A. McBride, and Donald Weise, eds. *Black Like Us: A Century of Lesbian, Gay, and Bisexual African American Fiction*. San Francisco: Cleis, 2002.

———. "Richard Bruce Nugent." In *Black Like Us: A Century of Lesbian, Gay, and Bisexual African American Fiction*. Edited by Devon W. Carbado, Dwight A. McBride, and Donald Weise, 73–74. San Francisco: Cleis, 2002.

———. "Wallace Thurman." In *Black Like Us: A Century of Lesbian, Gay, and Bisexual African American Fiction*. Edited by Devon W. Carbado, Dwight A. McBride, and Donald Weise, 63–64. San Francisco: Cleis, 2002.

Carby, Hazel V. *Cultures in Babylon: Black Britain and African America*. New York: Verso, 1999.

———. "'It Jus Be's Dat Way Sometimes': The Sexual Politics of Women's Blues." In *Unequal Sisters: A Multicultural Reader in U.S. Women's History*. 2nd ed. Edited by Ellen Carol Dubois and Vicki Ruiz, 238–49. New York: Routledge, 1994.

———. *Reconstructing Womanhood: The Emergence of the Afro-American Woman Novelist*. New York: Oxford University Press, 1987.

Chan, Jeffery Paul, Frank Chin, Lawson Fusao Inada, and Shawn Wong, eds. *The Big Aiiieeeee! An Anthology of Chinese American and Japanese American Literature*. New York: Meridian, 1991.

Chase, Cheryl. "Hermaphrodites with Attitude." GLQ 4, no. 2 (1998): 189–211.

Chauncey, George, Jr. "Christian Brotherhood or Sexual Perversion? Homosexual Identities and the Construction of Sexual Boundaries in the World War I Era." In *Hidden from History: Reclaiming the Gay and Lesbian Past*. Edited by Martin B. Duberman, Martha Vicinus, and George Chauncey Jr., 194–317. New York: New American Library, 1989.

———. *Gay New York: Gender, Urban Culture, and the Making of the Gay Male World, 1890–1940*. New York: Basic, 1994.

Cheng, Anne Anlin. "Skin Deep: Josephine Baker and the Colonial Fetish." *Camera Obscura* 69 (2008): 35–79.

Chevigny, Paul. *Gigs: Jazz and the Cabaret Laws in New York City*. New York: Routledge, 1991.

Chin, Frank. "Come All Ye Asian American Writers of the Real and the Fake." In *The Big Aiiieeeee! An Anthology of Chinese American and Japanese American Literature*. Edited by Jeffery Paul Chan, Frank Chin, Lawson Fusao Inada, and Shawn Wong, 1–93. New York: Meridian, 1991.

Chow, Rey. *Writing Diaspora: Tactics of Intervention in Contemporary Cultural Studies*. Bloomington: Indiana University Press, 1993.

Chuh, Kandice. *Imagine Otherwise: On Asian American Critique*. Durham, NC: Duke University Press, 2003.

Clément, Catherine. *Opera, or the Undoing of Women*. Translated by Betsy Wing. Minneapolis: University of Minnesota Press, 1988.

Cobb, Michael L. "Insolent Racing, Rough Narrative: The Harlem Renaissance's Impolite Queers." *Callaloo* 23, no. 1 (2000): 328–51.

Collins, Theresa M. *Otto Kahn: Art, Money, and Modern Time*. Chapel Hill: University of North Carolina Press, 2002.

Deleuze, Gilles. *Difference and Repetition*. Translated by Paul Patton. 1968. Reprint, New York: Columbia University Press, 1994.

Deleuze, Gilles, and Félix Guattari. *The Anti-Oedipus: Capitalism and Schizophrenia*. Translated by Robert Hurley, Mark Seem, and Helen R. Lane. Minneapolis: University of Minnesota Press, 1983.

Derrida, Jacques. *Archive Fever: A Freudian Impression*. Translated by Eric Prenowitz. Chicago: University of Chicago Press, 1998.

———. *A Derrida Reader: Between the Blinds*. Edited by Peggy Kamuf. Translated by Alan Bass. New York: Columbia University Press, 1991.

———. "Différance." Translated by Alan Bass. In *Critical Theory since 1965*. Edited by Hazard Adams and Leroy Searle, 120–36. Tallahassee: Florida State University Press, 1986.

———. *Of Grammatology*. Translated by Gayatri Chakravorty Spivak. Baltimore, MD: Johns Hopkins University Press, 1976.

Devor, Holly. FTM: *Female-to-Male Transsexuals in Society*. Bloomington: Indiana University Press, 1997.

Donovan, Brian. "The Peggy Joyce Scandals: Gold Diggers and Whiteness in Jazz-Age America." Paper presented at the Race and Ethnic Studies Institute, Texas A & M University, 5 February 2010.

Douglas, Ann. *Terrible Honesty: Mongrel Manhattan in the 1920s*. New York: Noonday, 1995.

Duberman, Martin B., Martha Vicinus, and George Chauncey Jr., eds. *Hidden from History: Reclaiming the Gay and Lesbian Past*. New York: New American Library, 1989.

Edwards, Brian T. *Morocco Bound: Disorienting America's Maghreb, from Casablanca to the Marrakech Express*. Durham, NC: Duke University Press, 2005.

Eng, David L. "In the Shadows of a Diva: Committing Homosexuality in David Henry Hwang's *M. Butterfly*." In *Asian American Sexualities: Dimensions of the Gay and Lesbian Experience*. Edited by Russell Leong, 131–52. New York: Routledge, 1996.

———. *Racial Castration: Managing Masculinity in Asian America*. Durham, NC: Duke University Press, 2001.

Eng, David L., and Alice Y. Hom, eds. *Q & A: Queer in Asian America*. Philadelphia: Temple University Press, 1998.

Erenberg, Lewis A. *Steppin' Out: New York Nightlife and the Transformation of American Culture, 1890–1930*. Westport, CT: Greenwood, 1981.

Ewen, David. *The Life and Death of Tin Pan Alley: The Golden Age of American Popular Music*. New York: Funk and Wagnalls, 1964.

Faderman, Lilian. *Odd Girls and Twilight Lovers: A History of Lesbian Life in Twentieth-Century America*. New York: Columbia University Press, 1991.

Fanon, Frantz. *A Dying Colonialism*. Translated by Haaken Chevalier. New York: Grove, 1988.

Fausto-Sterling, Anne. "The Five Sexes: Why Male and Female Are Not Enough." *Sciences* 33, no. 2 (March–April 1993): 20–24.

———. "How to Build a Man." In *The Gender/Sexuality Reader: Culture, History, Political Economy*. Edited by Roger N. Lancaster and Micaela di Leonardo, 244–48. New York: Routledge, 1997.

Ferguson, Roderick A. *Aberrations in Black: Toward a Queer of Color Critique*. Minneapolis: University of Minnesota Press, 2004.

Foucault, Michel. *The Birth of Biopolitics: Lectures at the Collège de France, 1978–1979*. Edited by Michel Senellart. Translated by Graham Burchell. New York: Palgrave Macmillan, 2008.

———. *Discipline and Punish: The Birth of the Prison*. Translated by Alan Sheridan. New York: Vintage, 1979.

———. *The History of Sexuality*. Vol. 1, *An Introduction*. Translated by Robert Hurley. New York: Vintage, 1990.

———. "Questions of Method." In *The Foucault Effect: Studies in Governmentality*. Edited by Graham Burchell, Colin Gordon, and Peter Miller. Translated by Colin Gordon, 73–86. Chicago: University of Chicago Press, 1991.

———. "What Is an Author?" In *Critical Theory since 1965*. Edited by Hazard Adams and Leroy Searle, 138–48. Tallahassee: Florida State University Press, 1986.

Franklin, Cynthia G. *Academic Lives: Memoir, Cultural Theory, and the University Today*. Athens: University of Georgia Press, 2009.

Freud, Sigmund. *Three Essays on the Theory of Sexuality*. With a foreword by Nancy J. Chodorow and an introductory essay by Steven Marcus. Edited and translated by James Strachey. New York: Basic, 2000.

Friedberg, Anne. *Window Shopping: Cinema and the Postmodern*. Berkeley: University of California Press, 1993.

Fung, Richard. "Looking for My Penis: The Eroticized Asian in Gay Video Porn." In *Q & A: Queer in Asian America*. Edited by David L. Eng and Alice Y. Hom, 115–34. Philadelphia: Temple University Press, 1998.

Fuss, Diana. *Identification Papers*. New York: Routledge, 1995.

Gaines, Kevin K. *American Africans in Ghana: Black Expatriates and the Civil Rights Era*. Chapel Hill: University of North Carolina Press, 2006.

Garber, Eric. "A Spectacle in Color: The Lesbian and Gay Subculture of Jazz Age

Harlem." In *Hidden from History: Reclaiming the Gay and Lesbian Past*. Edited by Martin B. Duberman, Martha Vicinus, and George Chauncey Jr., 318–31. New York: New American Library, 1989.

Garber, Marjorie. *Vested Interests: Cross-Dressing and Cultural Anxiety*. New York: Routledge, 1992.

———. *Vice Versa: Bisexuality and the Eroticism of Everyday Life*. New York: Touchstone, 1995.

Garcia, Matt. *A World of Its Own: Race, Labor, and Citrus in the Making of Greater Los Angeles, 1900–1970*. Chapel Hill: University of North Carolina Press, 2001.

Garrett, Charles Hiroshi. *Struggling to Define a Nation: American Music and the Twentieth Century*. Berkeley: University of California Press, 2008.

Gates, Henry Louis, Jr. "The Black Man's Burden." In *Fear of a Queer Planet: Queer Politics and Social Theory*. Edited by Michael Warner, 230–38. Minneapolis: University of Minnesota Press, 1993.

———. *The Signifying Monkey: A Theory of Afro-American Literary Criticism*. New York: Oxford University Press, 1988.

Gavin, James. *Intimate Nights: The Golden Age of New York Cabaret*. New York: Grove Weidenfeld, 1991.

Gewertz, Deborah, and Frederick Errington. "We Think Therefore They Are?: On Occidentalizing the World." In *Cultures of United States Imperialism*. Edited by Amy Kaplan and Donald E. Pease, 635–65. Durham, NC: Duke University Press, 1993.

Gikandi, Simon. "Picasso, Africa, and the Schemata of Difference." In *Beautiful/Ugly: African and Diaspora Aesthetics*. Edited by Sarah Nuttall, 30–59. Durham, NC: Duke University Press, 2006.

Gilmore, Ruth Wilson. *Golden Gulag: Prisons, Surplus, Crisis, and Opposition in Globalizing California*. Berkeley: University of California Press, 2007.

Gilroy, Paul. *The Black Atlantic: Modernity and Double Consciousness*. Cambridge, MA: Harvard University Press, 1993.

Glenn, Susan A. *Daughters of the Shtetl: Life and Labor in the Immigrant Generation*. Ithaca, NY: Cornell University Press, 1990.

Glick, Elisa. "Harlem's Queer Dandy: African-American Modernism and the Artifice of Blackness." *MFS* 49, no. 3 (2003): 414–42.

Goeser, Caroline. *Picturing the New Negro: Harlem Renaissance Print Culture and Modern Black Identity*. Lawrence: University Press of Kansas, 2007.

González, Jennifer A. *Subject to Display: Reframing Race in Contemporary Installation Art*. Cambridge, MA: MIT Press, 2008.

Gopinath, Gayatri. *Impossible Desires: Queer Diasporas and South Asian Public Cultures*. Durham, NC: Duke University Press, 2005.

Gordon, Linda. "Internal Colonialism and Gender." In *Haunted by Empire: Geographies of Intimacy in North American History*. Edited by Ann Laura Stoler, 427–51. Durham, NC: Duke University Press, 2006.

Gould, Stephen Jay. *The Mismeasure of Man*. New York: Norton, 1981.

Grewal, Inderpal. *Home and Harem: Nation, Gender, Empire, and the Cultures of Travel*. Durham, NC: Duke University Press, 1996.

Grewal, Inderpal, and Caren Kaplan. Introduction to *Scattered Hegemonies: Postmodernity and Transnational Feminist Practices*. Edited by Inderpal Grewal and Caren Kaplan, 1–33. Minneapolis: University of Minnesota Press, 1994.

Gubar, Susan. *Racechanges: White Skins, Black Face in American Culture*. New York: Oxford University Press, 1997.

Halberstam, Judith. *Female Masculinity*. Durham, NC: Duke University Press, 1998.

———. "Notes on Failure." Lecture at the University of Illinois, Urbana-Champaign, 14 April 2006.

———. *The Queer Art of Failure*. Durham, NC: Duke University Press, 2011.

Halberstam, Judith, and Del LaGrace Volcano. *The Drag King Book*. London: Serpent's Tail, 1999.

Hall, Christine C. Iijima, and Trude I. Cooke Turner. "The Diversity of Biracial Individuals: Asian-White and Asian-Minority Biracial Identity." In *The Sum of Our Parts: Mixed Heritage Asian Americans*. Edited by Teresa Williams-León and Cynthia L. Nakashima, 81–92. Philadelphia: Temple University Press, 2001.

Hall, Stuart. "The After-Life of Frantz Fanon: Why Fanon? Why Now? Why *Black Skin/White Masks*?" In *The Fact of Blackness: Frantz Fanon and Visual Representation*. Edited by Alan Read, 12–37. London: Institute of Contemporary Art, 1996.

———. "The Whites of Their Eyes." In *Gender, Race and Class in Media*. Edited by Gail Dines and Jean M. Humez, 18–22. Thousand Oaks, CA: Sage, 2010.

Haney-López, Ian F. *White by Law: The Legal Construction of Race*. New York: New York University Press, 1996.

Hansen, Miriam. *Babel and Babylon: Spectatorship in American Silent Film*. Cambridge, MA: Harvard University Press, 1991.

Hausman, Bernice L. *Changing Sex: Transsexualism, Technology, and the Idea of Gender*. Durham, NC: Duke University Press, 1995.

Heap, Chad. "The City as a Sexual Laboratory: The Queer Heritage of the Chicago School." *Qualitative Sociology* 26, no. 4 (2003): 457–87.

———. *Slumming: Sexual and Racial Encounters in American Nightlife, 1885–1940*. Chicago: University of Chicago Press, 2009.

Henderson, Mae G. "Josephine Baker and *La Revue Negre*: From Ethnography to Performance." *Text and Performance Quarterly* 23 (2003): 107–33.

———. "Portrait of Wallace Thurman." In *The Harlem Renaissance Remembered*. Edited by Arna Bontemps, 146–70. New York: Dodd, Mead, 1972.

Herring, Scott. *Queering the Underworld: Slumming, Literature, and the Undoing of Lesbian and Gay History*. Chicago: University of Chicago Press, 2007.

Holland, Sharon Patricia. *Raising the Dead: Readings of Death and (Black) Subjectivity*. Durham, NC: Duke University Press, 2000.

Hong, Grace Kyungwon, and Roderick A. Ferguson. Introduction to *Strange Affinities: The Gender and Sexual Politics of Comparative Racialization*. Edited by Grace

Kyungwon Hong and Roderick A. Ferguson, 1–22. Durham, NC: Duke University Press, 2011.

———, eds. *Strange Affinities: The Gender and Sexual Politics of Comparative Racialization*. Durham, NC: Duke University Press, 2011.

Huggins, Nathan Irvin. *The Harlem Renaissance*. New York: Oxford University Press, 1971.

———. Introduction to *Voices from the Harlem Renaissance*, ed. Nathan Irvin Huggins, 3–11. New York: Oxford University Press, 1976.

Huhndorf, Shari M. *Going Native: Indians in the American Cultural Imagination*. Ithaca, NY: Cornell University Press, 2001.

Hwang, David Henry. *M. Butterfly*. New York: Penguin, 1989.

Irigaray, Luce. *This Sex Which Is Not One*. Translated by Catherine Porter. Ithaca, NY: Cornell University Press, 1985.

Jacobs, Lea. *The Wages of Sin: Censorship and the Fallen Woman Film, 1928–1942*. Berkeley: University of California Press, 1995.

Jameson, Fredric. "Modernism and Imperialism." In Terry Eagleton, Fredric Jameson, and Edward W. Said, *Nationalism, Colonialism, and Literature*, 43–66. Minneapolis: University of Minnesota Press, 1990.

Johnson, Barbara. *The Wake of Deconstruction*. Cambridge, MA: Blackwell, 1994.

———. *A World of Difference*. Baltimore, MD: Johns Hopkins University Press, 1987.

Johnson, James H. *Listening in Paris: A Cultural History*. Berkeley: University of California Press, 1995.

Jones, Andrew. *Yellow Music: Media Culture and Colonial Modernity in the Chinese Jazz Age*. Durham, NC: Duke University Press, 2001.

Jordan, Winthrop. *White over Black: American Attitudes toward the Negro, 1550–1812*. Chapel Hill: University of North Carolina Press, 1968.

Jules-Rosette, Bennetta. *Josephine Baker in Art and Life: The Icon and the Image*. Urbana: University of Illinois Press, 2007.

Jun, Helen H. "Black Orientalism: Nineteenth-Century Narratives of Race and U.S. Citizenship." *American Quarterly* 58 (June 2006): 1047–66.

———. *Race for Citizenship: Black Orientalism and Asian Uplift from Pre-Emancipation to Neoliberal America*. New York: New York University Press, 2011.

Jung, Moon-Ho. *Coolies and Cane: Race, Labor, and Sugar in the Age of Emancipation*. Baltimore: Johns Hopkins University Press, 2006.

Jung, Moon-Kie. *Reworking Race: The Making of Hawaii's Interracial Labor Movement*. New York: Columbia University Press, 2006.

Kant, Immanuel. *Observations on the Feeling of the Beautiful and Sublime*. Translated by John T. Goldthwait. Berkeley: University of California Press, 1960.

Kaplan, Amy. *The Anarchy of Empire in the Making of U.S. Culture*. Cambridge, MA: Harvard University Press, 2002.

Kaplan, Amy, and Donald E. Pease, eds. *Cultures of United States Imperialism*. Durham, NC: Duke University Press, 1993.

Kaplan, Caren. *Questions of Travel: Postmodern Discourses of Displacement*. Durham, NC: Duke University Press, 1996.

Kelley, Robin D. G. *Freedom Dreams: The Black Radical Imagination*. Boston: Beacon, 2002.

———. "Notes on Deconstructing 'The Folk.'" *American Historical Review* 97, no. 5 (December 1992): 1400–1408.

Kellner, Bruce, ed. *The Harlem Renaissance: A Historical Dictionary for the Era*. New York: Methuen, 1984.

Kennedy, Elizabeth Lapovsky, and Madeline D. Davis. *Boots of Leather, Slippers of Gold: The History of a Lesbian Community*. New York: Penguin, 1993.

Kent, Rachel. "Time and Transformation in the Art of Yinka Shonibare MBE." In *Yinka Shonibare, MBE*. Edited by Rachel Kent, Robert Hobbs, and Anthony Downey, 12–23. New York: Prestel, 2008.

Kim, Daniel. *Writing Manhood in Black and Yellow: Ralph Ellison, Frank Chin, and the Literary Politics of Identity*. Stanford, CA: Stanford University Press, 2005.

Kim, Elaine H. "Asian Americans and Popular Culture." In *Dictionary of Asian American History*. Edited by Hyung-Chan Kim, 99–114. New York: Greenwood, 1986.

Kirschke, Amy Helene. *Aaron Douglas: Art, Race, and the Harlem Renaissance*. Jackson: University Press of Mississippi, 1995.

———. *Art in Crisis: W. E. B. Du Bois and the Struggle for African American Identity and Memory*. Bloomington: Indiana University Press, 2007.

Klopotek, Brian. "'I Guess Your Warrior Look Doesn't Work Every Time': Challenging Indian Masculinity in the Cinema." In *Across the Great Divide: Cultures of Manhood in the American West*. Edited by Matthew Basso, Laura McCall, and Dee Garceau, 251–74. New York: Routledge, 2001.

Knadler, Stephen. "Sweetback Style: Wallace Thurman and a Queer Harlem Renaissance." *MFS* 48, no. 4 (2002): 899–936.

Koestenbaum, Wayne. *The Queen's Throat: Opera, Homosexuality, and the Mystery of Desire*. New York: Vintage, 1994.

Kolodin, Irving. *The Story of the Metropolitan Opera, 1883–1950: A Candid History*. New York: Knopf, 1953.

Koritz, Amy. "Dancing the Orient for England: Maud Allen's *The Vision of Salome*." In *Meaning in Motion: New Cultural Studies of Dance*. Edited by Jane Desmond, 133–52. Durham, NC: Duke University Press, 1997.

Kurashige, Scott. *The Shifting Grounds of Race: Black and Japanese Americans in the Making of Multiethnic Los Angeles*. Princeton, NJ: Princeton University Press, 2010.

Lears, T. J. Jackson. *No Place of Grace: Antimodernism and the Transformation of American Culture, 1880–1920*. New York: Pantheon, 1981.

Lee, Robert. *Orientals: Asian Americans in Popular Culture*. Philadelphia: Temple University Press, 1999.

Lefebvre, Henri. *The Production of Space*. Translated by Donald Nicholson-Smith. Oxford: Blackwell, 1991.

Lewis, David Levering. *When Harlem Was in Vogue*. New York: Vintage, 1982.

Lipsitz, George. *American Studies in a Moment of Danger*. Minneapolis: University of Minnesota Press, 2011.

———. *Dangerous Crossroads: Popular Music, Postmodernism, and the Poetics of Place*. New York: Verso, 1994.

———. *Time Passages: Collective Memory and American Popular Culture*. Minneapolis: University of Minnesota Press, 1990.

Long, Alecia P. *The Great Southern Babylon: Sex, Race, and Respectability in New Orleans, 1865–1920*. Baton Rouge: Louisiana State University Press, 2004.

Lott, Eric. *Love and Theft: Blackface Minstrelsy and the American Working Class*. New York: Oxford University Press, 1993.

Lowe, Lisa. *Immigrant Acts: On Asian American Cultural Politics*. Durham, NC: Duke University Press, 1996.

———. "The Intimacies of Four Continents." In *Haunted by Empire: Geographies of Intimacy in North American History*. Edited by Ann Laura Stoler, 191–212. Durham, NC: Duke University Press, 2006.

Ma, Sheng-Mei. *Deathly Embrace: Orientalism and Asian American Identity*. Minneapolis: University of Minnesota Press, 2000.

Mahmood, Saba. *Politics of Piety: The Islamic Revival and the Feminist Subject*. Princeton, NJ: Princeton University Press, 2012.

Manalansan, Martin F., IV. *Global Divas: Filipino Gay Men in the Diaspora*. Durham, NC: Duke University Press, 2003.

Mangaoang, Gil. "From the 1970s to the 1990s." In *Asian American Sexualities: Dimensions of the Gay and Lesbian Experience*. Edited by Russell Leong, 101–11. New York: Routledge, 1996.

Marchand, Roland. *Advertising the American Dream: Making Way for Modernity, 1920–1940*. Berkeley: University of California Press, 1985.

Marchetti, Gina. *Romance and the "Yellow Peril": Race, Sex, and Discursive Strategies in Hollywood Fiction*. Berkeley: University of California Press, 1993.

Marez, Curtis. "The Other Addict: Reflections on Colonialism and Oscar Wilde's Opium Smoke Screen." ELH 64, no. 1 (1997): 257–87.

Massad, Joseph A. *Desiring Arabs*. Chicago: University of Chicago Press, 2007.

Massey, Doreen B. *Space, Place, and Gender*. Minneapolis: University of Minnesota Press, 1994.

Mbembe, Achille. *On the Postcolony*. Translated by A. M. Berrett, Janet Roitman, Murray Last, and Steven Rendall. Berkeley: University of California Press, 2001.

McAlister, Melani. *Epic Encounters: Culture, Media, and US Interests in the Middle East*. Berkeley: University of California Press, 2001.

McClary, Susan. *Feminine Endings: Music, Gender, and Sexuality*. Minneapolis: University of Minnesota Press, 1991.

———. *Georges Bizet: Carmen*. Cambridge: Cambridge University Press, 1992.

———. "Same as It Ever Was: Youth Culture and Music." In *Microphone Fiends: Youth Music and Youth Culture*. Edited by Andrew Ross and Tricia Rose, 29–40. New York: Routledge, 1994.

McClintock, Anne. *Imperial Leather: Race, Gender and Sexuality in the Colonial Contest*. New York: Routledge, 1995.

McClintock, Anne, Aamir Mufti, and Ella Shohat, eds. *Dangerous Liaisons: Gender, Nation, and Postcolonial Perspectives*. Minneapolis: University of Minnesota Press, 1997.

McDowell, Deborah E. Introduction to Nella Larsen, *Quicksand and Passing*. Edited by Deborah E. McDowell, ix–xxxii. New Brunswick, NJ: Rutgers University Press, 1986.

Mendoza, Victor. "A Queer Nomadology of Jessica Hagedorn's *Dogeaters*." *American Literature* 77, no. 4 (2005): 815–45.

Menefee, David W. *The First Female Stars: Women of the Silent Era*. Westport, CT: Praeger, 2004.

Merriam, Alan P., and Fradley H. Garner. "Jazz—the Word." In *The Jazz Cadence of American Culture*. Edited by Robert G. O'Meally, 7–31. 1960. Reprint, New York: Columbia University Press, 1998.

Meyerowitz, Joanne J. *Women Adrift: Independent Wage Earners in Chicago, 1880–1930*. Chicago: University of Chicago Press, 1988.

Miller, D. A. "Anal Rope." In *Inside/Out: Lesbian Theories, Gay Theories*. Edited by Diana Fuss, 119–41. New York: Routledge, 1991.

Miller, Monica. *Slaves to Fashion: Black Dandyism and the Styling of Black Diasporic Identity*. Durham, NC: Duke University Press, 2009.

Miller, Nina. *Making Love Modern: The Intimate Public Worlds of New York's Literary Women*. New York: Oxford University Press, 1999.

Mills, Charles W. "Racial Liberalism." *PMLA* 123 (October 2008): 1380–97.

Mitchell, Timothy. *Colonising Egypt*. Cambridge: Cambridge University Press, 1988.

———. *Rule of Experts: Egypt, Techno-Politics, Modernity*. Berkeley: University of California Press, 2002.

Mizejewski, Linda. *Ziegfeld Girl: Image and Icon in Culture and Cinema*. Durham, NC: Duke University Press, 1999.

Mullen, Bill V. *Afro-Orientalism*. Minneapolis: University of Minnesota Press, 2004.

Mumford, Kevin J. *Interzones: Black/White Sex Districts in Chicago and New York in the Early Twentieth Century*. New York: Columbia University Press, 1997.

Nakashima, Cynthia L. "An Invisible Monster: The Creation and Denial of Mixed-Race People in America." In *Racially Mixed People in America*. Edited by Maria P. P. Root, 162–80. Newbury Park, CA: Sage, 1992.

Nasaw, David. *Going Out: The Rise and Fall of Public Amusements*. New York: Basic, 1993.

Ngai, Mae M. *Impossible Subjects: Illegal Aliens and the Making of Modern America*. Princeton, NJ: Princeton University Press, 2004.

Ngô, Fiona I. B. "The Anxiety over Borders." In *Embodiments of Asian Pacific Islander*

Sexuality. Edited by Gina Masequesmay and Sean Metzger, 89–104. Lanham, MD: Lexington Press, 2008.

———. "A Chameleon's Fate: Transnational Mixed-Race Vietnamese Identities." *Amerasia Journal* 31, no. 2 (2005): 51–62.

Nguyen, Mimi Thi. "The Biopower of Beauty: Humanitarian Imperialisms and Global Feminisms in an Age of Terror." *Signs* 36, no. 2 (2011): 359–83.

Nyong'o, Tavia. "Punk'd Theory." *Social Text* 84–85, nos. 3–4 (2005): 19–34.

Ogren, Kathy. *The Jazz Revolution: Twenties America and the Meaning of Jazz.* New York: Oxford University Press, 1989.

Ordover, Nancy. *American Eugenics: Race, Queer Anatomy, and the Science of Nationalism.* Minneapolis: Minnesota University Press, 2003.

Osofsky, Gilbert. *Harlem: The Making of a Ghetto, Negro New York, 1890–1930.* 2nd ed., 1971. Reprint, Chicago: Ivan R. Dee, 1996.

Parreñas, Rhacel Salazar. "'White Trash' Meets the 'Little Brown Monkeys': The Taxi Dance Hall as a Site of Interracial and Gender Alliances between White Working Class Women and Filipino Immigrant Men in the 1920s and 30s." *Amerasia Journal* 24, no. 2 (1998): 115–34.

Peiss, Kathy. *Cheap Amusements: Working Women and Leisure in Turn-of-the-Century New York.* Philadelphia: Temple University Press, 1986.

Peretti, Burton W. *Nightclub City: Politics and Amusement in Manhattan.* Philadelphia: University of Pennsylvania Press, 2007.

Pfeiffer, Kathleen. Introduction to Carl Van Vechten, *Nigger Heaven*, ix–xxxix. 1926. Reprint, Urbana: University of Illinois Press, 2000.

Porter, Eric. *What Is This Thing Called Jazz? African American Musicians as Artists, Critics, and Activists.* Berkeley: University of California Press, 2002.

Powell, Richard J. *Black Art: A Cultural History.* 2nd ed. London: Thames and Hudson, 2002.

Prashad, Vijay. *Everybody Was Kung Fu Fighting: Afro-Asian Connections and the Myth of Cultural Purity.* Boston: Beacon, 2001.

Pratt, Mary Louise. *Imperial Eyes: Travel Writing and Transculturation.* New York: Routledge, 1992.

Puar, Jasbir, ed. "Queer Tourism: Geographies of Globalization." Special issue, GLQ 8, nos. 1–2 (2002).

Rana, Junaid. "The Story of Islamophobia." *Souls* 9, no. 2 (2007): 148–61.

Rancière, Jacques. *The Politics of Aesthetics: The Distribution of the Sensible.* Translated with an introduction by Gabriel Rockhill, afterword by Slavoj Žižek. London: Continuum, 2004.

Raphael-Hernandez, Heike, and Shannon Steen. *AfroAsian Encounters: Culture, History, Politics.* New York: New York University Press, 2006.

Reddy, Chandan. "Asian Diasporas, Neoliberalism, and Family: Reviewing the Case for Homosexual Asylum in the Context of Family Rights." *Social Text* 84–85, nos. 3–4 (2005): 101–19.

———. *Freedom with Violence: Race, Sexuality, and the US State*. Durham, NC: Duke University Press, 2012.

———. "Modern." In *Keywords for American Cultural Studies*. Edited by Bruce Burgett and Glenn Hendler, 160–63. New York: New York University Press, 2007.

Riley, Denise. *"Am I That Name?" Feminism and the Category of "Women" in History*. Minneapolis: University of Minnesota Press, 1990.

Roediger, David. *The Wages of Whiteness: Race and the Making of the American Working Class*. New York: Verso, 1991.

Ross, Marlon B. *Manning the Race: Reforming Black Men in the Jim Crow Era*. New York: New York University Press, 2004.

Said, Edward. *Culture and Imperialism*. New York: Vintage, 1993.

———. *Orientalism*. 1978. Reprint, New York: Vintage, 1994.

Scheper, Jeanne. "'Of la Baker, I Am a Disciple': The Diva Politics of Reception." *Camera Obscura* 65 (2007): 73–101.

Schneider, Mark Robert. *African Americans in the Jazz Age*. Lanham, MD: Rowman and Littlefield, 2006.

Schuyler, George S. *Black and Conservative*. New Rochelle, NY: Arlington House, 1966.

Schwarz, A. B. Christa. *Gay Voices of the Harlem Renaissance*. Bloomington: Indiana University Press, 2003.

Sedgwick, Eve Kosofsky. *Epistemology of the Closet*. Berkeley: University of California Press, 1990.

Shah, Nayan. *Contagious Divides: Epidemics and Race in San Francisco's Chinatown*. Berkeley: University of California Press, 2001.

Shohat, Ella. "Gender and Culture of Empire: Toward a Feminist Ethnography of the Cinema." In *Visions of the East: Orientalism in Film*. Edited by Matthew Bernstein and Gaylyn Studlar, 19–66. New Brunswick, NJ: Rutgers University Press, 1997.

———. *Taboo Memories, Diasporic Voices*. Durham, NC: Duke University Press, 2006.

Showalter, Elaine. *Sexual Anarchy: Gender and Culture at the Fin de Siècle*. New York: Virago, 1989.

Silva, Denise Ferreira da. *Toward a Global Idea of Race*. Minneapolis: University of Minnesota Press, 2007.

Singer, Barry. *Black and Blue: The Life and Lyrics of Andy Razaf*. New York: Schirmer, 1992.

Singh, Amritjit, and Daniel M. Scott III. "Excerpts from the Novels." In *The Collected Writings of Wallace Thurman: A Harlem Renaissance Reader*. Edited by Amritjit Singh and Daniel M. Scott III, 441–48. New Brunswick, NJ: Rutgers University Press, 2003.

Soja, Edward W. *Thirdspace: Journeys to Los Angeles and Other Real-and-Imagined Places*. Cambridge, MA: Blackwell, 1996.

Somerville, Siobhan B. "Passing through the Closet in Pauline E. Hopkins's *Contending Forces*." *American Literature* 69, no. 1 (1997): 139–66.

———. *Queering the Color Line: Race and the Invention of Homosexuality in American Culture*. Durham, NC: Duke University Press, 2000.

Stansell, Christine. *American Moderns: Bohemian New York and the Creation of a New Century*. New York: Henry Holt, 2000.

Stoler, Ann Laura. *Along the Archival Grain: Epistemic and Colonial Common Sense*. Princeton, NJ: Princeton University Press, 2009.

———. *Carnal Knowledge and Imperial Power: Race and the Intimate in Colonial Rule*. Berkeley: University of California Press, 2002.

———, ed. *Haunted by Empire: Geographies of Intimacy in North American History*. Durham, NC: Duke University Press, 2006.

———. "Tense and Tender Ties: The Politics of Comparison in North American History and (Post) Colonial Studies." In *Haunted by Empire: Geographies of Intimacy in North American History*. Edited by Ann Laura Stoler, 23–67. Durham, NC: Duke University Press, 2006.

Stoler, Ann Laura, and Carole McGranahan. "Introduction: Refiguring Imperial Terrains." In *Imperial Formations*. Edited by Ann Laura Stoler, Carole McGranahan, and Peter Perdue, 3–43. Santa Fe, NM: School for Advanced Research Press, 2007.

Stone, Sandy. "A Posttransesexual Manifesto." In *Body Guards: The Cultural Politics of Gender Ambiguity*. Edited by Julia Epstein and Kristina Straub, 280–304. New York: Routledge, 1991.

Stovall, Tyler Edward. *Paris Noir: African Americans in the City of Light*. Boston: Houghton Mifflin, 1996.

Studlar, Gaylyn. *The Mad Masquerade: Stardom and Masculinity in the Jazz Age*. New York: Columbia University Press, 1996.

———. "'Out-Salomeing Salome': Dance, the New Woman, and Fan Magazine Orientalism." In *Visions of the East: Orientalism in Film*. Edited by Matthew Bernstein and Gaylyn Studlar, 99–125. New Brunswick, NJ: Rutgers University Press, 1997.

Summers, Martin. *Manliness and Its Discontents: The Black Middle Class and the Transformation of Masculinity, 1900–1930*. Chapel Hill: University of North Carolina Press, 2004.

Susman, Warren I. *Culture as History: The Transformation of American Society in the Twentieth Century*. New York: Pantheon, 1973.

Takaki, Ronald. *Strangers from a Different Shore: A History of Asian Americans*. New York: Penguin, 1989.

Tawa, Nicholas E. *The Way to Tin Pan Alley: American Popular Song, 1866–1910*. New York: Schirmer, 1990.

Taylor, Diana. *The Archive and the Repertoire*. Durham, NC: Duke University Press, 2003.

Terry, Jennifer. "Anxious Slippages between 'Us' and 'Them': A Brief History of the Scientific Search for Homosexual Bodies." In *Deviant Bodies: Critical Perspectives of Difference in Science and Popular Culture*. Edited by Jennifer Terry and Jacqueline Urla, 129–69. Bloomington: Indiana University Press, 1995.

Tsing, Anna Lowenhaupt. *Friction: An Ethnography of Global Connection*. Princeton, NJ: Princeton University Press, 2005.

Tucker, Sherrie. "Together but Unequal: Dance Floor Democracy at the Hollywood

Canteen." Paper presented at the Annual Conference of the American Studies Association, Washington, DC, 5–8 November 2009.

———. "When Did Jazz Go Straight? A Queer Question for Jazz Studies." *Critical Studies in Improvisation* 4, no. 2 (2008): 1–16.

U.S. Department of Commerce, Bureau of the Census. *Thirteenth Census of the United States Taken in the Year 1910.* Vol. 3, *Population 1910: Reports by States, with Statistics for Counties, Cities and Other Civil Divisions, Nebraska-Wyoming, Alaska, Hawaii, and Porto Rico.* Washington: U.S. Government Printing Office, 1913.

———. *Fifteenth Census of the United States: 1930.* Vol. 3, part 2, *Population Reports by States, Showing the Composition and Characteristics of the Population for Counties, Cities, and Townships or Other Minor Civil Divisions, Montana-Wyoming.* Washington: U.S. Government Printing Office, 1932.

Valentine, David. *Imagining Transgender: An Ethnography of a Category.* Durham, NC: Duke University Press, 2007.

Valverde, Kieu-Linh Caroline. "From Dust to Gold: The Vietnamese Amerasian American Experience." In *Racially Mixed People in America.* Edited by Maria P. P. Root, 144–61. Newbury Park, CA: Sage, 1992.

Van Notten, Eleonore. "Wallace Thurman's Harlem Renaissance." PhD diss., Leiden University, 1994.

Vogel, Shane. *The Scene of Harlem Cabaret: Race, Sexuality, Performance.* Chicago: University of Chicago Press, 2009.

Voloshinov, V. N. "Critique of Saussurian Linguistics." In *The Bakhtin Reader: Selected Writings of Bakhtin, Medvedev, Voloshinov.* Edited by Pam Morris, 25–37. London: Arnold, 1994.

Volpp, Leti. "The Citizen and the Terrorist." In *September 11 in History: A Watershed Moment?* Edited by Mary L. Dudziak, 147–62. Durham, NC: Duke University Press, 2003.

Wall, Cheryl. *Women of the Harlem Renaissance.* Bloomington: Indiana University Press, 1995.

Watson, Steven. *The Harlem Renaissance: Hub of African-American Culture, 1920–1930.* New York: Pantheon, 1995.

Wiegman, Robyn. *American Anatomies: Theorizing Race and Gender.* Durham, NC: Duke University Press, 1995.

Wilentz, Sean. *Chants Democratic: New York City and the Rise of the American Working Class, 1788–1850.* New York: Oxford University Press, 1984.

Williams, Raymond. *Politics of Modernism: Against the New Conformists.* London: Verso, 2007.

Wintz, Cary D. *Black Culture and the Harlem Renaissance.* Houston, TX: Rice University Press, 1988.

Wirth, Thomas H. "Richard Bruce Nugent." *Black American Literature Forum* 19, no. 1 (1985): 16–17.

Wong, Yutian. *Choreographing Asian America.* Middlebury, CT: Wesleyan University Press, 2010.

Yoshihara, Mari. *Embracing the East: White Women and American Orientalism.* New York: Oxford University Press, 2003.

Young, Robert J. C. *Colonial Desire: Hybridity in Theory, Culture, and Race.* New York: Routledge, 1995.

Yu, Henry. *Thinking Orientals: Migration, Contact, and Exoticism in Modern America.* New York: Oxford University Press, 2001.

Zani, Philippe. Liner notes. Translated by Charlemagne. *Hawaii's Popular Songs: "Unforgettables," 1920–1930.* EPM Musique 995842, 1997, compact disc.

DISCOGRAPHY

Astaire, Fred. "Puttin' on the Ritz." Recorded in 1930. *The Roaring Twenties.* Intersound 1401, 1997, 4 compact discs.

Crumit, Frank. "Palesteena." Recorded in 1920. *The Roaring Twenties.* Intersound 1401, 1997, 4 compact discs.

Ellington, Duke. "Swingtime in Honolulu." Recorded 11 April 1938. *Cotton Club: A Nostalgia Collection.* Gallerie GALE 455, 2000, 2 compact discs.

Grainger, Porter. "Hula Blues." Recorded April 1924. *Porter Grainger in Chronological Order, 1923–1929.* RST Records JPCD-1521–2, 1995, compact disc.

Henderson, Fletcher. "He Wasn't Born in Araby, But He's a Sheikin' Fool." Recorded April 1924. *Fletcher Henderson and the Blues Singers.* Vol. 2, *1923–1924.* Document Records DOCD-S5343, 1995, compact disc.

Paul Biese Trio with Frank Crumit. "Chile Bean." Recorded in 1920. *1920: "Even Water's Getting Weaker."* Archeophone 9001A, 2004, compact disc.

Rudy Wiedoeft's Californians. "The Sheik of Araby." Recorded in 1921. *The Roaring Twenties.* Intersound 1401, 1997, 4 compact discs.

Smith, Bessie. "Foolish Man Blues." Recorded 27 October 1927. *Bessie Smith: The Complete Recordings.* Vol. 3. Columbia Records C2K47474, 1992, 2 compact discs.

Sol Ho'opp'i and His Novelty Quartet. "Hula Girl." Recorded 7 March 1927. *Chansons Populaires Hawaiiennes, 1920–1930.* EPM Musique 995842, 1997, compact disc.

Tucker, Sophie. "In Old King Tutankhamen's Day." Recorded in 1923. *The Roaring Twenties.* Waves 1400, 1997, 4 compact discs.

Waller, Fats. "In Harlem's Araby." Recorded May 1924. *The Complete Recorded Works, Volume 1.* JSP Records, JSP927A, 2007, 4 compact discs.

———. "The Sheik of Araby." Lyrics by Harry B. Smith, composed by Ted Snyder. Recorded in 1939. *Very Best of Fats Waller.* RCA B000050G8C, 2000, compact disc.

Webb, Chick. "Swinging on the Reservation." Recorded 29 October 1936. *Stomping at the Savoy.* Proper B000DNVRZ6, 2006, compact disc.

SHEET MUSIC

Berlin, Irving. "Araby." New York: Waterson, Berlin, and Snyder, 1915.

———. "From Here to Shanghai." New York: Waterson, Berlin, and Snyder, 1917.

———. "Puttin' on the Ritz." New York: Waterson, Berlin, and Snyder, 1929.

Onivas, D. "Burning Sands: An Answer to 'The Sheik.'" New York: Richmond-Robbins, 1922.

Smith, Harry B. (lyricist), Francis Wheeler (lyricist), and Ted Snyder (ccomposer). "The Sheik of Araby." New York: Waterson, Berlin, and Snyder, 1921.

Yellen, Jack (lyricist), and Milton Ager (composer). "Lovin' Sam (The Sheik of Alabam)." New York: Ager, Yellen, Bornstein, 1922.

FILMS, VIDEOS, AND DOCUMENTARIES

Heisler, Stuart, and Mark Sandrich, dirs. *Blue Skies*. 1946. Special ed., with *Birth of the Blues*, 1941. Universal City, CA: Paramount/Universal Studios, 2003. DVD.

Lee, Spike, dir. *Bamboozled*. Brooklyn, NY: Forty Acres and a Mule Filmworks/New Line Cinema, 2000. DVD.

Melford, George, dir. *The Sheik*. 1921. Special ed., with *The Son of the Sheik*, 1926. Chatsworth, CA: Paramount Pictures/Image Entertainment, 2002. DVD.

Riggs, Marlon, dir. *Color Adjustment*. San Francisco: California Newsreel, 2004. DVD.

Walsh, Raoul, dir. *The Thief of Baghdad: An Arabian Nights Fantasy*. 1924. Deluxe ed. Douglas Fairbanks Pictures/Kino Video, 2004. DVD.

INDEX

archives/archivists (*continued*)

Derrida on, 126, 134–35, 147; imperial selfhood and, 109–10, 121; instability of, 153; knowledge production and, 126–28, 134–35; meaning making through, 31, 147; national borders and, 122; queer black aesthetic production and, 112–13, 146–47; repertoire vs., 30–31, 126, 140; as simulacrum, 84; use of term, 30–31, 125–26

Around the World in New York (Bercovici), 16

Asian immigrants/Asian Americans: Chinese immigrants/Chinese Americans, 1, 3, 21, 22, 39, 197n45, 198n51; ethnic/racial categorization and, 204n49; Filipinos, 45–47, 65–66, 69, 203n39, 203n43, 204n45, 204n49, 211n111, 227n25; *flâneurie*, 12; interracial contacts with African Americans, 3–4, 213n30; masculinities, 46–48, 200n12, 211n111; misidentification of, 210n103; narratives of inclusion, 197n47

Bacon, Francis, 228n37
Baker, Josephine, 16
Bakhtin, Mikhail, 215n48
Bal Primitiv, 102–3
Bara, Theda, 54, 132, 222n28
Barber of Bagdad (Cornelius), 55
Barthes, Roland, 87
Bartky, Sandra Lee, 206n75
Baudrillard, Jean, 113
Beardsley, Aubrey, 81, 119, 141, 220n19
belly dancing, 2, 129–30, 135, 165, 177–78, 222n40
Bentley, Berenice Benson, 55
Bercovici, Konrad, 16
Berlin, Irving, 1, 155–56, 163–64, 197n45, 227nn17–18
Bhabha, Homi K., 111, 218n93
Birth of Politics (Foucault), 18, 136n31
black and tan clubs, 159–60, 222n40
black dandyism, 208n80, 213n28

blackface discourse, 163–64, 176, 207n76, 207n78, 228n37

blackness: archives of black women's subjectivity and, 137; black cosmopolitanism, 12–13, 31, 159–60, 163–64, 166, 175, 214n43; blackface discourse, 163–64, 176, 207n76, 207n78, 228n37; black orientalism, 95–97, 103–4, 107–8, 212n8; black subjectivity, 137, 158–59, 173–77, 180–81, 198n51; black/white dichotomy, 3–4, 13, 25–26, 103–4, 193n4, 195n15, 210n3, 210n5, 216n70; queer black aesthetics and, 24–25, 28–29, 73–77, 94, 95–97, 103–4, 112–13, 119–20, 146–47; referentiality of the black body, 30, 75–77, 82, 85–95. *See also* black womanhood; queer black aesthetic production

black subjectivity: Africanisms and, 173–77; of black womanhood, 137; competing narratives of subjectivity, 180–81; cosmopolitan aesthetics and, 175; diversification of, 198n51; geographic boundaries and, 158–59

black/white dichotomy, 3–4, 13, 25–26, 103–4, 193n4, 195n15, 210n3, 210n5, 216n70

black womanhood: black femininity, 62–70, 135–47; Black Salomé and, 135–39; as dancers, 59, 129, 222n40; as embodiment of distance, 139; imperial selfhood of, 17, 125; orientalisms and, 135–39; primitivisms and, 135–39, 159–60; respectability of, 139, 222n40. *See also* Walker, J. J.

Blue Skies (1946), 227n17

Boieldieu, François-Adrien, 55

borders/boundaries: black/white dichotomy and, 3–4, 13, 25–26, 103–4, 193n4, 195n15, 210n3, 210n5, 216n70; borderlands, 74, 212n7; comparative empire studies and, 22–23, 77–78, 121–25, 163; as contact zones, 13–14, 35–38, 45–46, 69–70; within dance halls,

3, 13–14, 35–36, 69–70, 112, 199n10, 204n45; distance/intimacy through, 7, 21–22, 133; embodiment of distance as, 139; gendered boundaries, 43–44, 51–52, 64, 135–39, 152; identity formation and, 15, 25–26, 29–30, 73–77, 85; immigration legislation and, 199n10, 200n13; imperial logic and, 26, 188–91; instability of, 13, 23, 25–26, 32, 48, 85–87, 115–16, 118–19; internal colonialism and, 22, 162–63, 166–70; jazz cultures and, 8, 43–45; marginalization and, 204n45; mixed-race bodies and, 63–65; multiracial spaces and, 44–48, 199n10; national boundaries, 21–22, 56–57, 119–20, 162–63; neighborhood delineations of, 3, 6, 8, 12–16; policing/surveillance of, 162, 166–67, 209n94; queer black aesthetics and, 24–25, 28–29, 73–77, 94, 95–97, 103–4, 119–20; racialization and, 3, 25–26, 28–29, 38, 64, 73–77, 107, 135–39, 152, 199n10; referentiality and, 76–77; remapping of, 166–70; sexual boundaries, 73–77, 105–6, 199n10; spatial discourse and, 20–23, 36–37, 51–52, 73–77, 135–39, 190; transformation/transgression of, 29–30, 43–48, 51–52, 57–59, 68–69, 79–80, 87, 89, 115, 118–19; unfixing of, 162, 166–67, 187–91; of urban spaces, 3, 12–14, 22–23, 57–59, 74, 162; use of term, 20, 36; veiling, 141–47. *See also* contact zone; spatial discourse
Bramen, Carrie Tirado, 12
Brancusi, Constantin, 100
Brody, Jennifer DeVere, 25
Brooks, Daphne Ann, 138, 223n44
Brown, Jayna, 138, 139, 176–77, 225n72
Bulosan, Carlos, 203n43, 204n45
"Burden of Black Womanhood" (Douglas), 228n35
Burton, Richard, 140
Butler, Judith, 205n59, 209n99
Byrd, Jodi, A., 181

cabarets, 44, 157, 195n20, 202n36
Cacho, Lisa Marie, 197n47, 209n94
California, 181–86
"Caliph of Bagdad, The" (Bentley), 55
Calloway, Cab, 1, 41, 198n51
Carby, Hazel V., 138, 199n9, 208n92
Caribbean/West Indian immigrants/Americans, 4, 10, 11–12, 35–36, 49, 56–58, 119, 196n28, 209n98
Carrington, Joyce, 159–60
Carter, Howard, 30, 156, 176, 179
Carter, Marion, 33–34, 44
Chase, J. Smeaton, 181–86
Chevigny, Paul, 202n36
Chicago, 9, 130, 201n19, 205n63
"Chinatown, My Chinatown" (Schwartz and Jerome), 198n51
Chinese immigrants/Chinese Americans, 1, 3, 21, 22, 39, 197n45, 198n51. *See also* Asian immigrants/Asian Americans
Chuh, Kandice, 188
City of Refuge (Fisher), 65
Clayton, Buck, 15
Clément, Catherine, 118
Cleopatra, 22–23, 103, 131–32, 171–72
Cleopatra's Night (Hadley), 22, 103
Cobb, Michael, 89–90, 110
Collins, Theresa M., 220n19
colonial discourse: ancient Egypt and, 176, 178–79; boundaries of internal colonialism, 22, 162–63, 166–70; civilizationist logic of, 168; cross-colonial narratives, 156–57; as destructive tourism, 168; domestic colonialization, 158–59; economies and, 161–63, 187–88; empire building, 4–5, 162, 214n43, 218n93; frontier mythologies, 34–35, 51, 184; of Harlem, 161–63; imperial discourse and, 181–85; indigenous populations and, 162–63; internal colonialism, 161–64; spatial discourse and, 181–86; tourism and, 159–60, 165–66, 181, 184–85
comedy shows, 133–34, 196n28, 207n78

Committee of Fourteen, 40–41, 50, 131–32, 201n20

comparative empire studies, 22–23, 77–78, 121–25, 163. *See also* borders/boundaries; internal colonialism; nationalist discourse

conquest discourse: anti-conquest discourse, 183, 229n55; civilizing tourism, 183; comparative empire studies and, 22–23, 77–78, 121–25, 163; domestic colonialism and, 158, 185–86; performance reception and, 132, 133–35; racialized contexts for, 22, 149, 158; sexualized conquests, 149, 188. *See also* colonial discourse

Conrad, Joseph, 168

contact zones: ambivalence/multiple meanings and, 218n93; borders/boundaries as, 13–14, 35–38, 45–46, 69–70; dance halls as, 13–14, 35–38, 69–70; as frontier mythology, 34–35, 51, 184; Harlem as, 162; homosexual contact and, 213n30; interracial contact, 3–4, 213n30; interzones, 199n10; as intimacy, 8–14, 27–32, 44–45, 133–34; jazz cultures as, 35–38, 163, 177–80; knowledge production through, 8; multiracial spaces as, 9–14, 35–38, 41–42, 44–45, 199n10; neighborhoods as, 13–15, 26, 31–32, 70; racialization practices and, 35–36; referentiality and, 26; as sexualized spaces, 42–43, 46–48; as spaces of possibility, 199n10; use of term, 35–36

coon shouters, 176, 207n76, 228n37

Cornelius, Peter, 55

cosmopolitanism: black cosmopolitanism, 12–13, 31, 159–60, 163–64, 166, 175, 214n43; imperial discourse and, 11–14, 21, 31–32, 39, 48, 49, 79; queer black aesthetics and, 88, 116–18; spatial discourse and, 175

costume balls, 102–3, 117–18

Covarrubias, Miguel, 93

Crisis magazine (cover illustration), 159–60

crossing performances, 36

Crumit, Frank, 138, 139, 176–77

Cuban migrants/Cuban Americans, 56–57, 203n39

dance forms: avant-garde innovations, 205n55; belly dancing, 2, 129–30, 135, 165, 177–78, 222n40; costuming and, 7, 62, 72, 102–3, 129–30, 132, 135, 143–44, 225n2; hoochy coochy, 1, 2, 3, 129–30, 178; orientalisms and, 205n55; shimmy, 129, 220n20

dance halls: black femininity and, 62–63; boundaries within, 3, 13–14, 33–34, 69–70, 112, 199n10, 204n45; as contact zone, 13–14, 35–38, 69–70; as democratic/disciplinary spaces, 112; immigrants and, 2–3, 13–14, 33–35, 37, 38–40, 44–48, 69–70, 203n43, 204n45; interracial sexuality, 35–38, 69–70; jazz cultures within, 41–44; marginalization and, 204n45; masculinities and, 62–63; racial labor and, 13; as racially border/bounded spaces, 3, 13–14, 33–34, 69–70, 112, 204n45; racial mixing within, 13–14, 33–35, 204n46; as sexual transgressive space, 13–14, 33–34, 37–38, 58–59, 69–70; in Thurman's *The Blacker the Berry. . . .*, 25, 37, 63–69, 104, 106, 215n57; vice legislation and, 14, 35–36, 40–41, 44, 69–70, 112, 195n20, 202n36; white woman and interracial relations within, 27, 33–34, 37, 57, 58–59, 204n48

Dancer, Harlem (VanDerZee), 135, 136

decadence, 29, 84–85, 88, 89–90, 112, 119–20, 166. *See also* morality

Delapazieux, Lucienne, 61

Deleuze, Gilles, 83, 113

Denny, Lorna, 61

Derrida, Jacques, 30, 111, 126, 134–35, 147, 191, 230n11

desire, 96, 149

Desiring Arabs (Mossad), 140

dialogisms, 215n48

différance, 191, 230n11

distance, 4, 16–18, 21–22, 23–26, 37–38, 100, 124, 211n2, 211n12. *See also* intimacy; spatial discourse

Dixie to Broadway (1924), 162

Donovan, Brian, 205n63

Douglas, Aaron, 99, 173–75, 176, 179, 180, 228n35

Douglas, Ann, 194n7, 216n71

drag performances, 36–37, 72–73, 100–101, 144–45, 152

Drawings for Mulattoes (Nugent), 97–103

Du Bois, W. E. B., 88, 159, 172, 214n43, 228n29

Ebony and Topaz (Johnson), 97

economies: of colonialism, 9–10; gold-digging, 47, 54–55, 132–33, 205n62, 221n27; impact of economic pressures on mobility of women, 52–53, 55–56; impact on social relations, 52; of interracial Harlem, 227n25; of U.S. economic and imperial power, 9–11, 34; vamp character and, 47, 54–55, 132–33, 205n62, 221n27

Edwards, Brian, 184

Egyptomania, 22–23, 103, 131–32, 171–80

Ellington, Duke, 1, 41

Ellis, Havelock, 61

Ellison, Ralph, 217n80

embodiment: black woman as embodiment of distance, 139; as borders/boundaries, 63–65; disciplining of female bodies, 206n75; gendered meanings of performance and, 201n23; mixed-race bodies as multiracial spaces, 63–69, 116; of orientalist discourse through Asian bodies, 79–80, 105; referentiality of the black body, 30, 75–77, 82, 85–95; self-definition of female bodies, 201n23; sexological discourse and, 27–28, 37–41, 66, 67, 86, 114–15

empire building, 4–5, 162, 214n43, 218n93

Endless Column (Brancusi), 100

Epic Encounters (McAllister), 122, 219n3

Erenberg, Lewis A., 222n32

eugenic sciences, 4, 14, 27, 38–40, 48, 62, 66, 200n16, 201n18, 201n19

Everybody Was Kung-Fu Fighting (Prashad), 193n4

exoticism, 15, 104, 127–28, 137, 140–41, 157–58, 169, 177–78

Faderman, Lillian, 209n102, 210n103

Fax, Elton, 196n28

Feinberg, Alex, 58, 59–61, 206n75, 207n78

femininities: agency through performance, 130, 222n36; black femininity, 62–63, 62–70, 135–47; through disciplining of bodies, 206n75; feminization of masculinities, 67, 96, 115, 151–52, 165–66, 180, 195n16, 216n66; *flâneurie* and, 195n16; gender ambiguity and, 125, 139–47; imperial discourse and, 129–31, 134–47, 229n53; modernity and, 11; race and, 62–70, 176–77; sexualization and, 54; white womanhood and, 47

Ferguson, Roderick A., 24, 52, 73–74, 85, 87, 158, 188–89, 190, 199n5, 200n14, 216n66, 226n9

Filipino Immigration to Continental United States and to Hawaii (Lasker), 204n49

Filipino migrants/Filipino Americans, 45–47, 65–66, 69, 203n39, 203n43, 204n45, 204n49, 211n111, 227n25

FIRE!! (cover illustration), 174–75

Fisher, Rudolph, 65

Fitzgerald, F. Scott, 10, 91

flâneurie, 12, 195n16

Flaubert, Gustave, 220n19

Foucault, Michel, 17, 18–19, 27, 41, 191, 202n34, 206n75, 212n14, 226n9

Hughes, Langston, 15, 71, 93, 171, 174, 195n22
Huhndorf, Shari, 184
"Hula Blues" (Grainger), 41
Hull, E. M., 22
Huysmans, Joris-Karl, 11, 81, 88, 91, 116, 119

immigrants/immigration: anti-immigration legislation and, 197n41; boundaries and, 199n10, 200n13; citizenship and, 189, 197n41, 197n47, 212n8; comedy routines and, 196n28; cross-racial allegiance and, 199n10, 200n13; dance halls and, 2–3, 13–14, 33–35, 37, 38–40, 44–48, 69–70, 203n43, 204n45; eugenics and, 14, 39–40, 200n16; jazz cultures and, 10, 37–38; Johnson-Reed Immigration Act of 1924, 38–39, 199n6, 200n16; permanent residency and, 197n41; sexological discourse and, 38–39, 201n18; whiteness and, 200n13
Immoralist (Gide), 140
imperial discourse: Chinatowns and, 1, 3, 21, 22, 39, 197n45, 198n51; colonialist discourse and, 181–85; connections/initimacies created by, 126, 132, 156–57; cosmopolitanism and, 11–14, 21, 31–32, 39, 48, 49, 79; domestic colonialism, 158–59; femininity and, 125–47; the imperial city, 8–14; imperialist fantasies, 159–71; indigenous peoples and, 184–85; New Negro movements and, 81–82, 158, 164–65, 172; oriental discourse through, 155–56; racial affinity and, 158–59; sexological discourse and, 69–70; westward expansion and, 34–35, 173–74, 181–86, 229n53
imperial logic: aesthetic production and, 6, 8, 11, 24–25, 37–38, 75, 85–86, 181, 186; ambivalence and, 11, 190–91, 218n93; antithetical modes of, 186; boundaries and, 26, 188–91; compet-

ing narratives of subjectivity, 180–81; contradictory aesthetic practices and, 111–12; crisis of referentiality and, 26–27; of domination, 161–62; of internal colonialism, 161–64; intimacy and, 7–8, 21–22, 82, 125, 152–53, 172, 185; knowledge formations and, 8, 23, 32, 188–91; as mode of meaning making, 4–5, 20–21, 64, 74, 190–91; modes of differential valuation and, 78–79; resistance discourse and, 36; spatial discourse and, 5–6, 17, 23–25, 122–23, 156–57, 190; structural importance of, 189–90; use of term, 5, 188; use of the palimpsest, 52, 188–91
imperial selfhood, 17, 107, 121, 125, 126–27, 185
Infants of the Spring (Thurman), 29, 63, 64, 84, 96, 104–11, 112, 114, 116–17
"In Harlem's Araby" (Grainger), 2, 6, 31–32, 41, 165–66, 224n65
"In Old King Tutankhamen's Day" (Tucker), 158, 173, 176–78, 179, 180
internal colonialism: borders/boundaries and, 22, 162–63, 166–70; colonial discourse, 161–64; economies and, 161–63, 187–88; through empire building, 162; frontier mythologies, 34–35, 51, 184; of Harlem, 160–64, 166–69; imperial logic of, 161–64; of neighborhoods, 160–64, 166–69; of New York City, 73, 87, 91–92, 161–64; queer of color critique and, 22, 31–32, 163, 189; spatial discourse of, 161–65; use of term, 31, 162–63
interracial relations: African American/Asian American, 3–4, 213n30; black/white dichotomy and, 3–4, 13, 25–26, 103–4, 193n4, 195n15, 210n3, 210n5, 216n70; within dance halls, 13–14, 33–35, 204n46; homosocial alliances, 213n30; interracial sexuality, 35–38, 69–70; meaning making and, 64; queerness and, 215n57; racial affinities/

Latino migrants/immigrants, 12–13, 34–35, 45, 56–57, 89, 93–96, 119, 203n39, 206n69
"Latins Are Lousy Lovers" (Norden), 206n69
Lawson, Louise, 54
Lears, T. J. Jackson, 194n7. *See also* Gordon, Vivian (Benita Bischoff)
Le Calife de Bagdad (Boieldieu), 55
Lee, Bruce, 193n4
Lefebvre, Henri, 19
legislation: cabaret laws, 44, 195n20, 202n36; Committee of Fourteen, 40–41, 50, 131–32, 201n20; immigration legislation, 4, 37–39, 197n41, 199n6, 199n10, 200n16, 201n18; morality and, 29, 84–85, 88, 89–90, 112, 119–20, 166; multiracial spaces as spaces of regulation, 14, 35–36, 38–44, 183, 199n10
lesbians, 205n63, 208n85
Leslie, Lew, 224n65
Lewis, David Levering, 163, 195n22, 215n57
liberation discourse, 190
Lipsitz, George, 189, 207n78
Locke, Alain, 82, 164
Lott, Eric, 207n78
Lowe, Lisa, 7, 136, 156, 190
Loza, Mireya, 215n62
Lulu Belle (1926), 163–64
Lunceford, Jimmie, 41

Madama Butterfly (Puccini), 29, 81, 103, 104, 110, 112, 119, 217n89
Marez, Curtis, 214n31
marginalization, 204n45
Mark Antony, 179–80
masculinities: Arab masculinities, 147–50; Asian immigrants/Asian Americans and, 46–48, 200n12, 211n111; black masculinities, 58–61, 62–63, 83–84, 143, 148, 180, 216n66; crimi-

nalization of men of color and, 56–61; dance halls and, 62–63; feminization of, 67, 96, 115, 151–52, 165–66, 180, 195n16, 216n66; *flâneurie* and, 195n16; masculine consumption and, 12, 195n16; masculinist desire, 229n53; orientalized masculinities, 55–56, 147–50, 180; queer black masculinities, 62–63, 83–85, 143, 211n110; racialized masculinities, 58–61, 62–63, 144, 200n12, 211n111, 216n66; white masculinities, 84–85
masquerade balls, 102–3, 117–18
Massad, Joseph, 140
Massey, Doreen B., 45
McAlister, Melani, 122, 219n3
McClary, Susan, 41, 201n23, 206n75, 221n27
McDowell, Deborah E., 213n17
McLaughlin, Andrew G., 52–53, 205n58
meaning making: through the archive, 147; through geographies of scale and aesthetics, 76; imperial logic as, 4–5, 20–21, 64, 74, 190–91; instability of, 110; interracial relations and, 64; knowledge formation and, 32; across national borders, 74; queer chaos of, 147; through spatial modes, 20–21; beyond U.S. borders, 193n4
Mendoza, Victor, 113–14
Menefee, David W., 222n28
Merriam, Alan P., 42
methodology, 187–91
Miller, Monica, 208n80
Miller, Nina, 141
Mills, Charles W., 19
mimesis, 83, 213n25
Minnie the Moocher, 1–2, 3, 17
"Minnie the Moocher" (Calloway), 1–23, 17, 21, 198n51
minstrelsy, 27, 53, 58–61, 176, 205n76, 207n76, 207n78, 228n37
"Misery" (Hughes), 174–75

97; reclamation of Africa and, 84, 158, 172–75, 228n34; respectability and, 143; as signifiers of freedom, 1; Thurman and, 143, 164. *See also* Nugent, Richard Bruce; Thurman, Wallace

New Orleans jazz, 197n46

New York City: African American migration to, 9–10, 52; Arab communities, 219n1; Asian immigrants/Americans in, 10, 12, 27, 34, 62–63; internal colonialism of, 73, 87, 91–92, 161–64; Jazz Age demographics of, 4–5, 9; Latino/ Caribbean immigrants/Americans in, 10, 34, 56–57; as modern metropole, 10–14, 34–35, 69–70; queer life within, 143–44; regulation of racial/sexual encounters, 44–48, 157–58, 195n20, 202n36; Vivian Gordon case, 49–61. *See also* Harlem; neighborhoods

Ngai, Mae M., 199n10

Nguyen, Mimi Thi, 93

Nigger Heaven (Van Vechten), 148, 150, 195n22, 225n69

Nijinsky, Vaslav, 217n88

No Place of Grace (Lears), 194n7

Norden, Helen Brown, 206n69

Nugent, Richard Bruce: Du Bois and, 88; emergent queer of color critique of, 29, 77–78, 81–85, 89, 97, 114; New Negro movement and, 81–82, 84, 97, 99, 114–19, 143; queer black aesthetic practices of, 29–30, 71–72, 83–84, 97–103, 110–19, 140; referentiality of the black body, 29–30, 75–77, 85–95; sexological discourse and, 81, 85–87, 97, 208n87; Thurman and, 87–88; use of orientalism, 29, 112–20, 141–47; use of primitivism, 29, 97–100

Nugent, Richard Bruce, works by: *Drawings for Mulattoes*, 97–103; "Geisha Man," 29–30, 78, 110–11, 112–19; *Naomi and Ruth*, 144, 146–47; *Opportunity* magazine (cover illustration), 71–72,

83–84; *Salome: Negrotesque I*, 141–43, 144; "Smoke, Lilies and Jade," 77, 87, 88–95, 116, 215n60, 215n62; *Untitled [Two Women]*, 144–46

Nyong'o, Tavia, 86, 212n5

Ogren, Kathy, 43

Old Lybia, 158

opera, 103–4, 110, 112, 114, 118, 129, 132, 217n88

Opportunity magazine (cover illustration), 71–73, 83–84

Ordover, Nancy, 39–40, 200n16, 201n18

orientalist discourse: Afro-Deco, 173–74; ambiguity and, 104–5; of Asia/Asian bodies, 79–80, 105; avant-garde dance movements and, 205n55; black orientalism, 95–97, 103–4, 107–8, 212n8; black women and, 135–39; through colonial analogies, 159–71; discourses of Araby within Harlem, 1–2, 155–59, 161, 164–71; as fantasy, 222n36; female performance and, 107, 121, 131–38; imperial selfhood and, 107, 121; jazz as signifier of, 170–71; through lyrics, 128–29, 149, 163–64, 176, 177, 179–80, 224n65; of musical language, 224n66; mutability of, 173–74; of nation, 79–80, 105, 159–71, 173–74, 182–85; opera and, 103–4; of perversion, 160–61; of queerness, 79–80, 84, 139–47; racial identification and, 157–58; sexological discourse and, 119–20; of sexual freedom, 160–61; through sexualizing discourse, 169–70, 266n6; as transgression, 107; use of term *orientalism*, 24; westward expansion and, 173–74, 182–85; women and, 135–39, 205n55, 221n24

Our Araby (Chase), 181–86

Pagan Rout, 62, 102

"Palesteena" (Crumit), 2, 127–29, 177, 224n66

palimpsest, 52, 188–91

Parreñas, Rhacel Salazar, 204n45

Peiss, Kathy, 49, 52

Peretti, Burton W., 205n58

performance: feminine agency through, 130, 222n36; gendered meanings of, 201n23; illocutionary force of music, 201n23; passing performances, 36–37, 213n17; repertoire, 30–31, 123, 125–26, 127, 134–35, 137, 140; respectability and, 222n40; self-definition and, 201n23. *See also* archives/archivists

Picasso, Pablo, 78, 143

Plantation Revue, 224n65

Play de Blues (Douglas), 174–75

policing/surveillance: of boundaries, 162, 166–67, 209n94; Committee of Fourteen, 40–41, 50, 131–32, 201n20; sexological discourse and, 27–28, 37–41, 61–62. *See also* vice legislation

Powell, Richard, 173–74

power relations: Foucault on, 196n31; interracial sexualities as narrative device, 199n9; knowledge formations and, 31, 122–24; multiple axes of power, 190; through reference, 156–57; spatial discourse and, 36–37; subjectivity formation and, 188; use of the palimpsest, 52, 188–91; of white interlopers in Harlem, 171

Prashad, Vijay, 193n4

Pratt, Mary Louise, 26, 35, 229n55

primitivism: African aesthetics and, 15–16, 83–85, 97, 159–60; African American subjectivity and, 17, 60–61, 72–73; as avant-garde culture, 29, 81–82; as black modernity, 119–20; black women and, 135–39; civilization vs., 97, 127–28; colonial aesthetics and, 11, 15–16; jazz cultures and, 42–43, 45, 58–59; mimesis, 83, 213n25; modernism and, 11, 15–16, 73, 97; New Negro movements and, 15–17, 29, 65, 71–72, 79–85, 97, 99, 172; oriental-

ism commingled with, 18–19, 29, 181; queer black aesthetic formation and, 75, 77–85, 97–98, 119–20; sexological discourse and, 62, 81, 85–87, 97; sexual freedom and, 42–43, 45, 58–59, 61, 72–73; as signifiers of Africa, 159–60

Puccini, Giacomo, 29, 81, 104, 112, 119, 217n89

Puerto Ricans/Puerto Rican migrants, 2–3, 10, 34, 47, 53, 56, 57, 203n39

"Puttin' On the Ritz" (Watson, Berlin, and Snyder), 163–64, 165, 227nn17–18

queer aesthetics: cosmopolitanism, 88, 116–18; death trope, 118–19; imperial logic and, 78–85, 217n88; masquerade balls, 102–3, 117–18; modernity and, 116–17, 139–47; use of term, 75, 219n119

queer black aesthetic production: borders/boundaries and, 24–25, 28–29, 73–77, 94, 95–97, 103–4, 119–20; chaos of meaning making, 147; comparative empire studies and, 77–78; cosmopolitanism and, 88, 116–18; European queer canon and, 29, 84–85, 89–90, 119–20; imperial logic and, 6, 8, 11, 24–25, 37–38, 75, 85–86, 181, 186, 217n88; through lyrics, 224n65; masculinities and, 62–63, 83–84, 143; New Negro movements and, 81–82, 84, 97; orientalism and, 95–96, 103–12, 119–20; primitivism and, 97–104; queer black writers, 214n46; queering of knowledge formation, 77–78, 85–87; queer subcultures of Harlem, 165–66; queer subjectivity, 165–66; racialized queering of words, 212n5; referentiality of the queer black body, 30, 75–77, 82, 85–95; spatial discourse and, 97–103

queerness: dance halls and, 62–63; deterritorialization and, 112–20; homosexual acts vs. homosexual identities, 211n110; homosexuality, 37–38, 39–40, 61–62, 63–64, 66, 67, 81, 211n110,

213n30; interracial relationships and, 215n57; literary disappearance of, 208n90; modernity and, 116–17, 139–47; queer art practices, 214n35; queer desire, 213n17; Salomé as, 139–47; sexological discourse and, 81, 85–87, 97, 101–2, 119–20; sheiks and, 224n65, 225n69; spatial discourse and, 80, 91, 103, 112–20

queer of color critique: gender/sexuality ambiguity, 22, 100, 101–2; identity formation, 97–100, 199n5; internal colonialism and, 22, 31–32, 163, 189; intimacy and, 24–25; national discourse and, 24–25, 31–32, 73–74, 78–79, 81–82; queer black aesthetic and, 29, 31–32, 77–79, 81–82, 84–85, 89, 100; temporal relations and, 97–103; use of term, 24–25, 73–74, 77, 199n5

Quicksand (Larsen), 79, 91, 213n15, 217n87

Race for Citizenship (Jun), 212n8
racial affinities/affiliation: between African Americans and Asia/Africa, 31, 179–81; collapse of time/space through, 180–81; geographic boundaries and, 158–59; racial intimacy, 22, 26–27, 42–43, 75–76, 138–39; temporal relations and, 7, 35, 173, 175, 180–81
racial ambiguity: mulattoes, 65–69, 98–104, 199n9, 208n89; racial illegibility, 104–5, 217n80; sexualization of mixed-race bodies, 210n106
racial discourse: black modernity, 97, 119–20; black/white dichotomy, 3–4, 13, 25–26, 103–4, 193n4, 195n15, 210n3, 210n5, 216n70; boundaries and, 3, 25–26, 28–29, 38, 64, 73–77, 105–6, 107, 135–39, 152, 199n10, 204n45; death and devaluation and, 188–90; embodiment of distance, 139; geographies of scale and, 157; interracial sexualities as narrative device, 199n9; legislation

and, 199n6; narratives of inclusion and, 197n47; orientalisms and, 157–58; polyvalent mobility of, 167–68; racial categorization of Filipinos, 204n49; racial intimacy, 22, 26–27, 42–43, 75–76, 138–39; racialized knowledge, 157; racialized masculinities, 58–61, 62–63, 144, 200n12, 211n111, 216n66; racialized queering of words, 212n5; racial logic of, 168; racial misidentification, 210n103; referentiality of the black body, 30, 75–77, 85–95; regulation and, 157; regulation and transgression of gender and, 199n5; regulation and transgression of sexuality and, 199n5; sexological discourse and, 39–40, 63–64, 66, 67; spatial discourse and, 3, 14–17, 27–29, 45–46, 123, 135–39, 164, 183; temporal relations and, 7, 35, 173, 175, 180–81; urban spaces and, 167–68, 201n19; use of palimpsest, 52, 188–91; violence and, 191

racial logics, 38, 168, 183–84
racial mixing: blackface discourse, 176, 205n76, 228n37; black/white dichotomy, 3–4, 13, 25–26, 103–4, 193n4, 195n15, 210n3, 210n5, 216n70; mixed-race embodiment as multiracial space, 63–69, 116; racial boundaries and, 3, 25–26, 28–29, 64; racial miscegenation, 36–37. *See also* interracial relations

Rancière, Jacques, 29, 32, 76, 77, 89, 91, 95, 120
Rapp, William Jourdan, 12–13, 16–17
Reddy, Chandan, 95, 118, 214n43, 217n87
referentiality: of the black body, 30, 75–77, 82, 85–95; contact zones and, 26; crisis of referentiality, 26–29, 30; imperial logic and, 26–27; instability of, 5–6, 16–17; queer identification and, 30, 75–77, 82, 85–95; queer orientalisms, 95–96, 103–5, 107–8, 110–12; queer primitivisms, 95–103; use of

referentiality (*continued*)
term, 5, 16–17, 76–78. *See also* ambiguity

Reiss, Winold, 228n35

repertoire, 30–31, 123, 125–26, 127, 134–35, 137, 140. *See also* archive; performance

resistance discourse, 36–37, 190

respectability, 143, 166–70, 222n40

Roediger, David, 207n78

Ross, Marlon B., 82

Rubaiyat (Khyyam), 157–58

Said, Edward, 84, 122, 134, 141

Salomé, 17, 30–31, 135–39, 220n19

Salomé (Strauss), 129–30

Salomé (Wilde), 122

Salome: Negrotesque I (Nugent), 141–43, 144

Save Me the Waltz (Fitzgerald), 80

scale, geographies of, 12, 18, 36–37, 38, 76, 78, 82, 114–15, 120, 133–34, 140, 157, 185

Schwarz, A. B. Christa, 87, 89, 115

Sedgwick, Eve Kosofsky, 84

sexological discourse: embodiment and, 27–28, 37–41, 66, 67, 86, 114–15; eugenics and, 201n18; gender formation and, 63–64, 66, 67, 209n101; homosexuality and, 37–38, 39–40, 61–62, 63–64, 66, 67, 81; immigrants/immigration and, 38–39, 201n18; imperial discourse and, 69–70; interracial relations and, 27–28, 37, 67; lesbianism and, 208n15; mixed-race bodies and, 27–28, 63–64, 209n101, 210n106; Nugent and, 81, 85–87, 97, 208n87; orientalist discourse and, 119–20; policing/surveillance and, 27–28, 37–41, 61–62; primitivism and, 62, 81, 85–87, 97; queerness and, 81, 85–87, 97, 101–2, 119–20; racial formation and, 39–40, 63–64, 66, 67; sexual formations and, 37–38, 61–62, 63–64, 66, 67, 81, 208n15; spatial relations and, 62, 170–71; temporal relations and, 62; Thurman and, 28, 63–64,

108–9, 208n87; vice legislation and, 27–28, 37–41, 61–62

sexual ambiguity, 36–37, 104–5, 208n15, 210n109

sexual formations: bisexuality, 36–37; borders/boundaries and, 73–77, 105–6, 199n10; geographies of scale and, 157; imperial selfhood and, 121; interracial sexualities as narrative device for, 199n9; intimacy, 22, 42–44, 100; knowledge formations and, 4, 90–92; narratives of inclusion and, 197n47; non-normativity of, 79–80; through orientalizing objects, 169–70; racial formation and, 199n5; repressive hypothesis of, 202n34; sexological discourse and, 37–38, 61–62, 63–64, 66, 67, 81, 208n15; sexual boundaries in multiracial spaces and, 44–48, 199n10; sexualization of mixed-race bodies, 27–28, 63–64, 209n101, 210n106; sexual regulation and, 157; of urban spaces, 201n19; use of orientalist fantasy, 22, 92, 104, 138–39, 149, 153, 170, 176–77, 222n36; vamp character, 47, 54–55, 132–33, 205n62, 221n27; white womanhood and, 49–54, 125–34

"Sheik of Araby" (Smith and Snyder), 147, 148–49, 223n61, 224n66

sheiks, 1, 15, 22, 30–31, 53, 92, 124–25, 147–52, 155–56, 180, 182, 185, 224n66, 225n2

Sheik, The (1921), 30, 92, 147, 148–49

Sheik, The (Hull), 22, 122, 147, 149

Shohat, Ella, 131, 173, 183, 216n70, 229n53

Shonibare, Yinka, 225n4

Shu, Lee, 48

Silva, Denise Ferreira da, 19

"Smoke, Lilies and Jade" (Nugent), 77, 87, 88–95, 116, 215n60, 215n62

Soja, Edward W., 199n10

Somerville, Siobhan B., 39, 63–64, 66, 67, 199n9, 201n18, 209n101

Soulouque, Faustin, 227n13

Wiedoeft, Rudy, 224n66

Wilde, Oscar, 82–83, 84, 89, 104, 106–7, 111, 116, 119, 144, 213n28, 214n31, 220n19

Wilentz, Sean, 207n78

Williams, Raymond, 11

Wirth, Thomas H., 72, 93, 111, 208n87, 215n59, 215n62

Wong, Yutian, 124, 205n55, 220n20

Wright, Richard, 24–25

Writing Manhood in Black and Yellow (Kim), 213n30

Wynn, Ed, 133

Yerkes, Robert M., 200n16

Young, Robert J. C., 229n1

Yu, Henry, 39